FRAGMENTED THOUGHTS
RANDOM DIRECTIONS

PATRICK D FERRIS

ALSO BY PATRICK D FERRIS

Larry and Giselle Series:

A Gypsy Romance

A Gypsy Engagement

A Gypsy Haunting

Terry Reid Mystery Series:

His Disciples Watch

His Disciples Sleep

His Disciples Deceive

Short Story Collection:

Fragmented Thoughts Random Directions

CONTENTS

FOREWORD

I'm very proud that Pat asked me to write the foreword for this book. There's a writers group in Fort St. John called the Writers of the Peace. Pat Ferris is a member of this group. They used to meet in the library every second Friday evening. I began attending their meetings in 2014.

I was new to Fort St. John and had just completed my first attempt at National Novel Writing Month. That takes place in November of every year. People all around the world dedicate themselves to producing fifty thousand words in thirty days. When the month was over I had succeeded in producing a small volume which could charitably be called a novel, but should never see the light of day.

When I discovered the Writers of the Peace I found a handful of aspiring writers, struggling to carve time from the rest of their lives to write. These people became my Companions on the Journey. There were also two treasures in the group, writers who had not only finished several books, but also released them into the world. Pat Ferris was one, Ronnie Roberts was the other.

In the years since then, these two veteran writers have given me advice, and encouragement, and taken me seriously. The greatest inspiration, though, came simply from watching them work. Write, publish, repeat. Write, publish, repeat. Simply to watch them go through the process many times, made it seem the goal was attainable. It was also a great education to see how they recovered from the banana peels that life threw in front of them. There are times in everyone's life when all they have are lemons. Life events happen that prevent us from writing, but, I know it's possible to power through them and recover because I have seen Pat and Ronnie do it several times.

This book is a collection of short stories by Pat Ferris. The title of the book is *Fragmented Thoughts - Random Directions*. The working title was *Pat's Shorts*. I encouraged him to stick with that title but I was overridden.

There are fifteen stories in this book and I could say something about each one. The opener, *Marcus*, is one of the best renderings of the Crossroads Legend that I've seen for a long time. I think it ranks right up there with the movie Angel heart. *Spencer's Ghost* is a great example of the *I See Dead People* genre of stories. What I will always remember about that story is how hard Pat had to work on it. For some reason the story wouldn't come and he almost abandoned it several times. We all cheered him on, helped him keep going and eventually he triumphed.

I could say something about each story, how it came to be and what it means to me. I'm not going to do that. Instead, I'm just going to say that these are short stories by a good man who loves history, cycling, and life in the North country. Spend some time with them, get to know Pat. Your time will be generously rewarded.

Oh yes, as you read these stories keep your eyes open for the ghost. I won't say that there's a ghost in every story, but Pat loves to throw one in whenever he can. Finding the ghost can be your *Where's Waldo* as you work your way through the book.

I envy you. You're in for a treat.

— Glenn Palmer, author of North Peace Blues

Fort St. John, 2019

MARCUS

He was an ant in a jar looking out at a little artificial world, trapped. Marcus never felt like the other kids, different, special, better. He was going somewhere but wasn't sure where.

Marcus Deering and his younger brother Elvin grew up together in their quiet, simple, tiny town of Adobe Arizona. Their parents were never judgmental of either of them, treating them with the same old-fashioned equality, sense of respect, and work ethic.

The family and the town routine never varied. The family hung out with the same people in town and at school. They attended their little town church each Sunday. Other than that, they never went anywhere or seemed to do anything. It was this crushing routine of blandness that Marcus hated.

Church, family and work. Their little religious enclave required no more, no less.

He looked around at the other boys in their school, all dressed in the same drab fashion—white shirts, long pants, suspenders. Their hair uniformly short, their faces scrubbed and shining. The girls wore dresses, no makeup, and invariably styled their hair in curls or pig tails. They all looked old-fashioned, straight out of a '50's sitcom, lost in time. Out of fashion never goes out of fashion in Adobe, Arizona.

Marcus stood alone as the defiant loner seeing himself as the sullen badass.

His young brother Elvin was the only one who would try to hang around with Marcus in the schoolyard. Elvin was quiet and kind, happy to embrace the simpler things. He'd once heard his parents whisper that Marcus was his half-brother by another father but didn't know what that meant.

Elvin was slower witted and smaller than his classmates, resulting in endless opportunities to be bullied and pushed around. This entertaining playground sport only compounded once the kids learned his older brother Marcus had no interest in protecting him. Elvin was fair game. Despite Elvin's sincere attempts to soften his older brother's self-imposed isolation, Marcus never missed an opportunity to embarrass or humiliate Elvin, taking perverse pleasure in reducing him to tears. Marcus was a self-centered jerk.

It was in the schoolyard in grade two when Elvin felt the full lash of his cruelty. He'd felt sick all morning, his belly churning and gurgling. "I don't feel so good Marcus. What'll I do?"

Marcus scowled at him. "Why do I care? I'm not wasting the last five minutes of lunch break on you when I could hang with Barbara, instead."

Elvin watched Marcus stomp away, trying not to swoon or barf. He staggered over by the swings waiting his turn but unsure if motion back and forth was a good idea. As he thought of it a sudden coughing fit grabbed him. It ended with a hard, retching gasp that caused him to fart. Bad idea. Horror of horrors he felt something hot start to fill up his shorts.

"Oh no!" he whimpered.

Swinging was replaced by awkward stares. The kids on the nearby swing saw the look of despair cross his face and soon smelled the disaster as confirmation. They'd all been there but not today.

Elvin looked around to see he was the center of attraction. The loud, cheerful playground was now as silent as a tomb. In desperation, he waddled over to his big brother Marcus to ask for help.

"Marcus! Ya gotta help me!" he pleaded. "I pooped my pants."

Marcus looked at his pant leg stain, growing by the second and took a sniff. "Did you really SHIT YOUR PANTS, Elvin?"

"Yes!" he sobbed.

Marcus replied by stepping back from Elvin, pointing to him. "Hey look everybody! Elvin shit his pants! Look, it's running down his leg!" Marcus made sure everyone in the playground saw it and was laughing.

Elvin was mortified. Poor Elvin was teased for months, afterwards. Nevertheless, Elvin adored Marcus and instantly forgave him which irritated Marcus more.

At home Marcus seldom missed a chance to point out to his parents how stupid their little town was or how pitiful their home and farm was. He bragged he would be a star athlete and a millionaire, someday. His parents simply listened and patiently waited for the weekend to arrive—they settled these issues in their own quiet way.

Saturday's were chore day and a time to do errands around the farm. When Marcus was being rebellious or just being mean to Elvin, which was constant, his dad assigned him a day or two of shoveling dirt, manure, grain, or picking rocks from the fields. After twelve hours hard physical labor Marcus was filthy, sore and hungry, choosing a bath and early bed after supper, over further conflict. He was a 'broken-in' mustang for a little while.

After Saturday it was church, which Marcus dreaded. They got up early, loaded into the van for the drive across the county to the church. There he was forced to sit and be quiet on the threat of another twelve-hour day with a shovel.

Marcus dreaded standing up and sitting down repeatedly while singing the same grim songs in their unimaginative drones. He hated preacher Rev. Gary Duke's lectures the most. All Marcus could think about was how unworldly the preacher was and how could he possibly know anything. He only knew their town of Adobe, escaping for a year to nearby New Mexico for religious indoctrination and then coming back like the prodigal son with a cheap toupee. How could he or anyone else in this shitty town know anything about the world and life, not having been anywhere?

Hicks and fools.

The only part Marcus liked was the church social, after the service. While his parents drank tea and talked about the crops and the weather, Marcus would check out the cutest of the church girls. A few were intrigued by his badass reputation. He learned early how to sweet talk them into sneaking off behind one of the church buildings for some kissing or other such monkey business. The girls would have to explain grass and twigs in their panties when they got home.

Barbara Stellina was his favourite. He sometimes thought her a kindred spirit, like him, restless and rebellious. He would see her sullenly killing time in the parking lot. There was no mistaking her hot figure making her cheap, worn dress look far better than it could with anyone else. A gem.

Such was the dull life of Marcus Deering, hick farm kid, now in his early teens.

It all changed one Sunday as the family drove home from church, pausing at a rural stop sign in the middle of nowhere. There had been a spectacular accident at this corner a few days earlier, so the locals were actually stopping at the stop sign, looking, instead of barreling through—though, undoubtedly, after a few weeks as the memory of the accident faded, they would likely relapse into their normal behaviour. Caution right now.

It was a hot and humid day, so all the windows were rolled down. His parents were too cheap to buy an air-conditioned vehicle, considering it a needless luxury, even in Arizona. Marcus gazed off into the distance, frowning in surprise at encountering something blessedly different on the horizon. Off and over to the right a slow moving, peculiar, bumble of color and glitter, headed for the intersection. He slid higher in his seat as it came closer. Something about them made him more excited than he had ever been.

This must be one of those pro biking teams!

Against a hot, dull desert background shot a brilliant blaze of color, pomp and coolness, a sensational cycling team pouring through the intersection, so close he imagined he could hear their breathing, could feel the air move as they passed, cooling his clammy skin.

The group moved swiftly and precisely, ten riders, all riding double file, inches away from each other. Impossible to maintain! How did they not crash, fall, smear their bodies across the hot pavement? The hazard of their closeness seemed to be of no concern to them.

Marcus read a few of the names on the jerseys—Shimano, Mavic, Pirelli—as they flashed by, all elegantly printed with stylized European logos. They pedaled elegantly, effortlessly. The shocking colored clothing they wore matched and form-fitted perfectly as did their special sunglasses, matching helmets and bicycles. The bike tires made an amazing hissing sound as they buzzed over the hot asphalt. The riders exuded an aloof coolness, totally ignoring the dull van with arrogance and pretention. The elite. Not one rider wasted a glance on the Deering family vehicle or its amazed occupants.

He was entranced by this slowly moving spectacle, fascinated by their efficient rhythm and sense of cool. They were as different to the people in his bumpkin town as it was possible to be. He knew he had to become one of *those* cyclists, someday, somehow.

His family watched the bike riders in awe, as if they were robots flying in from Mars, then started laughing and pointing at them.

"Look at them funny bike riders," said Elvin, giggling at the sight.

His parents joined in. "Couldn't deliver a newspaper on them skinny tires."

Marcus ignored them, not wanting to miss a single sound, sight or smell of the riders as they passed, savouring every moment. In just seconds they were gone, leaving Marcus's dismal rural world of farmyards, trees and quiet country roads behind them. Leaving Marcus behind them.

As soon as Marcus got home, he poured through the yellow pages for phone numbers of bike shops in Tucson, then made a few calls. One of them helpfully gave him some names of local bike clubs to contact. He called and found out how he could join and where the next event took place.

Couldn't be difficult. He had to join them and show them how great he could be.

Using a tired, old road bike he found in the barn and resurrected, he came out and tried the first race. The other club riders snickered at him when he arrived at the start line. His bike was clearly a cheap clunker from another era, his clothing merely cut off shorts and a t-shirt, capped off with a loaner hockey helmet and running shoes. Marcus looked and felt like the biggest hick on the planet among the spandex greyhounds with their designer sunglasses, perched on gloriously elegant, handmade bikes. He was used to teasing others and not being teased himself. He stuck out like a dog turd in a punch bowl. Calming himself, he thought this race was just for recreational riders, so it was a moderate distance of twenty-five miles on a rolling hilly circuit.

Easy for me. I got this.

Just when he thought he couldn't take any more stress, someone shouted 'go!' The thirty riders around him clicked their shoes into their special step-in pedals and the group sped away from him. He fumbled as he lost time shoving his runners into the ancient old toe clips and straps. Finally, he had them in, relieved, he poured on the power and caught back up to all the riders.

At first Marcus was a bit winded, struggling to keep up. He wisely caught his breath, soon brashly passing everyone on the left and took to the front, stupidly towing the group along behind him. He was sure he was winning because he was in the lead—it wasn't until after the race that he learned all the other riders were getting a free ride drafting behind him, waiting. Maybe they were laughing at him.

He was determined to crush them.

The other riders were impressed the new kid on the crappy bike was as strong as a moose and almost as experienced. They left him behind in the dust as soon as they got close to the finish. Marcus went from first to thirtieth in five seconds. Dead last. *He* was the one crushed!

He rode home in tears, not understanding why he had done so badly. He went from believing he was the strongest rider but wound up dead last. Marcus didn't stick around to hear the other riders asking "Who was the new kid with legs of steel? He could have beat us all if he had a brain and a proper bike."

Monday at school, he quickly learned everyone knew he'd come last in the race. Their teasing only made him more determined than ever. Cycling had unearthed a burning sense of desire and urgency in him he had never felt before. This was the first outlet he'd found for all his longings and desires for escape. It became the focal point in his life.

But for a lucky meeting, his dreams may have all come to nothing.

Tuesday night, a club cycling coach phoned and asked to come and see him, impressed at Marcus's strength in last Sunday's race. She told him her name was Julie Bates, then surprised him by telling him that with a little polishing she thought he could do very well. She even offered to loan him one of her old race bikes. Marcus accepted her offer on the spot and arranged to meet Julie in person the next evening at his house. Only years later would he realize how important this coach and bike loan would be.

He was so excited that he could hardly concentrate all day at school. Time crawled by. Finally, the ordeal was over and he raced home, wolfed down supper and waited for the coach to arrive. The knock at the door came at seven p.m. Opening the door, Marcus and his family found Julie standing on the porch beside the loaner racing bike.

"Hi Marcus. Mr. and Mrs. Deering. My name is Julie Bates and I'm the bike club coach. Marcus, you did very well last Sunday. I think you could do even better with a few tips and a different bike."

Marcus rushed outside to see her. Julie looked like the classic cyclist, all dressed up in form fitting spandex featuring the name 'Bates Bikes'. She was mid-height, thin, tanned and fit looking. He also noticed how pretty she was with long brown hair, striking blue eyes, and old—maybe in her late thirties? She had a bag in one hand, and leaned the bike on a porch chair behind her.

"Here's a bike for you to use for a while. It is an older machine but is much better than what you are using, no offense."

His parents and Elvin came out and sat on the porch swing as

Marcus checked out the bike, trying unsuccessfully to tamp down his excitement. "Wow!" was all Marcus could say, over and over again. The bike was painted silver and had chromed forks and looked beautifully elegant. He read the name out loud, "Cinelli?"

"It's Italian and pronounced 'Shin-Ellie'" she corrected gently. "It's a ten-year-old Italian machine with 18 speed gears but it works well enough and is still fairly light by today's standards. It needs cleaning and polishing but I'm sure you can deal with that. I also have a pair of proper biking shoes for you." She glanced at his feet then gave him the bag from under her arm. "They might be a bit big but should do the job. And there's a pair of cycling shorts, jersey and cycling helmet inside, too. They should fit, alright. Go and try them on. Remember to wash the clothing every single time you use them."

Marcus took the clothing from Julie and rushed into the bathroom peeling his shirt off as he sped through the living room. Once wearing the biking gear, he gazed at the bathroom mirror marveling at the strange clothing, running his hands up and down the smooth fabric. They felt completely good, like he'd finally found his proper attire at long last. It felt wonderful and fast just standing there except for the chamois pad in his crotch. That was weird.

Soon he was back outside admiring the bike.

Julie gave him a quick lesson on shifting and how the step-in pedals and shoes worked. "Use both brakes at the same time, see? Pump up these tires twice a week to a hundred psi. Here's how the funny presta valve works to do that. Oil this chain when it gets shiny. Hop on the seat and let's adjust the seat height. Helmet and gloves go on like this."

He was spellbound. It was like getting the instructions for flying a space shuttle.

Then they were off for a short bike ride. They rode around the paved loop in the little town side-by-side, with Julie providing an endless stream of helpful instructions like—"Look up, where you want to go... Lean into the corner, outside pedal down like this... Eye contact with car drivers... Get your feet out of the pedal clips *before* you stop or you'll tip over and skin your knee."

He was impressed how effortlessly she handled her bike and how close she rode to him. None of his wobbles and miscues seemed to concern her as she guided him along. She introduced 'drafting' or the art of following other riders for speed and efficiency, the secret weapon of cycling. She gave a short explanation on how to ride in a bunch, sprint and breakaway. It was a lot of information for one evening but Marcus soaked it up like a sponge. Soon the lesson was over, and Julie drove away, leaving Marcus with his newfound treasure of cycling gear and a bike.

All this new information was overwhelming, but he'd never admit it.

After a bath, Marcus carefully hand-washed his new-to-him biking clothes and then sat with his parents, babbling on about next Sunday's race. He was full of ideas about what he would do. He could see his parents had no real idea what he was talking about, but still— they *did* pretend to listen before his dad returned to reading the newspaper and his Mom to her knitting.

While Marcus and their parents were talking, Elvin secretly took the new bike downstairs into the workshop. He busily cleaned, waxed and polished the bike until it looked like new. The chrome sparkled and the paint shone. Even the old black shoes were restored and polished to a brilliant shine.

As soon as he was done Elvin brought it back upstairs, put it in their shared bedroom, and waited to see his brother's reaction. When Marcus walked into the room, he looked the bike over critically and muttered, "If it doesn't work perfect, I'm gonna kick your ass," before flopping down on his bed and laid there, wide awake, his mind racing with possibilities.

A knob even when he's happy thought Elvin, surprised and disappointed at not getting any acknowledgement or thanks but brushed it off to be soon forgotten. Marcus was Marcus.

Downstairs his parents sat in the living room, his dad looking at the newspaper and his mom sewing socks. Their old clock ticked to mark the silence as was their evening custom after a long, hard day.

"The bike stuff might be good for Marcus," his mom offered quietly.

"Could be. Might have to do the Saturday barn chores myself from now on," Dad said.

"It'll be worth it."

"...hope so."

It was another long boring day at Marcus's hick school as he counted down the minutes to don his new spandex and ride his bike. Marcus shoveled down his evening dinner, dressed in his bike gear and was off training in the neighborhood. The weather was hot, sunny and windless. A perfect night to ride. He rode up the school hill a couple of times, swooped around every corner he could find and did a few little sprint finishes at all the road signs he could find. It was fabulous to feel the wind in his face with a nimble bike under him, willingly obeying his every command. Glorious. He couldn't get enough of that amazing bike. It was the most incredible thing he ever had between his legs.

That was until he saw Barbara Stellina standing in her front yard. Her cute body was squished into a small two-piece robin's egg blue bathing suit bought before she started to fill out. The bikini color complimented her dark Mediterranean complexion perfectly, breasts straining the tiny top, the little knot in the front hanging together for dear life.

Marcus was mesmerized. She never dressed like this for church.

She called to him as soon as she saw him. "Hey, Marcus. Is that you in that bike outfit?" She smiled invitingly, walking up to him as he stopped on his bike. His eyes drank in her every move.

She looked smoking hot! As smoothly as he could, Marcus rolled his bike beside her on the road and came to a full stop for a grand entrance. It would have worked if he hadn't forgotten he had the newfangled 'click-in' shoes and cleats. He struggled to get his feet out from his bike at a dead stop, failing.

"Shit..." he mumbled, gracelessly tipping over, landing hard on the pavement with his knee and elbow. He was careful to make sure no damage happened to the precious bike. Skin grows back for free, but bike parts were expensive!

Barbara rushed to him to help. Her warm, plump breasts rushed at his face as she tried to disentangle his feet from the pedals. She was wearing some kind of sunscreen, maybe, that made her skin shiny and smelled really good. Her hair brushed his face and her big sympathetic brown eyes blinked down at him as he lay there, helplessly. There was a split second where neither spoke, then, they managed to get his feet clicked out after a few seconds. When Marcus finally stood up, he felt foolish.

She noticed blood dribbling down his leg. "Oh my gosh! You're bleeding! Come to the house and let's clean that up right away! Here, I'll take your bike."

She wheeled his bike towards her house while Marcus clunked and clicked along behind her in the awkward, stiff-soled cycling shoes, watching her curly long brown hair trailing down her back, past her bikini tie strap leading down to her plump, round bottom.

"It's not bad. Just a couple of scratches," he grunted. His injuries forgotten, he could not help but suck in how good she looked in her swimsuit. No tired pink Sunday dress today!

Barbara was the same age as Marcus, but she was a bit of a rebel and *did* like the boys. He knew very well he was enough of a "bad boy" to interest her as compared to the bland unworldly farm kids around town.

Barbara wasn't unaware of what was going on around her. Her older sisters were unhappily married off, one-by-one. When the men weren't around, she heard them bitterly complain of early marriage, banishment to bear numerous anonymous children and unceasing maid work. They all spoke of missed opportunities in the big city. At one gathering her oldest sister Emma teased her, "You're next Barb. They already have Jeb picked out for you. Remember to walk two steps behind him."

Barbara wasn't stupid. She knew she would become just another baby machine and dumpy looking farmers' wife until the day she died. This was her chance to play around a little. Barbara was more interested in entertainment than being betrothed. She had a mind of her own.

Marcus sat on the couch in the living room with his trusty bike standing in the mud room while Barbara rummaged around in the bathroom for bandages. The family terrier 'Pookie' sat on the carpet in front of Marcus, watching him intensely with beady little eyes, growling whenever Marcus moved.

"I don't think your dog likes me," he called to Barb, not taking his eyes off the mutt.

"Oh, don't worry about him. He's just guarding the house while Mom's at work. She's on night shift at the wheat elevator," she called out, coming out of the bathroom with a handful of bandages. She quickly patched the bleeding knee up. "Better?"

"Yeah. Thanks Barb." Marcus smiled.

She gave him a big wet kiss as a reply and plopped a handful of condoms down on the coffee table. Wow. She yanked the string on her tight bikini top allowing her breasts to make a grand entrance and was on top of him like a cat, kissing, purring and licking. Marcus was almost overwhelmed.

A dream come true.

They were mating animals in heat, continuing to have sex for what seemed like hours. Barbara was inventive and energetic as they moved around the couch, floor, chairs and padded bar stools. His knee hurt but he would not admit it. He was in exquisite pleasure, never wanting it to end.

Two hours flashed by as if it was just seconds. The intense, single-minded passion had both Marcus's and Barbara's full attention. It was as if it was a dream sequence.

They did have an audience who was mystified at the proceedings. 'Pookie' watched every minute of it in fascination and amusement, without a blink. Every time Barbara giggled or squealed, the dog barked and growled threateningly. To Marcus's disgust, Pookie ran behind him and licked his legs and feet whenever he could.

"Get outta here, you stupid dog!" Marcus hissed.

Pookie looked at him, puzzled, then snapped up the discarded used condoms on the tabletop. Gulp!

"Noooooo!!" cried Marcus.

Pookie looked at him, licking his lips and coughing.

Show stopper.

"Will those make him sick?" Marcus asked. He was not so much concerned about the dog's health as what appeared in his leavings in a day or two. If her Mom saw it that could be hard to explain.

"Oh, dogs can eat anything, silly. I'll walk him for the next few days," Barbara giggled, putting her arms around Marcus and pulling him back down on the couch. He had time for one more kiss.

Marcus could see it was getting dark and he had yet to ride home. It was a school night. "Gotta go."

"Are you sure you can't stay all night," Barbara asked breathlessly.

"Sorry, but my parents will wonder where I am," he said.

They sat, side-by-side on the couch for a few minutes before Marcus stood and dressed. She then stood and made a show of putting on a wispy, short bedtime top.

Breathtaking.

"With a body like that you could rule the world."

"Think so, Marcus?" she whispered huskily, playing up his attention.

"You are the most beautiful girl I have ever seen, better looking than most movie stars." Marcus said it like he meant it, which surprised even him. Sincerity wasn't his thing.

Barbara stood for a second with a look of surprise, blushing at his profound compliment. "That's... that's... so sweet." She gave him an affectionate hug and kiss. "You come back to see me real soon Marcus Deering."

"I just might do that," Marcus replied, meaning it.

He said his goodbyes, hopped on his bike and headed home, which wasn't far away. On the ride he thought about Barbara and their wild evening. It was a night to remember.

He was home and through the door and headed for a shower. Hopefully his folks wouldn't grill him over tonight's shenanigans.

"Did you have a nice ride, Marcus?" his mom called up to him.

"You have no idea, Mom," Marcus mumbled, fighting to hide the huge, silly smile on his face. "Best ride, ever."

He trained like a demon all that week. Sunday, he feigned sickness to skip church. As soon as his family left, he popped out of bed, quickly dressed and appeared at the local bike race at ten a.m., barely.

The other riders didn't make the connection between last week's hick and today's road warrior. This time Marcus was armed with some training, Julie's coaching tips, a better bike, a new sense of confidence and no relation to the cycling bumpkin of last week.

After quickly signing on, he climbed on his bike and drifted into the crowd of cyclists, invisible. The starter yelled, "go!" The group started the road race and quickly accelerated up to speed. After a few minutes he realized at a glance, where he should be and what he should do in this race. Julie said: *Front is best and back is death.*

This was a revelation.

He worked through the riders like he was swimming through a school of fish and was soon with the front three leaders. Marcus then stood on his pedals and rode away. He easily came in first, minutes ahead of the puffing, sweating, and embarrassed pack of riders.

The other riders were shocked at how this inexperienced rider could beat them so easily. They made various excuses—some even made veiled cheating allegations which were immediately squelched by the race referee.

Who was this new guy? Parents and friends were shocked and impressed by this "Boy Wonder".

His parents were also impressed, glad to see Marcus had finally found something he was good at. They relented and allowed him to skip church for racing. He had their acceptance.

He went on to have an impressive season. It didn't take long until news of this exceptional "natural" cyclist got around. Offers of new bikes and equipment rolled in before he knew it. Soon Marcus had the bike and clothing to make him look like the latest bike racer. His natural ability allowed him to race larger and larger events.

He went from top junior to top elite, flying up the ranks—from Zero to Hero in seven years.

He always made sure he travelled with his team to avoid traveling to a race in the embarrassing family van. He ignored his family whenever a race was close to his hometown. Cycling was his ticket out and he was not going to bring any small-town memories with him. His family ceased to exist for Marcus—his parents knew this; Elvin did not.

And then Marcus became a real, live European Pro rider.

Marcus thought back to his first truly big win, becoming the champion of all the world. He stood on top of the podium, looking down on everyone with tears streaming down his face. Everyone was in tears. His competitors looked up at him with tears of envy, anger and disappointment. Marcus had stolen their dreams and crushed their hearts.

His magic moment.

Marcus never tired of thinking back to that day. He was the king. There was no other way to describe it. His win came as a huge surprise to everyone. It was a lucky, lone escape with bad weather and distracted teams only paying attention to each other. Just a no hoper, brash, mouthy American. While the cats fought amongst themselves, the mouse got away in the rain.

Once he had a few minutes lead, the pack was unable to catch him in time. Coming across the finish line, alone with his hands held high in air, was a glorious feeling! He remembered it so well. It made him smile and his adrenaline pump.

He didn't care that back home in America few noticed his triumph. They thought of cycling as obscure as yak racing. Bike riders were peculiar looking athletes, attired in skin-tight spandex, doing strange things on bicycles. It was as out of place as ice hockey was in Egypt or curling in Brazil. Bizarre.

Despite the public's lack of interest, a few American cyclists could be as hardcore and obsessed as anything across the pond where cycling was the rage and passion. They were willing to toil through the local low budget so-called professional ranks with the hopes of moving up to real pro teams, to make their fame and fortune—realize their professional dreams.

Marcus Deering became one such successful American rider.

After he won the Worlds, a Dutch team was so impressed they hired him on the spot as their team leader. ProTour! He received a lot more money, new bikes, new equipment and raced two hundred fifty of the best races in the world in his first year.

All this was pretty heady stuff for a twenty-one-year-old.

Marcus proved he was no flash in the pan by picking up some wins in the early season one-day classics. These were the 'hard' races of the early spring in cold rain, greasy roads, crashes and mud. He proved he was up to the challenge.

His team had him do a few early stages of the Tour de France in each of those two years, asking him to drop out to spare him from the dreaded mountains. Climbing the Alps was not good for a young rider and Marcus was not used to riding as a stage racer quite yet.

The next year, his team director promised. He would be the leader of the team for the greatest sporting event in the world.

Marcus lived the nomadic life of a professional athlete in Europe. It was a constant stream of various hotel rooms that went with two hundred and fifty races, from February to October. There was a different language to deal with every week in the international melting pot that cycling had become.

He was a stranger in a strange land, but he thrived on it.

Everyone knew who he was. Groupie's threw themselves at the riders, vying for their attentions in much the same way they did for American Basketball players and other pro sports back home.

He made a hundred grand a year, which was decent for a sport like cycling. A Tour De France win could turn that into million-dollar contracts with endorsements. There was no place to go but up as he became more established, faster and better known.

At the end of each season he moved back to his Tucson mountain home in the USA for the winter. Marcus made sure it was a beautiful house with his old, hated home-town of Adobe barely in the distance, way down below. He could look at it and scoff with derision whenever he wanted.

It was back to American food with his good old fashion American drawl. He rode his mountain bike on the trails and ate his meals in local restaurants in relative obscurity. Nobody in the States knew or cared who Marcus Deering was. Who cared about those spandex-wearing weirdos, anyway?

Finally, he had the life he always wanted but there was a chilling setback on the horizon, heading his way.

The setback started subtly. He began getting odd pains and unexplained weakness. Normal fatigue never went away as it should have, making recovery from training and racing a little more difficult with each race. He did his best to ignore it, thinking it was a passing ache or pain from the long, hard racing season. While towelling off after a shower one day, in the mirror he spied a large, funny looking mole on his back and finally gave in and went to the doctor. He was pretty sure the mole was something new, but his back was not an area he regularly looked at and his various girlfriends were never around long enough to make that judgement.

Cancer!

A doctor had it pegged at an aggressive form of skin cancer from sun exposure while cycling all those years. This cancer was serious and spreading rapidly.

Sorry, terminal.

They told him there was no hope—"Get your affairs in order". They thought he might last until February and it was already January. Sorry. Then came the line of quacks claiming a secret potion—for a price.

He wearily stood in the window of his home thinking cancer was a terrible way to die. Doctors milked away his hopes and money with stories of a promising discovery here and a chancy a new medication there. Marcus soon had very little left.

It still pissed him off thinking about how his fortunes dropped. His Dutch team quickly rid him from their roster—a sick rider was an expensive liability. Few professional teams of any sport tolerate a lame duck athlete on their team. It cost them time and money.

There were a dozen riders waiting to take his spot for a fraction of his wage.

The normal drill was—meet with the athlete, show the contract everyone signed, noting the fine print saying not riding meant termination and give the rider the boot. This time, they got him to sign the waiver to be rid of him from his hospital bed after he'd received the latest futile operation. *Wake up! Sign here!* It was like signing a deathbed confession, humiliating and cheap.

That also meant he no longer received the bonus free European medical insurance. As soon as his prospects dried up, he was forced to return to his origins back in the USA, home of the free, land of the brave—with the highest medical premiums in the world that absolutely did not covering Marcus. You pay for your medical out of your own pocket or die. Free enterprise. Business was business and nothing personal.

If he were a millionaire he could have cared less but he wasn't.

Dying was a long, painful road and he could already see the end. Death was just around the corner. Painfully, he shuffled to the front door of his house in time to see the backend of a heavily loaded postman making his rounds. Undoubtedly medical bills and the latest tests confirmed he had only weeks to live and "Be sure to pay us before you expire".

People around him quickly cut their ties with him. In the past, Marcus had proven to be a tiresome glory hound at best and a cruel egomaniac at worst. Asshole. Nobody hung around him by choice. His good-bye letters were more like "good riddance". His life was winding down even though he was relatively young.

His younger brother Elvin was the only one who showed concern these days, but Marcus screened out his calls. He despised Elvin's embarrassing small-town bumpkin life, annoyed at how his little brother insisted on staying, seemingly content, in the town he'd grown up in, now looking after their aging parents. Elvin still slept in the same bedroom in the family home that he'd shared with Marcus years ago.

Elvin explained his reasoning—this way he could help his parents along with the farm and the house. It was live at home *with them* or put them "into a home"—and that he could not bear. Seeing their parents still independent was the source of Elvin's happiness and all else was secondary.

Elvin's talent proved to be in carpentry. There was nothing he couldn't manufacture and build out of wood. He renovated most of the houses in the area and he was the first one people called when they needed help. Elvin felt great satisfaction at a job well done...

Bored already, Marcus swept these thoughts of his brother from his mind and settled instead on reviewing fond memories from his own life. He enjoyed thinking back to those early days of cycling and his time with Barbara. Those were the days. Though he struggled against it, these pleasant thoughts were soon ended when another wave of nausea swept over him and he fought the urge to throw up. There was not much left to vomit, anyway.

He could eat very little these days. He'd always been skinny but now he was down to just skin and bones. Even his hair was gone. Now it was a struggle to lurch dizzily from one empty room to another in his house.

Marcus would sell his soul to get better and to ride his bike, again. "What's my shitty soul worth these days?" he snorted out loud.

All he had to look forward to was wasting away at the tender age of twenty-three. The obituaries of some newspaper might report the death of an ex-world champion in an obscure sport. The article would be in the fine print, buried in the back pages. Who cared who Marcus What's-His-Name was, anyway, the guy who got bumped from Jimmy Kimmel for the Hula Hoop inventor.

He felt crushed, watching his life ebb away and there was nothing he could do. Utterly alone, he waited to meet his maker. He gazed out the window with tears rolling down his cheeks. Death in a few weeks was all he was certain of. Who would even find his body? Would some workman or a postman complain about the bad smell or mail not being picked up? Would the police or a bill collector forced open his door to find his emaciated body? It was all so dreadful, wretched and as humiliating as it could possibly be.

Helpless to change anything, Marcus sat, awaiting the end. At least oblivion was better than these awful remains of a life he suffered through. Marcus dozed off, slumped in the chair, dreaming of getting his life back and hoping this was all just a nightmare.

Windy draft. Cold. Marcus awoke with a start. He could see the screen door off the snowy sun deck was open and a chilling breeze coursed through the house. Slowly and painfully he struggled to his feet, swaying for a moment, testing to see if he could stay upright before attempting to move. Stooped over, he dragged his feet slowly, step by uncertain step, across the carpet and shut the door, ignoring the errant snow that had escaped inside.

"Damned wind," he mumbled to himself.

"Feeling lonely and abandoned, Marcus?" said a cheery female voice from behind him.

Marcus turned painfully around in surprise, despite his nausea and dizziness. Seated in a nearby chair was his old childhood sweetheart Barbara Stellina!

He stared at her in disbelief. Her face, her exquisite body, her beautiful eye lashes were the same as when he'd known her so many years ago. It was as if she hadn't aged a second but her warm and friendly gaze had changed into something hidden and perhaps... sinister? Were the cancer drugs making him see things?

He gazed at Barbara in wonderment. She was formally dressed in a perfect old-fashioned long black Sunday dress. It had a tight, high neck, as if she came from a special church ceremony. She had a little round hat on her perfect hair to match her shiny black shoes. Her deathly white pale face was heavily made up. Unusual for her. Was that a tiny black veil?

Marcus snapped out of his morbid thoughts and asked, "Are you really... Barbara?"

Something about this person claiming to be Barbara was different. Her stony gaze was unblinking, calm and confident with a powerful eye contact that seemed bottomless, searching for something in his soul. Pitiless.

She assessed Marcus with a chilling laser focus. "My image is whatever you wish it to be. In this case it's... Barbara Stellina. Is this offensive?"

"Not at all. We were..." he stopped, uncertain. "Barbara and I were... great pals, years ago."

"Were you...intimate?" Barbara asked, with a knowing smile, eyes on him intensely.

"Well, yes, on occasion."

"Ah." She seemed barely interested.

"Aren't you... Barbara?"

Her answer was a harsh cackle.

"What?" His mind reeled. "You — you aren't Barbara?"

"No, I'm not. I'm a stranger here to help."

"A stranger? Then *who* are you?"

Barbara spoke without emotion. Matter-of-factly. "Who I am depends on your point of view. I could be death, or I could be your second chance."

It took some seconds as Marcus grasped the monstrous purpose of her appearance. "H-how did you get in here? How - how do you know me?" stuttered Marcus, breaking out in a chilling sweat.

"Let's say I can get around when and where I please. And you could say I know everybody, including you," 'Barbara' replied, her smile mirthless.

"Why are you here?" asked Marcus shakily. "What if I called the police?"

"Go ahead and make the call. I'll be gone when they get here, and you will be dead in sixteen days." Barbara tilted her head slyly. "Maybe I'm not even here?"

Marcus gulped as he considered calling the police on this weirdo but wasn't so sure he could operate his cell phone. He was so shaky and weak—was Barbara a drug hallucination? A waking dream? He stood in stunned silence, hardly believing what he was seeing and hearing. Maybe this will pass. Marcus slowly raised his hand and weakly slapped his own cheeks. Nothing changed. Barbara sat in the chair, watching him sweat and totter around, confused and anxious, slapping his own cheeks, mumbling to himself.

Finally, Marcus pulled himself together and croaked, "Are you still here?"

"I never left."

"So?"

"Marcus; you will be dead in sixteen days and they'll find your stinking corpse sixty-four days later. Your body will be dumped in a pauper's grave because only the single person who cared for you knows of your death while the rest hate you. What's the glory in that, Mr. Deering? An anonymous hole in the ground to weed over and Marcus Deering will be forgotten for millennia." She paused, considering. "I can show you on your TV if you're interested."

"No! What will happen to... my soul?" Marcus asked, barely making it to the nearest chair before his legs gave out.

Barbara watched him, then shrugged. "That's not my department, as they say. Where do you suspect it will go?"

Marcus was short of breath. "I'd like to think my soul goes to heaven. I *did* go to church."

"A community, personal deeds and friends are the judges of how a life is lived, not just standing in a designated building once a week. I have an endless supply of "godly" ministers and church goers feeding the furnaces. Trust me—Hell will never freeze over."

"So maybe I'm headed... south... instead? Does it really matter?"

Barbara gently shrugged, unblinking. "It matters not to me where you'll go, right now. Think of what could be, Marcus. Think!"

"Do you have an alternative to... my imminent death?"

"Yes, I do. I came with a proposition, Marcus. I'm the answer to your hopes and dreams. You'll be rich and famous. A celebrity... household name."

Marcus waited for a minute and asked, fearing the answer. "What do *you* want in return?"

She smiled boldly. "It's not what I want; it's what I *require* from you."

Marcus swallowed hard. "What... is it?"

"Come-come, Marcus. Are you a fool? You can only truly own one thing... your soul!"

Marcus paled further under her powerful gaze. "Um...so you are...the..."

Barbara's eyes glowered and her voice rose in power and depth, roaring, shaking the windows all around him, rattling the china in the cupboards, sending his wall-mounted pictures crashing to the floor. *"Do you wish me to grow horns and a tail? Spit fire?"*

Marcus shrank into his seat, terrified.

She calmed and smiled sweetly, coyly, just like Barbara always had in his memories. "As I said, I am here to help. I have resources you can't imagine. You can be healed as good as new and be able to go on to unimagined success beyond your wildest dreams, top of the world for ten years. At the end of those ten years, we meet again, back at Tisdale Park in your old hometown. You remember Tisdale Park, don't you? You got up to all sorts of shenanigans in that park, if what my people tell me is correct."

Marcus shuttered at the idea his life was so well known in this way, but quickly shook it away to think clearly for a few seconds. He was a dead man, waiting to fall down and be buried. Another ten years to live? What choice did he have? He shifted forward, balanced precariously on the edge of his chair, swaying weakly.

"You take my soul in Tisdale Park in ten years?"

"That's the deal. Take it or leave it."

"Why Tisdale Park?"

"I like it there. The roses will be out. Do you prefer the Wal-Mart parking lot?"

He bleated, "Tisdale is fine. Yes. Let's do it."

"Was that *yes*, Marcus Deering?" she asked, sounding surprised, slowly standing imperiously.

He paused. "Yes...yes, I-I did say yes," he confirmed, nodding, gasping, forcing the last of his strength into his legs to stand, to reach out and grasp her hand.

She put her warm sweet hand into his. "Congratulations," she said, leaning into his face with a warm kiss, like the old days, when they were lovers.

For a moment he felt like a young man again. Barbara's sweet kiss warmed his heart. Her lips slid over his cheek, her tongue licking gentle circles on his ear, surprising him. She started playfully sucking his ear lobe then bit it hard, savagely, with sharp teeth. Chomp!

"Ouch! What are you doing!" he shouted, stepping back and putting his hand to his ear, feeling warm wetness. Looking at his hand he was shocked to see it was bloody.

"Tasty!" Barbara declared, languidly licking his blood off her lips and teeth, savoring. "Gentleman shake hands—a blood bond is forever." She laughed at him.

Horrified, Marcus stared at the blood on his hand with a sinking dread this pact could never be changed. He stuttered, "N-now what?"

"You do nothing. Go on with your life and I'll do the rest."

"For how long?"

"Ten years. You can be the person you always wanted to be, for better or worse," she answered matter-of-factly, rising to her feet. "I must go."

Marcus looked at her, mystified.

She smiled. "You received the gift of life at no cost to you...at least monetary. Some men and women use this gift for redemption, humanity, to make a better world. One became a nun. I'm having a tough time getting payment from that one but we have many lawyers working on it."

Marcus would have laughed if the joke had been made by anyone else. "I can imagine."

"What will be your legacy, Marcus?"

He squirmed under her scrutiny. "I... don't know."

She nodded, turned and headed for the sun deck door, reaching for the knob but hesitated and turned back. "A caution to you... fine print if you will. This isn't super-powers. The bus will kill you if you get run over. Be smart."

"I'll keep that in mind."

Barbara looked him in the eye. "Are you not curious *why* I look like your old love Barbara Stellina?"

Marcus was already shaking his head, "*No...no.*" He was afraid of the answer.

Barbara reached to her forehead and wiped away a bit of makeup, revealing a bloody bullet hole in her skull. She made a point of standing close to him while sticking her finger in the hole.

Marcus leaned back, scrambling to catch his balance, horrified at the sight. "G-get away from me!"

"A reminder. Barbara took your advice and got out of that little town. We made a deal and she became a notorious stripper and got shot right here. I got her early. Choose wisely Marcus."

"No..."

"If you'd taken an interest and come to her funeral, you'd have recognized her funeral dress. Do you like it?" Barbara closed her eyes and stood motionless.

"Nooooo!" Marcus collapsed to the floor in horror and lost himself.

He awoke on his floor, shaking. What had he done... or had it really happened? He turned his head, searching his surroundings fearfully, his gaze landing on Barbara's little black hat and veil lying on the carpet beside him. He shuddered in revulsion, knowing it was all true.

After crawling to the couch to get back on his feet, he limped over to close the sundeck door to keep out the blowing snow, then dragged himself into his bedroom. He fell onto the bed and had the best sleep he'd had for months. Waking up was a bonus.

He felt hungry and didn't throw up.

A miracle coming or just a nightmare?

Starting the next day Marcus felt the deadly cancerous effects leaving him. He felt better and looked better every day.

His doctors patted each other on the backs for saving his life, offering gigantic medical bills. Marcus laughed and threw them back in their faces. He stopped all the chemo drugs. "Someone" was looking after him. It was an amazing recovery, any way you looked at it.

Marcus resumed cycling within the month. After six months of sickness his legs had no strength and his body no endurance. He was being passed on the hill by the slowest riders. Marcus was so appalled and disgusted that he pulled over into a ditch and cried.

Was this as good as he got? Had "Barbara" tricked him, given him a fate much worse than death? But his weight and strength came back over the next six months, at a steady but unremarkable rate so as not to raise suspicion. Who'd believe his "soul" story, anyway?

As he trained, he was able to ride more and more miles. It was a slow improvement at first but started to pick up gains, finally riding with his team and eventually keeping up. He had never appreciated his strength and skill until it was gone. The smell and sight of the scenery, the sounds of the bike tires on the road and the birds in the trees were all sweeter this second time around.

He found himself being friendly and gracious to his team-mates, at least for a little while.

That spring he did a couple of North American races with excellent results. Initially, he was considered damaged goods so some team directors were cautious about signing him, despite his promising early season. Possibilities. He won Beauce and Gila. Teams started approaching him once again to see what he could do in Europe.

His big break came in early April. The AVIA-Ford team took a chance on him and signed him up for a low base salary with "bonuses"—cycling-team speak for "you only get paid when you win something for our team". Marcus made sure he won something very soon.

A close third overall finish in an Italian stage race shook up the cycling establishment. Was Marcus Deering too good to be true?

It took Marcus a few years, but his name was on everyone's lips now. Team offers poured in, but he stuck with AVIA-Ford—they'd promised he'd be a direct advisor to team management. Marcus was now able to influence who was selected for the team, equipment, sponsors and what races they attended.

The boss.

Manufacturers from all over the world lined up with gifts of the latest bikes and clothing. They built custom machines for him, to ensure he'd win the big races as well as the Tour De France on their equipment.

Marcus and his team did very well, right from the start of that new season. He had an eye for a talented team and knew "doctors" who tinkered with their riders' physiology to make them faster and tireless. His riders were well paid and ordered to perform and ask no questions about what was given to them.

Other riders called his doctored team "The Vampires".

After five years of re-climbing the cycling ladder with a lot of success and publicity, Marcus finally won the big one, the Tour De France—and in a brilliant fashion. He stayed in contact with the top two leaders, then beat them on the last mountain stage to steal the lead, sealing it with a win in the final time-trial. The cycling world was amazed but still skeptical. Some of the best hadn't ridden this year. A soft win.

Marcus could hardly believe it himself, standing on the podium with the Tour Trophy. It was a dream! The entire world looked up at him on the podium and on TV as the winner of the greatest bike race in the world. The bands played, the President of France shook his hand and Paris looked at him with envy.

Pity it was not a Frenchman but what can you do?

After a solid road season Marcus was ready for his Tour defense. This year's Tour was considered a showdown of the best. Anyone who was anyone would be there. Past winners and future stars intended on making the Tour very difficult for this brash American to repeat his "easy" win.

Marcus and his powerful team repeated the Tour to win by an even more convincing margin. He stood atop the podium with his trophy held high over his head feeling a pride and confidence he'd never felt before. He felt like the all-powerful master of all he surveyed.

He was their Adonis.

His life was even more spectacularly successful after that second Tour win. American TV talk show hosts sought him out, he did movie cameos and was recognized on the street all over the states. Marcus was the star of the land—there was nothing he couldn't do, and he did anything he could have imagined.

His churning publicity machine made Marcus a household name, earning him tens of millions of dollars in endorsements for everything from high-end running shoes to men's deodorant. With Marcus Deerings' name attached, the sponsor's products sales soared, guaranteed.

Catherine, his girlfriend, was a movie star featured regularly in Playboy and porn movies. She was utterly beautiful in every way, especially when they were alone. In private, she had an unexpected sweet graciousness that made their time together very special. The truth was, she reminded him of Barbara, but he'd never admit it. Despite her beauty and faithfulness, he slyly watched for other girls on the side.

Even National Enquirer magazine snooped around and did a story on him running around the night clubs in the off season. There were many women who couldn't drop their pants fast enough for the rich and famous Marcus Deering.

He now had a view of the world very few could imagine. Movie stars, Senators, even Presidents made sure they had a photo taken with Marcus. "Who's that man standing with Marcus Deering?" "Oh, that's the President!" Marcus Deering was the king and he had his loyal subjects to do his bidding.

He won everything worth winning efficiently and ruthlessly.

This was his sixth Tour De France since he'd beat cancer. He'd won the first five handily but this one felt different. Something about this one made him uneasy.

It was months past the deadline "Barbara" had set for him to pay up, so he made sure he was never alone to avoid facing her. *Keep moving* was his plan, *never go home, never linger long*—where he was certain she would be waiting for him. It was working so far...

Marcus was on the edge of something he'd never thought he'd be able to do—*six* Tour wins— achieving the impossible. He'd won yesterday's Tour De France stage by 30 seconds. If he could hold that to Sunday's final sprint stage, then the Tour was his. Fail on Friday's climbing stage and it was over.

All Tour De France races were tough and unique, three weeks of racing almost every day. The time used on each day's race, called a stage, accumulated for the total event. The rider with the lowest total time was the winner.

This year's race was not going as well as he had hoped—his team was having trouble with riders crashing and wearing out far too early. Nor were they excited about helping him win, a grumbling under their breath growing in volume on how he treated them. Unhappy Vampires. His faithful lieutenant, Kerry Hampton, was tired of being the butt of all Marcus complaints about their team's performance. Things were not going well at AVIA-Ford.

Most disturbing of all was what Marcus witnessed in yesterday's stage. While riding through an avalanche of fans in a midsized French town, he was almost certain he'd caught sight of Barbara in the crowd, clan in her funeral dress, angrily pointing her finger at him. Marcus had something that belonged to her and she wanted it badly.

There was no more denying it—their ten-year anniversary was past.

He knew he was on borrowed time—what harm could it cause? Push it to its limit, go another year or so? It wasn't like she could kill him off, as far as he knew, anyway. Could she?

Right now, he had bigger fish to fry. Concentrate. Marcus had to think how he'd approach tomorrow's stage. The truth was, Thursday's race had worn him down to a nub and his entire team was exhausted. Freddie and Benito specialized in the steep mountain climbs, but Freddie was badly bruised from a crash and Benito, an older rider, was fading fast, his days numbered. Kerry was valiantly pulling Marcus in the big stages but just didn't have the juice like he used to. Younger horses were needed.

Both Benito and Kerry would be replaced with younger, stronger riders next year, but for now, they had no idea of Marcus's future plans for them. They'd be abandoned like race-horses with broken legs.

Sensing weakness, Marcus's competitors would be ready to pounce. They'd make their plans about leading the pack into the hills, stringing out riders for miles. The last climbing stage was up the steep and final Alp D'Huez. On those slopes a dozen of the worlds' elite would work together to rid themselves of that pompous jerk Marcus Deering when he was alone and vulnerable.

He knew he needed help. It was not that his body or fitness was failing him. He was still as good as any other top rider. He needed a boost, an overdrive, something that could allow him a vital thirty seconds jump.

All sports have their drugs of choice and cycling was no different with EPO being their "go juice". Cycling officials ruthlessly tested for it but some years the so called "doctors" were a step ahead—and the dopers held the Jersey in Paris.

Marcus had a "friend" of his team doctor had access to EPO, the cyclist endurance drug of choice. A cyclist was a red blood cell cardio machine and EPO artificially re-built it. The problem was the dope control commissaire would get the rider's urine sample and ship it to the lab right after the race and the rider would be busted and banned for five years, second offense twenty years. Gotcha!

Most EPO comes from China, Marcus knew, so it was made with little in the way of regulations, tracing or government interest. Better yet, the US and WADA, the World Anti-Doping Agency authorities have little contact with the manufacturers so their supplier web would remain a secret.

The team doctor arranged for a meeting between Marcus and the EPO supplier in the back of a nearby hotel to discuss the details. Marcus's doctor told him, for a price, this batch could be special and untraceable. It would be put in Marcus's own bag of blood he had previously saved for just such an occasion. That bag would contain a special masking agent that would allow the EPO to be untraceable when the test was done—there was no present testing method that could make a positive finding—this version of EPO masking was brand-new on the market.

Only one drawback—it had to be kept cool or it *would* become traceable.

The doctor stressed the importance protecting the transfusion—refrigeration at 30 degrees. Once the blood/EPO bag was safely inside a specialized fridge, nobody must open it until exactly thirty minutes before race time, when Marcus would receive the transfusion from the "doctor" and hurry to the race start. The timeline was tight. The transfusion's magical effects would wear off as the race continued. Any failure in this procedure and all would be lost, and Marcus would be paraded around as a drug cheat.

It was all arranged. The "doctor" would have a little fridge containing the blood/EPO bag installed in Marcus's room and safely taped shut, tonight at six p.m. while the team was at supper. This "Vitamin Fridge" would be placed next to his regular room fridge, which contained his energy drinks and milk. But, Marcus really needed someone to guard that fridge and keep their mouth shut.

Who could be trusted with this magic potion?

Marcus would have to think about the best way to keep and guard the fridge with his dope, have the "doc" administer it to him within the time period and get to the race start. Deep in thought, he left the room for the team bus. He jumped and cringed when he heard a familiar shout behind him. His loser brother Elvin! How was he even here?

"Hey Marcus!" gushed Elvin, eyes glowing with pride for his big brother. "How are you doing?"

"Fine, Elvin," grumbled Marcus, looking already for an escape.

"Isn't this the most amazing event, ever?"

Marcus walked away from him, already feeling weighed down by Elvin's cloying adoration.

Elvin was his only brother—and still such a hick!

———

Elvin knew he wasn't the sharpest tool in the shed, knew he didn't get out of their little hometown nearly often enough. So he was a bit "unworldly"? It didn't bother him. It didn't even bother him when Marcus was sometimes mean to him in front of friends and family. Elvin guessed it was because to Marcus, Elvin represented all that Marcus despised about their humble beginnings. A reminder. That was okay—everyone had their personal hang-ups.

Elvin didn't mind when Marcus never called him—or returned his calls. When the hometown folks asked after Marcus, Elvin's ready reply would be, "Oh, he's crazy busy training" or "He must be out of cell range". The truth was Marcus could do no wrong as far as Elvin was concerned.

For years now, it was one of Elvin's great wishes to watch his big brother ride the Tour. He followed every minute of it, on TV, and read as many magazines about it as he could find. Finally, he decided he had to go to France and see this amazing race for himself. He saved money from his carpentry earnings, lived at home and spent very little. It would be a trip of a lifetime! Nobody could talk him out of it, and oh, did they try—especially their parents. Elvin was not to be deterred.

Elvin's parents were worried—they'd had seen the animosity between Marcus and Elvin from an early age. Marcus always had his head in the clouds and was not going to stay and be a 'hick' in a small town, while little Elvin hung on his brother's every word. As soon as he could, Marcus made good his escape through cycling, while young Elvin stayed far behind.

His parents called their famous son, Marcus Deering as often as they could, to hear how he was doing, trying to connect, but Marcus could hardly be bothered returning their messages. They endured it wordlessly, like solid quiet parents do. They felt their kids had some growing up to do and let them go about it with minimal fuss or nagging.

Meanwhile, Elvin went to a travel agent and told them he wanted to see his big brother at the Tour!

The travel agent set him up on a Tour De France all-inclusive and here he was, watching his big brother in the biggest sporting spectacle on earth. Now that he was here, in person, he could see it was even bigger than he'd ever imagined.

———

M arcus was horrified when Elvin showed up at the race start! The last thing he wanted was to be tour guide for his little brother!

At first, he avoided Elvin like the plague. That worked for a while but it was obvious he'd hurt his little brother's feelings. Even *his* ice-cold heart could see it in Elvin's face.

When Elvin hugged Marcus on his Thursday stages' triumph, almost in tears in front of all the TV cameras, Marcus was horribly embarrassed. He *never* showed emotion at these big races! "Some other time, Elvin! I'm kinda busy right now," Marcus said through clenched teeth, pushing him back into the crowd, before he turned determinedly back to the interviewer.

Dozens of "Tour hero" interviews followed, with all the predictable questions. He tried hard to address each as if this was the first time the unoriginal question had been asked. "Will the French press ever leave you alone?" or "What do you say to the charges that you doped to win?" Marcus answered each question in turn, clearly and professionally, not letting them under his skin. Then, suddenly, in the middle of the gazillionth boring interview, he had a stroke of genius. He broke into a huge grin and looked around at the media people, seeing them for the first time as if they were his best friends. Graciously and quickly, he ended the interview with the excuse he needed to return to his team bus.

Elvin could be the guardian of his little bag of "insurance" for tomorrow's stage! There was no one better for the job!

He knew he needed to make amends with Elvin to make this happen. The media crowd moved on to some of the other riders, allowing Marcus to make his way the team bus where he showered and got cleaned up. As was his habit, after the shower, he paid special attention to his toenails, shaved any hair off his legs that was appearing and checked himself for saddle sores.

Soon he was lounging in a comfy chair with a recovery drink and a banana. "A cyclist never stood when he could sit and never sat if he could lie down". Life was good. Marcus looked over at Kerry Hampton, who'd had an especially hard day and looked fried.

Kerry Hampton slouched on the bench, changing into dry clothes very slowly. He was truly spent. It had been another very hard day in the service of the famous Marcus Deering and Marcus knew Kerry was the team rider who gave the most effort each and every day. Kerry's word was his bond and all the other riders looked up to him. This pissed Marcus off to no end. Who was paying the bills on this team, anyway?

When Marcus won, he loved basking in the glory, sharing how brilliant he was. But when he didn't win, he always made sure to lay the blame where it belonged—with the team—always through Kerry. There was no love lost between them, but Kerry did always show a professional courtesy.

"Kerry! Do me a favor before you go back to the hotel?" asked Marcus.

———

"Sure," replied Kerry. *Uh–oh!*
"At the end of the block you'll see Elvin. Bring him over here for me."

"Sure... Anything wrong?" asked Kerry suspiciously.

"Just bring him. He's on the curb."

Kerry raised his eyebrows and grimaced. "Shall do." Stifling a groan, he pushed stiffly from his seat, and was off, ambling out of the bus and down the block.

Kerry knew Elvin from Marcus's years rising in the amateur ranks. Elvin was rarely far behind, helping pass out water and food, driving and doing anything that needed to be done. Marcus invariably treated him shabbily, like he was some sort of valet or peon. Kerry was an only child and would have loved to have a brother or a sister.

Kerry could see Elvin ahead on the curb. He looked crushed. Kerry recalled Marcus dismissing his beamingly proud younger brother and shook his head. Marcus could be such an asshole, sometimes—even most of the time, for that matter.

He eased down to sit beside Elvin on the curb. "Hey, Elvin. How's it going?"

Elvin glanced up and quickly mopped his tears off his face with his hands. He seemed relieved to see a friendly face.

"Hi Kerry. I guess I screwed up. Marcus isn't very happy with me. Maybe I shouldn't have come all this way—but it's the *Tour De France* and *my big brother* is in it!" He shrugged his shoulders and added forlornly, "I just had to see it at least once."

"It's ok, Elvin. You just caught Marcus at a bad time, that's all. I'm sure it isn't a huge deal," Kerry lied.

"It's like Marcus is embarrassed to have me here—he doesn't introduce me to his team or his friends or anything. When he sees me in the crowd, his eyes just skip over me, like I'm nobody. The only reason I know *you* is because I've known you since before Marcus made pro."

Kerry remembered a long time ago when *he* was the top rider and Marcus was the newest rising star. He also remembered the utterly devoted little brother Elvin had been, following Marcus everywhere. He'd thought Elvin was a sweet, kind kid, doing everything he could to help in his own, awkward way, which, of course, drove Marcus crazy.

Marcus had always been a prima donna, and on many occasions, just a prick. The world revolved around him and he loved it. A hick little brother was no asset to someone as pretentious as Marcus.

Kerry remembered back to a time when a TV camera crew did an interview with Elvin, at the Tour of California. Elvin gushed for the camera about how proud he was and how he thought Marcus was the best bike rider in the world. He added that the French press should leave his brother alone! Marcus had been horrified and forbid Elvin to ever speak to the media again. Elvin went home after that and had stayed away from Marcus and his cycling events for years—until now—finally deciding to come and watch, try one more time.

"Elvin, Marcus feels like a knob, the way he treated you back there and he's really sorry," Kerry lied again, "and he wants you to come on back to the team bus and see him. What do you say?" Kerry felt awful, lying like this. He might just be setting up Elvin for a fall, but there was always the chance Marcus had finally had a change of heart but that was unlikely.

"Marcus wants to see me?" Elvin asked, surprised.

"That's what he told me," Kerry assured. "Come on, let's go see him."

Kerry was hoping this was not some new way to humiliate Elvin. Pay cheque or no pay cheque, Kerry was getting tired of performing for the famous Marcus Deering.

They both walked over to the team bus and it was very obvious that Elvin was immediately impressed. He might have expected an old Greyhound or a school bus and this was a luxury bus for rock stars!

Marcus was at the back—a king on his throne, surrounded by women, jesters and advisors. He waved Elvin forward with a friendly smile, dismissing Kerry and the rest with a casual wave of the hand.

Kerry was not sad to go. *Will I go to hell for this?*

———

"Hi Elvin, sorry for losing my cool back there. I was baked and they were badgering me with a bunch of stupid questions," Marcus began.

"It's ok, Marcus, you're under a lot of pressure. You're doing well, right?" Elvin rushed to reply, clearly thrilled to be here talking to a rich and famous person, his brother the famous Marcus Deering.

"Yeah, I have a little lead going into the final Alp stage," Marcus answered, watching his brother's face carefully. "It's going to be tough. My team is worn out, and the other teams are all gunning for me.

We'll know by this time, tomorrow." Marcus ended with a weary smile. He was happy to see Elvin ate it up. Perfect.

"Well, this is awesome to see you in action! I've never to Europe before, and now, because of you, I'm here!" grinned Elvin.

Marcus glanced around the bus to make sure nobody heard what he was about to say. "Elvin, I need a bit of help and I don't know who to trust," he said with an air of conspiracy.

"Gosh Marcus, you can count on me!" said Elvin.

"I knew I could." Marcus smiled. "Let's meet over at my room—#22—across the street there, in maybe an hour?"

An hour later, Marcus was touring his little brother through his room, mending fences. This was working out so well… He almost felt a pang of guilt.

"Wow! This is a really nice room for France!" declared Elvin, "My room's a dump compared to this!"

"Yeah, you just have to know a few people to get something decent over here," Marcus agreed smugly.

"So, all I have to do is keep this little fridge closed and sealed. Don't let anyone else open it, right? There's a regular fridge next to it you can use," Elvin recited.

"That's all you have to do."

"Or your vitamins will go bad and you'll lose the stage, tomorrow?"

"Correct."

"I'll guard it with my life, Marcus!" Elvin vowed vehemently.

"I did tape the door shut so there will be no mistaking it for the other fridge and we can make sure it did not get opened," Marcus pointed out.

"So, I'll just hang out until you get back. Are you going to be late?"

"Yes, I have a late team meeting so don't wait up. Use this room and sleep here, tonight, and I'll have the other one. I'll try not to wake you up when I get back." Marcus's "team meeting" was with a couple of cute podium girls. Losing a bit of sweat and bodily fluids always made Marcus a bit faster on the climbs. He cheated on Catherine all the time. So what?

"Sure thing," assured Elvin. "See you later."

Marcus was out the door and off to see the girls. Podium Girls were forbidden to go out with bike riders, but Marcus wasn't hemmed in by that archaic rule. As past Tour champ, he suspected the girls had a soft spot for him and he was going to find out if it was true.

They were very accommodating.

Back at the room, Elvin had the TV on and was going through the channels. They were all in French, with nothing for him to watch. Elvin looked at the clock and saw it was only seven p.m., but he was still on Adobe, Arizona time. Tired, he laid on the comfortable bed, closed his eyes and went fast asleep. He awoke with a start, looking immediately at the little special fridge. It was still taped shut and all looked well.

The small bedside clock was flashing zeros. Must have been a power surge. He checked the lights—the bedside lamp went on just fine. He listened for the fridge—still humming quietly in the corner. All good. He reset the clock to match his watch, then got up, showered and went to bed. He woke again at two-thirty a.m. when Marcus arrived and stumbled into the other room. Sleepily Elvin wondered why Marcus would be out so late on the night of an important stage like the Alps. One thing for sure—his brother had confidence.

Elvin awoke at eight o'clock in the morning and looked over at the fridge. The tape was still in place, untouched so all was well. He brushed his teeth, dressed and was ready for the day's exciting climax to the Tour. Tentatively, he tapped on Marcus's door. "Hey, Marcus. All's well—the fridge is still taped up."

"Huh?" Marcus grunted. "Oh—yeah—good!"

"Breakfast?" asked Elvin, hoping Marcus would invite him to eat with him. It would be cool to meet the team.

"Uh, no. I'll sleep in for a while. Race start isn't 'til eleven. Catch up with you, later," he mumbled.

The brush off. Like always. Elvin left, closing the door behind him. Why had he thought this would be any different? Still, he made his way to the race staging area early, eager despite it all to be part of history in the making not knowing how close Marcus was to losing it all.

This was the crucial stage for Marcus's challenge of Tour De France. It was long, hot, hilly and as tough as it got and his team was hurting and could barely keep up. The race commentators were having a field day with Marcus's narrow lead and his razor thin lead.

The king is dead!

"His team is a shambles!" pronounced the Spanish commentator.

"Marcus Deering is vulnerable and alone, ready for the slaughter", declared the French press, thrilled to see the American take a beating, finally. Seeing an American win the Tour rankled the French to their very core. There had not been a French winner in decades and nor was there a likely contender on the horizon, either. Still, they would rather any nationality but an American win "their" race.

Even the American press was nervous. "We shall see if Marcus Deering can marshal his once mighty team to dominate this stage," they proclaimed hopefully. Not likely.

"I wonder where Mr. Deering is?" mused the Belgium TV commentator with a knowing wink. "The race start is only twenty minutes away and there's no sign of him!"

———

M arcus Deering was in a strange hotel room, all too aware of what the hour was. "Fuck, Doc, why is this taking so long! I have the race of my life in twenty-five minutes!!" he blurted.

Marcus was fully dressed in his bike clothing, lying on the bed. The bag of special blood was hanging beside him on the room coat rack.

"Relax; this transfusion is taking a bit longer than I thought. Lay still so it'll run in faster!" assured the "doctor". "Seems thick. Hmmm... Odd." He gently squeezed the bag.

Finally, the precious IV bag was drained and Marcus was on his feet and rushing to the door.

The "Doctor" clutched his arm. "Hey! Where's my payment?"

"It's in the envelope, by the bed." Marcus shook him off and raced out the door.

The crowd broke out in cheers and whistles, but some booed as Marcus rode up to the start, threading his way straight to the head of the race, resplendent in his yellow leader's jersey, alongside his suspicious team.

"Nice of you to join us!" Kerry whispered sharply. "Busy with the podium girls?"

"Remember who signs your pay cheque," Marcus countered under his breath as he smiled and waved to the crowd.

The announcer shouted over the growing din, "Are all the riders ready for the start of Stage 19 of the Tour De France?" The crowd roared in response.

"This is the toughest stage! Two hundred kilometers including *one* Category One Climb and *two* Above Category Climbs! The finish line is on the Alpe D'Huez!"

It seemed it would be impossible, but the crowd roared even louder. Hundreds—maybe thousands—of colourful flags, from countries all around the world whipped and snapped above the fray.

"Go!"

The crowd exploded in cheers as 120 riders left the start line, the residue of the 190 who'd started two and a half weeks before. The pace was an easy cruise for the first sixty kilometers. Most riders were tired, bruised, cut, and beaten up. One rider barely survived being run off the road into a wire fence. He was tough and stayed in the race as a point of honor, regardless of how far back he was.

The first climb was their wakeup call, twenty kilometers long and steep. Massive crowds of rabid fans jammed each side of the road, where they had been camped for days—a drunken beach party and exuberant Halloween party combination waiting for the Tour to pass. These fans hailed from all over the world, had been drinking for days in their sweltering little campers and tents, packed tight like sardines to secure a seat for the event. Though some dressed in normal street clothes, more wore outrageous costumes for the occasion, while others stripped down to scanty and alarming Borat suits, proudly parading their "assets". It was a crazed cross section of humanity, dying to see their cycling heroes positioned so close they could reach out and touch the riders which they did at every opportunity. A creepy Halloween groupie's ball.

At the Tour De France anywhere from fifteen to twenty million people show up in person to stand and watch the three-week event going by, while another two hundred million watch it on TV. The Tour was free. What other sport was there where you could stand a foot or two away, breathe the same air as your cycling favorite, absolutely free of charge?

Fans being this close to the competitors was a good and bad thing for the riders. Fans could push their favorites up the hill, if given half a chance, or pour cooling water on their backs. They could run alongside the riders, screaming encouragement in their faces.

If the fans *don't* like a rider, they curse and spit on them as they pass. A rider might even get punched. It was like riding through a packed mall during a Christmas sale. All this was done as the riders suffer in the heat, up a ten percent grade mountain trying to maintain focus on the race. They battled their way through that pulsing gauntlet of fans every inch of the way with more than a few racers lashing out at fans as they passed.

European riders knew how to deal with these crowds when cycling through and the crowds responded by melting away before them, seldom interfering with their progress. The more generous pro riders might advise the new professional riders—Neo-pros—to just ride like the crowd wasn't even there. Ride like there is no madness and chaos in front of you. A mirage.

Easier said than done.

Marcus and the pack started on the new hill with the screaming fan chaos all around them. There were faces, close up, shouting, running alongside. The road in front of them was painted with names of the riders in all languages, encouraging them. After five kilometers the pack was dwindling—the screaming fans were not. Marcus's enemies had their riders on the front of the line, forcing the pace. The weak dropped by the dozen, to make their way to the finish as best they could. All the struggling riders knew was they must keep within ten percent of the winners' time or they would be eliminated from the race!

The sweat poured down Marcus's face while he dodged elbows, screaming fans clutching at him, patting his back, shoving water bottles in his face. This raucous crowd shouting in his ears barely gave Marcus and the other riders enough room to pass. A drunken ragged gauntlet.

"Hey, watch it! Get away!" shouted the rider beside him, suddenly hooked on a purse strap of something, yanking him over. Marcus was lucky not to get mixed up in the crash.

In the chaos Kerry valiantly kept Marcus near the front of the pack and in contention. His other team riders had wilted and were gone. Smelling vulnerability like a shark smells blood, the other teams kept up the cruel pace. Top of the first hill and the pack was burnt down from one hundred and twenty to twenty-five riders. Marcus and Kerry were still there with Marcus feeling surprisingly strong as his "Go Juice" kept him feeling fresh as a daisy and strong as a gorilla. Magic.

A few riders who'd been dropped had managed to catch back up on the hair-raising descent, bringing the group back up to thirty riders. The next long climb beat that number down to fifteen. One by one, the riders slowly drifted off the back of the little string to disappear in the noisy crowd of following cars, honking horns, screaming spectators and chaos. The front runners held together. After one last downhill the pack number was back up to twenty—all who were was left to challenge the last twenty-five mile climb up to Alpe d'Huez.

Every cyclist in the world knew that Alpe d'Huez was the ultimate selection, today. Alpe d'Huez would decide who won and who lost the Tour. All Marcus had to do was stick to whoever the leader was and his thirty-second lead was safe. Contenders would have to attack him and gain at least thirty-one seconds on Marcus to take over the Tour, but he stuck to them like glue. Three and a half billion people breathlessly watch this drama on TV while twelve million wild spectators crowded the racecourse and the slopes of the climbs to watch in person, some so close they could touch the riders.

Alpe d'Huez is a notorious climb with twenty-one bends, ending up on the treeless slopes of a ski hill. The average climb is an eight percent and fourteen km climb, which is hard on riders who've already have done twenty days of racing plus five hours, today. If all went well, the winner would do the final climb in about forty minutes.

Marcus Deering's main rivals were Leif Parsons of Australia, in second place, thirty seconds back and Mig Ramierez of Spain, forty seconds back, both with two of their strong team riders remaining with them. Marcus had a thirty second lead but only had one rider left with him, Kerry, who was clearly struggling.

The group of fifteen riders hit the bottom of Alpe D'Huez at speed, left from the previous downhill. Both Parsons and Ramierez team riders hit the front and drove the pace, in hopes of dropping Marcus and gaining a lead on him. They would keep the pace fast for as long as they could, then drop off, forgotten. Their team leaders would be safely in the draft, enjoying being towed along until about the midpoint of the Alpe when they would pull away from Marcus, winning the stage and the Tour.

That was the plan.

Marcus Deering and Kerry could see that strategy and knew they had to counter. The key was to stay in the line with the other team riders, see if they burn out, then follow their team leaders.

The fans were going wild on the narrow road to the top of the mountain. They ran alongside the riders shouting and shaking their fists like they were at the football game of the century and the winning goal had just happened.

At the halfway point of the hill the Parson's and Ramirez's lead riders were clearly hurting. As they fell away, their team leaders took over with a vengeance, rapidly pulling away from the little group of riders. The pack disintegrated with riders struggling along in ones and twos falling away like leaves in a blistering hot wind. Parsons and

Ramierez drove on as planned but Marcus Deering clung stubbornly onto them.

That was not in *their* plan.

By the halfway point of the climb, the pace returned to normal, the sense of urgency crumbling. Marcus had been expected to be doomed by the acceleration yet remained with them, unscathed. Easy. Now it was his turn to try a few accelerations. His rival duo had spent it all, so he went to the right, up shifting into a faster gear, stood on his pedals and stomped hard. He alternately pulled right and left on his bars, mashing the pedals and pulling hard on the upstroke. This allows a rider to generate more power and speed but took more energy. Today, Marcus had power to burn.

The crowd sensed something important was happening and surged for a look, barely getting out of the way in time, the police fighting to keep the crowds back.

Marcus pulled away like an angel, flying away from them all, smiling. Witnesses were amazed. He kept going, eventually gaining a two-minute advantage on his rivals, throwing his hands in the air at the finish with joy!

He'd won the legendary Alpe d'Huez stage *and* his sixth Tour De France! Unheard of!

The last stage into Paris was largely ceremonial. The riders drank champagne and mugged for the cameras. The sprinters dueled it out for the final win. They all got on the podium for the final awarding of the Tour De France trophy and the big winner's cheque, which traditionally the winner split among his team. Hopefully Marcus wouldn't forget again, this year. Tacky and cruel.

And the winners all got to go to the medical trailer to give a urine sample to make sure there was no funny stuff that gave them an unfair advantage. Marcus the winner, especially, was tested. It would be months before the results came back, but Marcus wasn't worried.

A forgotten, ignored face in the milling crowd, Elvin, was thrilled Marcus won his record sixth straight Tour.

———

I t had been a grand summer after his Tour win. Marcus took home a million francs which he finally distributed among his team as per tradition. Kerry demanded it or a lawsuit would follow.

He had to stay ahead of "Barbara" so he kept moving, laughing to himself at how clever he was.

Marcus received millions of dollars to show and ride various races all over Europe. He even did some six-day track races. Sponsors lined up for him to give endorsements for everything from bicycle parts to shaving cream. One even trotted him out as the spokesperson for Parkinson's campaigns but there were some grumblings of doubt about how much the sponsor actually passed down to research after Marcus's "fees" were paid. No matter—it was all about great publicity.

Marcus took February off from racing. He went to his winter rental in Arizona and did some training and recovery. The winter weather in Tucson was a nice change. There was no pressure to do a series of races like there would have been if he'd wintered in the south of France. He could just do as he pleased in relative anonymity.

He hadn't seen or heard from "Barbara" for weeks. She must have given up on payment.

There was also some time for Catherine now, his semi-forgotten and neglected girlfriend. They had been going out for almost a year but with his full racing schedule, he rarely saw her. Texts, emails and phone calls were often their only contact for weeks. She was sweet but not the smartest.

Catherine tried very hard to please him by cooking for him and spending time with him. She even let him meet some of her Playboy Mansion girlfriends, going as far as to finally agree to some wild group sex that Marcus insisted upon. She told him it made her feel empty and cold.

Eventually, Marcus became bored with his Playboy Bunny girl-friend. She was a knockout to look at and have sex with. Her breasts were huge and perfect, she had the nose and face that had been masterfully designed and built, an exquisite figure with long legs, and an ass that was perfection. Cosmetic surgeons had renovated

Catherine from a cute, shy, tall, flat chested Swedish-American girl to a perfect "10". There was not a scar to be found anywhere and Marcus had looked closely on numerous occasions.

Marcus came to the conclusion Catherine was the world's best sex toy and about as interesting to talk to—her body more a tribute to her doctors than to herself. He'd always teased her about it, saying they should have enhanced her brain, but now he couldn't ignore it. After a last satisfying make-out session, he informed her he was breaking it off. She blinked back at him in shock, still holding a sheet to cover her nakedness. It was plainly obvious the girl hadn't seen it coming. How stupid was she?

"But..." She glanced around the bed. "We just..."

"Look at yourself—you're nothing but a fake everything. You're a dumb blond, medically made up to look like a movie star—the only thing they missed; the only thing that mattered—was your mind."

She stood up, naked, and pulled on the dress he'd so recently peeled off, then faced him coolly, her expression abruptly condescending. "Well Marcus, that also goes for bike riders who use dope to win races...and talk in their sleep!" She gazed deep into his eyes so there would be no mistaking her meaning.

Burn.

Marcus stood frozen, aware his mouth was open, shocked. He only came out of his stupor when he heard the front door slam behind her. He broke out in a sudden sweat. Would she tell anyone? Nah. She wouldn't tell anyone. No one would believe her anyway. Would they?

To quell his nerves, Marcus called up his director and suggested they do the Tour of the Gila in New Mexico with the team as a winter training camp and kick off for the racing season. It would be great publicity for the AVIA-Ford team in the USA. There would be some good teams as well as some decent amateurs to fill in some roster spots left over from Kerry's departure. It was time for some fun in the USA.

The marketing people made Marcus the center of attraction at the "Gila". It was a parade and he was king. People requested autographs everywhere. Naturally, Marcus received "start" money, a cash payment to bring world cycling publicity with him to the race. He was only too happy to oblige. His bank account was so full it was splitting at the seams.

The Gila race was surprisingly fast for his team. Half the racers were the Professionals, already established and the other half were riders with everything to prove and nothing to lose. A hungry rider would take the chance that a pro would never consider.

Marcus was still getting used to some of the new team members, what with half of his old team getting the boot and a new batch of riders eagerly signed on. He was holding his own in the top ten waiting for the later, longer stages to pounce and take the lead.

On the night of the prologue, Marcus was just getting back to his room after a satisfying liaison with a local girl. When he walked in the room and flicked on the light, he was shocked to see Barbara sitting on the couch in his hotel room. His heart sank.

"B-Barbara?"

"I see you remember me, Marcus," she said, without a trace of emotion, still wearing the same funeral outfit, taunting him... haunting him.

"What do you want?" he stammered.

"What do I want?" Barbara glowered at him, ready to spit fire. "I want your soul!"

"But - but I've barely lived! You can't have me *yet*."

"Barely lived? Let's list off what I've given you. Let's start with your life, shall we? Ten and a half years ago, you were a dead man. I allowed you to live and amass riches and fame beyond your wildest dreams. And now it's time to pay the devil his due, as the old saying goes."

"But I'm not ready to die, yet. I have more goals to achieve, more people to reach with my charity rides!" Marcus pleaded.

"Charity? Is that what you're calling it?" Her eyes burned into his.

"Well, yes. It's important to give people hope," said Marcus humbly. "I have more work to do."

"The only work you do is for yourself, Marcus. Your time is up. I expect you tomorrow. Make it a good one." Her tone was icy.

"Good one? You mean I have to... take my own life?"

"Very perceptive. We collect souls but can't bump folks off for them. Against the rules according to our legal people and... ahem... God knows Hell is full of lawyers. Some of them claim to know you and are looking forward to seeing you again."

Marcus swallowed hard. "How shall I... do myself in?"

"Any way you want—I have no preference. Suit yourself—if you dare. The clock is ticking and I have a reach that will surprise you." She vanished.

Marcus stood there and shook, then collapsed on the bed in anguish, moaning out loud, not caring how he sounded, then stopped. She hadn't said where; he could slip away like he had before, couldn't he? Yes, he knew his day of reckoning was coming but he would not go quietly. He would wring every drop of life he could from the time he had left.

Marcus raced at Gila for two more stages, enjoying the races like never before. Maybe "Barbara" would let him be, for a little while longer.

Maybe if he *actually* gave the money to charity this time, he could buy himself more time? Can't take it with you.

Marcus rode stage five of Gila, soaking in the adulation of the crowds of cheering spectators. He was the center of their world and he reveled in it. A shout got his attention.

"Hey you! Number one-fourteen!" the commissaire official waved to him grimly. "Stop right here."

A ball of anger welled up inside of Marcus. "What's the problem!" he demanded.

The commissaire official rudely shoved aside the few on-lookers between himself and Marcus. "You tested positive for doping at the Tour de France on your first sample," the stern-face official hissed at him. Swiftly he stripped off Marcus's jersey number, removed the GPS transponder from his bike and barked, "Your second sample will be tested as confirmation. You're suspended until the results are back."

Marcus was horrified. Only then did it dawn on him this area was full of spectators of all ages, all stunned silent, their eyes large, their expressions reproachful. As he looked along the rows, his face burned red with shame, the people lowered their "Marcus" flags. Three kids dropped theirs on the road and turned away. One of them, a boy, called out, "Dopers suck!"

Everywhere his eyes darted, it was the same until his eyes caught a woman dressed in a tight black dress. Barbara! Her gaze burned into his as she grinned. He felt the sting of her mighty reach. Quickly he dropped his bike, covered his face with his hands and loped to the team vehicle while the mechanic grabbed his bike and hung it on the roof rack.

As Marcus slumped in the back seat, devastated, Rory, his long-time team director shook his head and spoke. "A doping charge means you are off the team and off the payroll. I'll expect you to pick up your stuff and get another room on your dime!"

From the number one rider in the world to number one heel.

Marcus dragged himself to his room, stripped off his gear, letting each garment drop onto the floor. It took several minutes to rouse himself to step in the shower, numbly feeling the water cascading over him. He barely felt it. What just happened here? How in the world had the EPO been detected? It was fool-proof—he'd done everything right! He had used it many times with no positive results—this was simply not possible.

Then he thought of Elvin, the one he'd trusted to guard his EPO that night.

Elvin screwed me!

Soaking wet Marcus stormed out of the shower, grabbed his phone and tapped in a long unused phone number. A friendly, surprised voice answered.

"Hey, Marcus, I haven't heard from you for months! Still riding that Tour win wave?" gushed Elvin, obviously thrilled to hear from him.

"Elvin, shut up and listen to me! The Tour! What did you do to that bag in the fridge you were guarding?" Marcus shouted, not caring who heard him.

"I... er... nothing... What—what bag? You never said a bag of anything. I made sure nobody got into *the fridge*. What happened, Marcus?" Elvin ended feebly. "Please, tell me."

"Listen up, you fucking hick! I don't ever want to see you again! You let the fridge quit and cooked the bag I had in there! You screwed my life!" screamed Marcus. He ended the call, then looked to the door —someone was pounding on it. "Hey, Marcus! How about a story for Cycling International!"

"Fuck off!"

Looking out the window he saw media cars rolling up, gathering around his hotel, vultures sniffing out the stink of his unbelievable winning streak, microphones and shoulder cams at the ready to record every sordid detail. How much had they caught of his phone call? How did they get wind of this so fast? That night Marcus threw his phone in a toilet and was on a plane back to France to escape the American media, gnawing at him like wolves with a bone.

———

E lvin was horrified beyond belief at what he'd done—or hadn't done for his brother. That fridge… what had happened? He tried calling Marcus back, but the calls wouldn't go through.

Giving up after two days, Elvin opened his computer and called up the cycling news site himself to learn what had happened. The sensational news was everywhere, posting about Marcus Deering failing the dope test from his sixth Tour win. The story added that Deering had now failed the second test, so it was undeniable—Deering was guilty as charged. The big networks picked it up. ABC News asked the President about it and he just shook his head and said, "I thought Deering was okay but he's a doper."

Marcus had said "a bag". "I never saw any bag," Elvin mumbled.

Then it dawned on Elvin what had been that sealed fridge—Elvin had been guarding *a blood transfusion bag* for Marcus for the important stage the next day.

Marcus's dope cache was in a *blood bag!*

Elvin knew then that *he* somehow had caused Marcus to fail that test. He wasn't sure how, but it had to be something to do with the fridge in France. He'd screwed up and ruined his brother's life. It was his fault and his alone. He went out to the big old abandoned barn where he and Marcus used to play in simpler times and quietly hung himself.

———

At first, Marcus couldn't sleep. Drug headlines shouted at him, taunted him, repulsed him in constant nightmares. His ex, Catherine stood laughing at him in one, calling him the biggest hypocrite in history. He awoke, sweating and groaning. Eventually he nodded off again, exhausted, only to have Catherine laughing at him again, this time calling him a two-timing cheating hypocrite, followed by Kerry and his team-mates showing up to scream and shoved him around. "Where's our win money!" He couldn't take it anymore.

Next day Marcus tottered into a pharmacy and picked up some cheap, heavy duty sleeping pills guaranteed to keep him under for eight hours. Finally, some sleep, he thought. Deep, deep drugged sleep.

Now when he slept, he didn't see any of his cycling buddies, Catherine or news people at all. Peace. Barbara, however, now appeared in his dream, smiling, just like the old days.

She said "Hi Marcus. Look who we have for a guest," and pointed to her right.

His mind's eye saw a ten-year-old boy that looked a lot like Elvin… could it be…He *was* Elvin, kneeling inside the mouth of a cave that belched flame and smoke. He cried out "Help me Marcus! Why are they doing this to me? You've gotta help me!"

In this nightmare he looked to Barbara, "What are you doing to my brother? Elvin doesn't belong there!"

"He just arrived. We have him on loan until you replace him."

"Can't be—!" He awoke in a bath of cold sweat. It was just a dream, right? Stress—lack of sleep. He grabbed the remote and turned on the TV, raising the volume, needing voices to ease his lingering nightmare images. A few dreary commercials calmed him. He stood up, leaning on a nearby stand then wobbled his way to the bathroom and sat.

Elvin's story blared from the TV.

"Late last night, the body of Elvin Deering, brother of disgraced cycling star Marcus Deering, was discovered hanging in an old barn on the family property. Apparently, he had committed suicide some hours earlier leaving a heartfelt note taking blame for his brothers doping allegations and said this was too much to bear as he loved his older brother so much. The coroner is still investigating."

Marcus threw up in the nearby tub. He was not only a sport cheater but now responsible for his loyal brother's death. His world was crashing down. Every story was more lurid than the last and they kept on coming, horrible and endless.

His parents left tearful messages pleading for him come home for Elvin's funeral but he didn't respond. He couldn't face it; he couldn't face them. He knew it was his parent's way to forgive but everyone in his hometown would rightfully vilify him as the scumbag cheater who caused Elvin's death. Instead, Marcus went out and drank until the bar bouncer tossed him out on the street.

The next morning he awoke in his hotel room, surprised to find he'd made it back at all. He closed his eyes, contemplating a couple of aspirins to ease his pounding headache.

A voice shook him to his core. "You aren't going quietly, are you, Marcus Deering?"

His face twisted with rage. "No! I'm *not* and I don't see *what* you can do about it!" Marcus staggered to his feet and peered groggily around the darkened room for "Barbara". His mouth fell open when he saw it was "Elvin"!

"Hey 'bro!" Elvin greeted him with a mean, wolfish grin.

Marcus collapsed to his knees, sobbing and crying. He choked out, "Elvin! Is this a joke? I thought you were dead! What are you doing to me?"

"Doing to you? It really is all about you isn't it? Poor Marcus," "Elvin" teased fiendishly.

"I thought…"

"Of course, I'm dead you idiot! I'm glad you recognized me! I thought you'd like to say hi to Elvin instead of Barbara. See? Elvin still has his funeral clothes on and some make-up, too. Want to see the rope burns?"

"No!" Marcus moaned, scrambling away on all fours, horrified beyond anything he could imagine. Here was someone who could show up as both Barbara and Elvin with ease. Who was next? He fought to compose himself, needing his wits about him—this would be the most important conversation of his life.

"You asked me what I can do about it?" sneered "Elvin" angrily. "You'd be AMAZED! Are you even curious why your greedy dope plan didn't work out and how you got caught?"

"H-how did you know about that?"

"It seems there was a perfectly timed power failure that caused your sample to become detectable. Hmmm. Think Sherlock."

"Power failure?"

"Elvin did his job. It was *me* who cut the power to that fridge for two hours, enough to spoil your dope's invisibility," "Elvin" assured. "Not that you care about Elvin, anyway. He was innocent, you moron. He *kept* his word."

Marcus huddled there, while the enormity of what had happened sank in. Then he screamed, spittle flying from his mouth, "Get out! Get out!"

"What's wrong? Not working out like you planned? Whose fault is that?" "Elvin" grinned savagely. "I gave you ten more years that you *did not have,* and you fucked it up! And here you are stealing more time. You're a greedy, greedy man. How do you think people will remember you after you're gone, now?"

"I-I think they will remember m-me for my c-charity work," Marcus offered unconvincingly.

"Remember you? They'll think of you the same way they think of O.J. Simpson! I can hardly wait to see *him*! Now there's a man who can help you stoke the fires for eternity." "Elvin" roared with laughter, his eyes blazing. "And all his lawyers!"

"I'm just not ready to die, yet, that's all," Marcus finally whispered.

"You've had more than your share of life. Be a man about it, for once." With that "Elvin" smiled and started walking out. Just before the door he turned to Marcus and said, "I know what you're thinking, Marcus: How much worse can I make this?" He pulled his collar down so Marcus could see the neck rope burns. "Do you remember the nightmare you had about Elvin in Hell? All true! Your sweet little brother is with us on a temporary stay, stoking the fires."

"No-o-o!"

"How long he stays is up to you."

"You're keeping Elvin hostage?"

"Are you such a greedy fool? *Of course*, we'll keep him as hostage!" "Elvin's" voice rattled the doors and windows and as Marcus quivered on the floor. "Seems there's some fine print in your contract that says we can keep a relative for an unpaid soul, so too bad for Elvin. O.J.'s lawyers were very helpful. Not that you care..."

Marcus climbed unsteadily to his feet and stood, pale and stunned, barely whispering, "I'm coming ... soon."

"Elvin" nodded and vanished.

Marcus was besieged, hounded by the media as he fought his way through the French airport to catch his flight back to the states, but he had no choice. He had to go home, where he'd made that evil deal so long ago. Maybe his old town minister could save him. A man from God could talk to the evil stranger, on Marcus's behalf, could he not?

Reverend Gary Duke was an old family friend. He'd been the family minister for years and knew Marcus well. Marcus knew Gary heard him laughing behind his back at every opportunity yet here Marcus was kissing Gary's feet, begging for mercy.

Reverend Gary Duke was the first person Marcus phoned when he got back. "I have a tall tale for you and a million-dollar donation for you and your church. Meet me at Tisdale Park."

Gary agreed with reservations.

Meeting with ministers always made Marcus nervous. They always seemed to crowd into his personal space a bit too much, kept the handshake going twice as long as necessary, all the while looking deep into his eyes with an unblinking gaze. Ministers were like mechanics looking intently at something broken, trying to figure out how it worked and what caused it to fail.

———

At the appointed hour Reverend Gary Duke sat on the bench in Tisdale Park awaiting Marcus. He was skeptical of the strange request by this child of the Deerings, faithful and elderly followers of his church. Their son Elvin's passing was a dreadful event caused by his older brother Marcus, their wayward man-child. Marcus was their village "Icarus", who flew too close to the sun and was now falling to earth clutching at anything he could on his way down. Foolish, vain and arrogant.

But rich and stupid—and the church *was* in need of a new roof.

In the distance he saw an older, fatigued Marcus cycling towards him, head bowed, eyes puffy. Gary sat up a little and waved him over.

Marcus stuck out his hand like he was reaching for someone to pull him up. "Reverend Duke! I'm so glad to see you."

They shook hands earnestly and silently.

"Sit, Marcus and tell me your troubles."

Marcus climbed off his garish colored bike and sat down beside him on the old unpainted bench, awkwardly, hesitantly.

Gary was speechless for a few seconds having the famous bike racer Marcus Deering, dressed up in his spandex finery with an exquisitely made French bicycle. Clownish, he thought. Gary broke the ice, feeling he had the upper hand. "So, Marcus, things seem to be going badly for you, these days. I'm so sorry about Elvin's passing. I was at his funeral. Pity you could not attend. I think everyone was watching for you." He studied Marcus's expression for any sign of genuine remorse. Was his remorse replaced by fear?

"I thought the inevitable publicity would ruin the funeral," Marcus lied.

Bullshit. "So, what can I do for you this morning, Marcus? Want me to take your confessions, forgive you or...?" Rev. Duke asked, remembering his role here. He could see Marcus was nervous.

"It's a long story. Do you remember when I was dying from cancer, ten and a half years ago?" Marcus asked, obviously uncomfortably.

"I do—and I also remember thinking about the call for Last Rites for you. You recovered. It was indeed an example of God's Miracles."

Marcus looked around suspiciously. "There is a bit more to the story, Gary. Just when it looked like I was doomed to death, I had a visit from an odd... stranger... Who said everything would be well—if I accepted his help."

"His?"

"Um... the man... below..."

Gary's eyebrows shot way up. "You're kidding, right?"

"I wish I was."

"Assuming there is such a thing, you're saying you made a pact... with the Devil?" Gary blurted before he could help himself, shocked. "Assuming you're not delusional." *Clearly Nuts.*

"I don't know what to say. This stranger appears and disappears. He knows more about me than anyone. I'm at a loss as to what to do about him," pleaded Marcus, real tears streaming down his cheeks.

This from the callous Marcus Deering—it was disconcerting to say the least.

"Could you talk to him for me? Please? I'm begging you."

Rev. Gary sat for a few minutes, struggling to understand what he was being asked to do. Part of him wanted to assist while the other half thought psychiatric help was needed. He decided the best course of action was to play along and see where it led. Marcus was falling apart and maybe keeping up this charade would help him. "Alright. Where do I find this stranger?"

"Uh... I don't know. He just turns up... But he *did* say I should meet him back here when my time was up."

"Ah. You aren't putting me on, are you, Marcus? This isn't some reality TV stunt, is it?" Rev. Gary grinned like a fool while glancing around for hidden cameras.

Marcus's cold white face stopped Gary's search, told him Marcus was deadly serious. "I know this sounds crazy, Reverend, but please believe me. Could... could I go out for a bike ride to clear my head, and you hang out here and see if... *He...* turns up?"

Now Gary was both sceptical and intrigued. *He wants me to stay here while he goes and rides his bike?* Watching Marcus's worried face, Rev. Gary caved. What was an afternoon in the park on a sunny day? Not a bad thing. And it was obvious Marcus was coming unhinged. Gary owed it to Elvin, at the least. "How will I know it's... Him?"

"There will be no doubt when... *He...* arrives."

"Ah, of course." Gary sighed and nodded. "Go ahead and I shall wait and see."

"I'll ride up to that little hill right there and you can call me when you're done."

"Sure," he agreed somewhat disbelieving, then watched Marcus ride away.

And the minister did wait. After a while he daydreamed in the warm sun on the park bench. It was so serene and pleasant. He closed his eyes and relaxed. Getting paid to nap.

A disturbing voice jolted him awake. "Are you here to plead for Marcus Deering's soul?"

Gary glanced all around, his gaze snagging and stopping at a familiar looking man sitting near him. Couldn't be. "Hal? Hal Cramp?" he breathed in astonishment. "H-how can you be here? You're—you're *dead!*"

"I'm not Hal, as you knew him. I thought I'd appear as a friendly face."

Gary was stunned, disbelieving.

Hal continued, "Still got that "thing" going with your church secretary? You always did have a wandering eye."

Gary squirmed in his seat, completely unnerved at seeing an old friend and mentor—long *dead* —alive and speaking to him, with information only he and Bernice knew. "H-how could you know that?"

"Can I say you and Hal have some skirt chasing... history... despite your sacred trust."

"If you are the—" The more Gary thought, the more the implications smacked him in the face. "Is Hal... *down... there?*"

"Hal" sighed. "Everyone goes somewhere, Gary. You of all people should know that."

"Assuming you're the real deal, which I doubt, I am a man of God and look after the welfare of my congregation," said the Reverend, fighting for calm himself, "and for the record, I think you're a scam artist attempting to extort money from Marcus Deering!"

"Really? So why are you here for Mr. Deering's benefit when you don't visit the elderly and dying patrons of your church? Rather have a beer with your friends, instead? Too busy with the rich patrons? Deering promised payment, did he not?"

Rev. Gary reddened.

"Hal" stretched his arms along the back of the bench and gazed around. "You have it pretty nice around here, Gary. You do as you please, visit who you feel like and strut around like you're someone important." He turned to Gary suddenly, his eyes drilling into his. "The truth is, you don't think much of your church or congregation, now, do you? You think you're better than this fleabag town and its citizens."

Gary swallowed hard.

"Bit of marriage trouble, Rev. Duke?" the stranger queried with a leading drawl.

Gary stammering, "How could you possibly know that?"

"I know most everything."

The reverend looked confused about what to do.

"Get out of here, Mr. Duke! This is not your concern. *Go now!* It will be your turn to see me soon enough!" "Hal's" eyes blazed, his voice cracked like thunder, shaking Gary profoundly.

Gary leaped from the park bench and ran to his car as fast as his stubby, chubby legs would carry him. He drove away with a chirp of the tires, glancing repeatedly in his rear-view mirror the entire way home.

Marcus watched the little conference from a few blocks away, saw

Rev. Gary suddenly leap from the bench and scurry to his car, fleeing like lightning bolts bounced off his feet.

The meeting was over and Marcus guessed his last chance was gone.

Defeated, he turned his bike around and went to his big house up on the hill—the house he'd spent years looking down at his home town of Adobe, Arizona with scorn. He entered through the garage and made his way to his room. Once there, and with meticulous care, he dressed in his favourite cycling gear, his winner's Tour De France jersey, shorts and socks, watching his reflection in the mirror as he did. When he was satisfied, he collected his shoes and bike in the garage then he rolled back out the door.

No helmet for this ride.

His favourite ride was the long and winding Diamond Hill. If he got very low, sometimes he could attain speeds of sixty miles an hour going down. Breathtaking. He leaned into each corner as far as he could, inches from the pavement.

He loved the feel of speed. The wind blew through his hair and across his face. His eyes watered, even under the designer glasses. Hands low on the bars and crouching his legs in, he could get a bit more speed. Leaning on the corners was the best part. Looking far ahead, he could see the right turn coming at the bottom of the hill. Safely holding this corner would have been a piece of cake at his present fifty miles per hour.

He made a tricky right-hand corner on the bridge at the bottom of the hill without using his brakes, tribute to his God given talent as a bike rider. He looked carefully ahead and saw the next corner was a familiar gentler right. There was a big truck coming towards him in the left lane. It was at that moment, Marcus decided that he would not hold the corner. He gracefully slipped over the centerline, into the path of the truck. That face of the truck driver was the last thing Marcus would see.

———

The truck driver was headed home with a Kenworth tandem and empty trailer. Light and empty, he could make it up the hill at a decent speed if he could get around the corner at sixty-miles an hour, which was a speed he could handle. He leaned into the steering wheel and dropped a gear, anticipating the increasing grade.

Is that a bike rider coming down the hill like a speeding bullet? Absently, he wondered if the rider would be able to hold the corner at the speed he was traveling.

Shit! In a flash the bike rider blew across the lane into the front of his truck. BOOM!

It was like the truck had hit a deer with bits of his grill flying into the windshield.

The ambulance was on the scene within minutes. There were traces of a bicycle, yes, but there was no rider to rescue—not even enough to identify. Blood, guts and the remains of a bicycle mashed into the truck grill.

"There's gonna be Hell to pay over this," the driver said to no one in particular.

The attending medics and patrolman thought the truck driver wasn't nearly as concerned as he should have been. They shrugged it off, getting the body from the grill and, on to the gurney and settled into the back of the ambulance.

The patrolman was first out of the ambulance, grateful for some fresh air. "Where did that truck go? It's gone!"

The medics joined him, looking around for the truck, too. Vanished.

"Geez. Did either of you recognize that driver?" the annoyed patrolman asked the mystified medics.

One of the medics looked at him and nodded, "He looked kinda like a picture of someone I saw in TV last night. Something about guarding dope for his brother."

"I saw it too!" said the other medic. "His name was Elvin Deering."

TRENCH CAKE

Everyone had gone to the party except for Erika who was stuck babysitting her ancient Grandmother. Erika's tea was cold, and the only edible item left on the little table in front of her was Christmas cake.

"I hate Christmas cake, Grandma. Who eats this stuff, anyway?"

Her Grandma looked at her, sadly. "You'd be surprised."

"This sounds like a grandma story about the old days," Erika said, smiling, sitting back in her chair. Grandma Morgan stories about the old days could be interesting.

"So long ago, when I was your age, Christmas cake represented hope."

Erika sat for a moment trying to imagine how a block of stodgy cake with nuts and berries could possibly be considered hopeful.

"Really? In what way?"

"You have to picture the world I lived in. It was 1944 and we lived on the Prairies after a decade of depression. What have you heard about the depression, Erika?"

"We heard all about it in school. Dirt storms and a stock market crash."

"That's part of it but have you heard what happened to the average citizen?"

"No."

"We were on the farm and there was very little rain for years. The topsoil that was our livelihood just blew away in the wind. Nobody had any money. Luckily we managed to have our own little gardens to keep our bellies filled."

"So you couldn't buy any food in those days?"

"We hardly had a penny to buy anything. We traded or grew what we needed. My dad took the engine out of our old car and changed it into a wagon because he couldn't afford to get it fixed or buy gas for it."

"So, this story is about Christmas cake, right?"

"Sorry. I'm prattling on. In 1939 Canada was at War and most of our young men marched away to fight. They stayed at their overseas posts so nobody came home very often. We just knew they were out there because the army preacher hadn't come by to tell us they were dead yet."

"No news was the best news. Oh no..."

"My dad and two brothers were in the conflict. My grandparents looked after us and the farm. My grandmother used to say Christmas cake was 'Hope'."

"Hope?"

"Yes, hope. She'd been through the Great War, WW1. I remember she'd say it's time to make Christmas cake to send to the men. She said, 'I'm feeling sad, so it's time'. She'd ask me to help make it while telling me a story."

"Like you're telling me, now?"

"Yes. She'd scramble around to find glazed fruit, raisins, peel, nuts she'd hidden away and combine it with flour, molasses and any other ingredients she could find. We baked it all and then had to soak it in rum and cheesecloth to preserve it. It wasn't easy in those days. She'd spend all afternoon making this special cake. She'd specially cut it into three parts and get it ready to send overseas."

"Why was it 'Hope?"

"When she was done, she looked at me and said 'I hoped I could find enough ingredients to make this cake—and we did. She said, "I'm hoping it will make its way across the Atlantic and the ship won't be sunk. If it makes it to the port and it makes it to my Dad and my brothers, wherever they may be". And 'I hope they are alive to eat it and think of us, standing here in this kitchen baking it just for them'."

"You were thinking of them and they were thinking of you, Grandma? They could take their minds away from the awful things they were experiencing for a moment to imagine us baking for them at home, here in this kitchen."

"So Christmas Cake was 'Hope' for you and your grandma and your family."

"Yes, Christmas cake will always be 'Hope' for me," her Grandma replied gently, a slow tear running down her cheek.

A FARMERS RANT

E rika and the Morgan's all sat at the picnic table having lunch, overlooking the big, winding river, nursing ice cold drinks on a gloriously hot day. It had been a long but successful harvest. Lawrence Senior and Larry looked very tired. Jo-Anne and Giselle were watching their men, sun burnt and stooped after many long hours.

"Thank-you, son. I could not have done all this without you."

"Glad to help, Dad."

"Now, if we only get some cooperation from the rail companies and some prices, we'll get by."

Jo-Anne sighed, "Here comes another 'Lawrence, the annoyed farmer' rant."

Instead, Larry spoke up and recited the rant by memory, complete with a few added silly theatrics of his own. "I'm getting too old for this. After twenty years of ups and downs, I'm not sure I can do this anymore. I mean, I can, but I don't know if I'm up to it. I know the roller coaster cycle of it all. You stand around all winter waiting for the snows to melt, fields to dry, and get a late snow or rain. You shell out a ton of money you don't have for new equipment, seed, fertilizer and hired hands and you wait... and wait... sometimes to late spring. Finally, there is a break in the weather, and you hustle out to seed the fields. Then the tractor shits out... the part is unavailable for two weeks... the hired hand's old aunt in Nova Scotia dies and he leaves for two weeks. You stand there in perfect weather for weeks with your blood pressure going through the roof. Finally, the part for the tractor comes, the farmhand returns and then it snows. You wait and wait, snapping at everyone who shows any sympathy. Finally, the seeding is done after two weeks of sleepless days and nights. You can sigh a sigh of relief. Then you hope the weather is decent, but it rains all spring and the seed in the field starts to rot. Some survive. Then the sun comes out and dries the shit out of everything. Luckily, you get by with a decent fall harvest...a bit dry but you will at least get your investment back and pay off some loans from the bank. Everything worth keeping is in the bins. Then you wait to sell the crop. The marketing board is gone so you try to sell your own stuff and answer calls while harvesting. Finally, you get a buyer, call the railroad to get a grain car only to find out they have none available 'cuz the eco folks in the cities stopped the pipelines. The rail companies can make twice the money moving oil than they get for moving grain for cheap farmers. So, you wait and the grain prices go down as the farmers nearer the cities get their crop in and flood the market. It's December before you get to sell your crop and now at a discount. At year's end you find you did not make ends meet so it's back to the bank for an extension of your loan. Maybe next year will be better or it'll be the year I subdivide the land to developers and finally make some money!"

Everyone sat in stunned silence until Lawrence senior stood up grinning, "Exactly!" and gave Larry a hug while Jo-Anne and Giselle shook their heads in disgust.

COASTAL QUEEN

The view of the ocean surf, superb yard layout and lush gardens of the rambling spacious home could not soften the blow of this dreaded day. She froze in horror as she heard the front door knob rattling and clicking insistently. A key finally turned successfully in the lock and the door swung open.

The open door exposed a worn, tired looking older, scruffy, unshaven man bearing a giant filthy hockey bag. He was big, over-weight, wearing dirty jeans and a grimy jacket proclaiming some motor-cycle manufacturer, all topped off with a filthy hat on his balding head. His craggy face, big belly and gnarled hands would put him at about sixty years old.

She quickly blocked his entry with a scowl.

They stood face-to-face regarding each other rather like a pair of rival alley cats. Breaking away from her glare he slowly glanced around the pristine living room, the carefully placed beautiful furniture then settled his eyes back on the well-tanned older woman in front of him, attired in perfectly matched yoga wear, designer glasses, leather sandals and jewelry. His eyes searched hers for some trace of recognition or spark of affection and found none.

"What are you doing here, Les?" she asked him suspiciously, arms crossed.

"They canceled the Mac job, so I thought I'd come home early," he offered defensively. "I couldn't call. We were out of phone range way out there. I have no other place to go."

Annoyed, she charged, "You were supposed to be gone for work for another month. I have plans. I suppose you had some drinks with your pals."

"I might have but so what? This is my home, too. Last time I looked my fat pay cheques were still paying the bills around here while you live in luxury. You were too uppity to stay living in little Standhope, remember? That hick town wasn't good enough for you... Angie!"

His words stung. She had no comeback and it was time to retreat. She carefully walked up to him and kissed his cheek but as reluctantly as if he was a statue covered with pigeon shit.

At last he cracked a reluctant smile, "That's more like it. I see you missed me, *Angelique!*" he said sarcastically.

Turning away she replied, "Yes, well, we will just have to fit you in, I suppose. Drop those dirty clothes right there so you do not get my beautiful crème carpet dirty."

It was at that moment Les felt like a piece of salami hanging in a jewelry store window, out of place and unwanted. After disrobing under her irritated gaze he stood naked in front of her, beat up work clothes at his feet, feeling ashamed and embarrassed, wishing he was anywhere else but his home.

"Go and clean up," she commanded. Disgusted, she scooped his clothing up as if they were full of excrement, shoving it all into a black garbage bag, not offering to wash it. All of his worldly work possessions were unceremoniously shoved into the closet on a shoe shelf. It was as if she was enduring a stray dog for the day.

Sometime later Les reappeared. He was showered, shaven, sported a smell of cologne, was well dressed, newly dignified and presentable to his irritated wife of thirty-two years.

She looked him over carefully before grunting a sound that could pass for approval. "Don't be asking me for food or sex. I have to go for a stroll in the park and then golf at the club at one-thirty. No, you are not invited."

Hurt, he stood for a few moments watching her speak before sadly sighing, "What has happened to us, Angie? We used to be so in love. We had to be close to each other every minute. Now I'm just a stranger in your life."

After some thought she finally said, "I'm sorry Les. I guess this arrangement works too well. I live here where I can have a life away from the old hometown, friends and relatives. My life is my own after toiling for everyone else for so long. This is my perfect life in my perfect home. Back home I was just Angie from down the street in a shabby little house but I'm 'Angelique' down here. I have one of the best houses in this area. I'm special. "

Les added miserably, "This arrangement was supposed to include me. I was going to work wherever I had to and send you the big bucks. You were to look after this – your dream home for our retire-ment. So here I am the migrant worker living a sort of homeless life in camps while you live in luxury. I have to schedule my visits down here! I'm just a nuisance now. You seem to have forgotten about me, Angelique or are you still Angie?"

She winced on hearing her old nickname, sighed and reached out her hand to his. "Walk with me Les—like we used to—before we drifted apart."

SPENCER'S GHOST

A Snowy Highway

The dreary and tedious winter had long since worn out its welcome. It had been cold and snowy every day it seemed, and was snowing hard again, snowflakes having a mesmerizing effect in the Cunningham's headlights, reducing visibility to almost nothing. Stopping wasn't an option. The highway was far too narrow to safely move to the side of the road to wait out the storm, *if* they could see where the edge of the road was; plus, they were only a few miles from home now—they were committed. Jeff said nothing as his wife Carol concentrated on the road. Their little Mustang car was cool and fast when it was dry but being light and high powered was not the best when road conditions were slippery and dangerous.

"These roads are awful, Jeff. I hate it. It's a good thing Mrs. Wright was willing to walk Spencer home from school," Carol murmured, struggling to keep the car under control. The center lines were no longer visible.

Silent for a moment, Jeff said, "I applied for my old job at the Agassiz Prison. It… it looks good that I might even get back in."

Caught by surprise Carol said, "Back to being a jail guard? Why? I thought you were happy working on the railroad?"

"It was fun for a while but I'm tired of the hours, supervising people, fooling with train schedules and all that crap. Back at the Agassiz jail, I just show up for work, get paid and go home. We'll get a house nearby. That way it's not much of a commute and cheaper than Vancouver. And," he added pointedly, "No snow. What do you say?"

"I need to think about this, Jeff," Carol said, stunned.

"It's already arranged. It's a done deal," he announced.

Shocked, Carol half-turned toward him, losing her death grip on the steering wheel for a split second too long.

A forty-ton logging truck popped out of the swirling snow, flattening the little car as if it were a tube of cardboard.

The logging truck driver was unhurt but knew something awful had been crushed beneath his wheels. He scrambled out into the blinding snow and crawled under the big truck's tires. Steaming blood ran from the flattened car and pooled on the icy road. The driver had seen a lot in his forty years of driving but was not prepared for this. On his hands and knees, he began to cry.

———

Carol and Jeff Cunningham's nine-year-old son Spencer found it odd his mom wasn't home when he arrived from school. At first, he busied himself in his room with homework and watched TV a bit, but by five, he was sitting at the kitchen table, waiting and getting scared.

It was seven–thirty before Susan Frey, a social worker, and a police officer knocked on the Cunninghams' front door. Identification of the victims had been slow; the drive in the blizzard was difficult, making them later than they would have liked.

There was no reply to their urgent knocking.

They could still see the remnants of Spencer's footprints just outside the doorway, so they knew he was in there. Susan had once heard Carol say in conversation that she, and all of Brandon Lake, left spare front-door keys under their welcome mats. She lifted up the mat and found the key as predicted. Opening the door with it, she saw at once there was smoke belching from the oven. She ran inside to turn it off. Grabbing a dishtowel, she pulled a big metal pan out, dropping it onto the counter with a clatter. It was the charred remains of a pot-roast, and what could have been three potatoes and five carrots. She flipped the overhead fan on high, then turned, her gaze catching on a colourful collection of a child's artwork stuck to the fridge. It broke her heart.

Spencer was seated at the table between his parents' places, where his plate, fork, spoon and goofy plastic cartoon cup had been carefully placed before him. There was a flower arrangement in the center of the table, a basket of buns and salt and pepper shakers shaped like smiling bears. The police officer crouched down beside him.

Spencer looked very small with his big black glasses, clutching a worn, one-eyed elephant in his arms. He was as white as a ghost. "I didn't know how to shut off the oven. Mommy says I mustn't touch it," he whispered.

Susan came to Spencer's other side. "It's alright, Spencer. Remember me? I knew your parents. We met at the picnic at the lake last year."

Spencer nodded and nudged his glasses back up on his nose. "Where's my Mommy and Daddy?"

Overwhelmed by sadness, Susan picked him up and held him, tears streaming down her face.

The Visitor

Susan Frey arrived unannounced at the Alexanders the next day. Beth Alexander invited her in out of the weather and fed her a steaming cup of tea. Susan was initially silent about the boy, confining herself to her tea and making small talk. When she felt enough time had elapsed, she told Beth the sad tale of Jeff and Carol Cunningham, both killed in a car accident, the day before. Beth and Joe both knew the Cunningham's from the BCR shop where Joe worked, so the news was especially shocking. Spencer wasn't with them at the time, thank God. He was staying at the local hospital for a few days while Susan found a place for him to live, temporarily. She wanted Spencer to keep going to his regular school so his routine would remain the same.

Susan said, "Didn't I see you and Joe with Spencer at the Railco barbeque?"

"Yes, Jeff was Joe's boss at Railco. I wouldn't say we saw a lot of each other, but we did get together from time to time. And yes, we did spend time with Spencer... poor kid."

Susan considered her words before speaking. "We don't have any place for Spencer out here and he needs someone who knows him. I don't want to totally alienate him by sending him away to Vancouver. He has school and his teachers here, so this would be a good place for him at this terrible time. I could set you up as a temporary foster home, Beth."

Beth considered before speaking. "This – this is unexpected. I'd have to talk it over with Joe, first."

Susan sipped her tea, letting Beth take in all the information. "Do you know if Jeff and Carol had any relatives?"

"I don't believe they did. As far as I know their parents are deceased and they didn't have any brothers or sisters. It was a small family on both sides. Carol said Spencer would be carrying on the Cunningham name, single-handedly," Beth said.

"That's what we found, too. We were hoping some relative were available but no luck," Susan said.

"So, how exactly do we become a foster home?"

"I have the forms to fill out and you're done. We could speed this up so it's done in a few days. I do appreciate this, Beth. This is a bad time for all of us, but I'm desperate to get him placed."

"That poor boy! It's the least we can do for Jeff and Carol."

Later that very night, Beth explained the situation to Joe and he was in complete agreement. They spent the balance of the evening setting up the guest room for Spencer who would arrive the next day.

What do you say to a nine-year-old orphan?

That Friday afternoon, Susan brought Spencer straight from school to the Alexander's. Spencer got out of her car, with a little old-fashioned suitcase which appeared to hold all his belongings. Beth and Joe could feel his overpowering sadness. One look at his innocent, honest expression almost brought them both to tears. They could see both Jeff and Carol in his face. He was all by himself in the world and was now being presented to them. He was wholly at their mercy. It was a crushing responsibility the Alexanders felt they were ill-equipped to handle. They just wanted to run up to him and hug this poor boy but it was not their place. He looked like he had cried all he could until there was nothing left but emptiness. He stood before them, his pale face downcast, his arms slack by his sides, a tiny statue of sadness.

Susan placed her arm over Spencer's slumped shoulders and guided him towards the Alexanders. Joe and Beth smiled and put on a brave face, but they too felt overwhelmingly sad. Beth reached out and gently shook Spencer's limp hand, then invited him inside the house. When Susan was satisfied Spencer would fit in, she said her goodbyes, and drove away. Watching her out the front window, Spencer tracked her car down the driveway and around the corner until it vanished from sight. It looked to Beth as if Spencer believed with Sue's departure, the whole world had deserted him.

———

The Alexanders showed Spencer around the busy farmyard. He perked up a little when a broken-down horse clumped over to him and pushed its hairy muzzle in his neck. "Buckles" was happy to see anyone and could be depended upon to nudge them in hopes of a carrot.

Rags the dog was next to approach Spencer, wagging his skinny tail. He was fat, old and friendly, always looking for a pat on the head or, better yet, a handout.

The mule was aloof and would not come to say hello at all. He just suspiciously walked around in the snow observing the tour. It was his job to guard the farm which he did all the time. Beth told Spencer she had named him "Joe" because she thought the mule looked like her husband when he hadn't shaved for a few days. Joe was mildly amused.

The ducks and chickens interested Spencer as they cluttered, quacked and clucked, approaching every obstacle like a comedy troupe, full of excitement, gabbling and squabbling among themselves. After a few minutes and a brief smile, his interest in their antics soon faded. In spite of Joe and Beth's best efforts to make him feel at home, Spencer had a crushing sense of sadness and no one he trusted to share it with.

His room at the Alexander's was nice and bright with a colorful bed, chest of drawers and a pillow. Beth took his clothes from his suitcase and put them in the drawers of the wooden dresser. His stuffed toys were put on top of the bed, including battered Ed the elephant.

The room should have been great, but things were missing. He realized that it was the small stuff he'd barely noticed before. His old room had had some pictures of him on his bedside stand, of his mom and dad, along with a few old birthday cards, gifts, and special toys. They wove together the story of him and his parents and all the things they'd done together. There was nothing here like that and never would be again. Soon tears were streaming down his face. He saw that Beth was crying too. She held him tight and just this time, he let her.

The first few weeks living with Joe and Beth were hard but is seemed the Alexanders were up to the challenge. They worked tirelessly to cheer him up. There was nothing Beth wouldn't make, cook or do if he could muster up a smile in response, which he found himself trying to do more often than he'd like, for her sake, even if it was fake. She tried so hard, he felt bad it didn't make him feel better.

As the days and weeks went by, some of his new chores started to feel good to him, like feeding the horse, mule, ducks and the chickens. He liked the way the animals crowded around him when he spread out their food. They scratched, clucked and quacked at each other in barnyard chaos. It was times like these that his smiles weren't fake.

Each day, the school bus would come by the farm to take Spencer to school. The other kids and the teachers were nice to him but he stayed mostly to himself. His marks were steady. Homework was never a problem; he worked just as hard as he did before.

One Saturday afternoon Joe, Beth and Spencer went on a spring picnic. The weather was pleasant so they went off to a nearby lake for a bit of sightseeing and wildlife watching. They built a fire, roasted some hotdogs on home-cut sticks and drank hot chocolate. Later, they went to the edge of the lake to watch for ducks and beavers. Spencer threw rocks out on the thin ice which still covered parts of the lake. The rocks made a high-pitched pinging noise as they bounced and echoed across the wide area. Spencer had never heard such a crazy, eerie sound.

As they stood quietly at the lake shore, a breeze came up. Rippling waves crossed the lake, disturbing the thin layer of surface ice. Then one large sheet of ice began moving across the lake, hitting against another large sheet, then slid up on top of it before moving away. The sliding sound of the ice layers produced the most magical sound Spencer had ever heard. They seemed to sing, squeal and chime. He knew he would never forget that sound.

It was a pretty good day.

Spencer had been with the Alexanders for almost a year. The teachers were pleased and the social worker was happy with his adjustments. Sometimes he felt sad, but the Alexanders would get him to do a few chores to bring him out of the funk and back into his new routine. They showed him every day they liked having him around.

Spring and summer came and went, followed by a glorious fall. Spencer and the Alexanders were constantly out and about getting wood for the stove, feed for the little farmyard troupe and planning for the coming winter. Joe came up with a set of cross-country skis for each of them, and a toboggan. When the snow arrived, they'd head out to the local ski trails every weekend followed by a hair raising toboggan run down the hill. He loved the feeling of speed as they bounced and scraped on the ice and snow with complete abandon, him and Joe screaming and laughing all the way.

Of all his chores, chopping wood was the one he most admired.

It was a grown-up job, one that showed him Joe trusted him. This trust was a new experience for Spencer, one he wanted to earn and keep. And there was the fact that splitting and hacking away on a block of wood appealed to all boys. He jumped at every chance to chop wood. Joe and Beth had been nervous about it at the start, but he'd persisted until they finally gave in. Joe methodically showed him how to chop while being careful not to hit his hands or feet. It was only after Joe was confident that Spencer took the task seriously and would be careful, that he allowed him to take over the task.

Spencer would split the firewood with a hatchet on a piece of an old fence post. He'd select a large piece of wood, too big for the stove, balance it on the chopping block, then swing the hatchet high over his head and bring it down on the wood, splitting it in two. He loved the stretching of his muscles, the satisfying splitting sound as the wood cracked apart, the growing evidence of his hard work piled up in the wheel barrow, all soon to be warming them in the house.

It was a rainy Saturday morning. The woodpile was soaked. Spencer was working on a particularly awkward piece of wood from a tree root that wouldn't stand up by itself. The hatchet bounced off instead of biting into the wood. Frustrated, he changed hands, which did no good at all. Before throwing the chunk of root back into the pile as useless, he gave it one last whack. The hatchet glanced off the slimy wood and went where it was not supposed to go, buried into the mitt on his left hand.

Everything stopped.

The hatchet had sliced through his mitt, and stuck into the wooden stump, cementing the mitt to the block. In horror, he looked at the damaged left mitten, with the hole and bit of blood that splashed in crimson droplets across the snow. He knocked the hatchet aside and gently pulled his hand free of the mitt. There was only a bloody stump where his finger had been.

He opened his mouth and screamed.

Then he saw the finger, lying beside his boot in the snow, bloody at its base, white at its tip. It was so small and so very large, both at the same time. He kept looking in horror at the bleeding hand with the missing finger and screamed and screamed.

Joe came running, followed by Beth. When they saw his hand and the finger in the snow, there was a lot more screaming and commotion.

At the house, Beth quickly bandaged his hand up to stop the bleeding. Joe called the hospital to say they were coming before scooping Spencer up and half-running toward the Jeep. He set Spencer into the backseat, with Beth climbing in after, gathering Spencer's quaking body against her for the ride to the hospital. Through the whole trip all Spencer registered was the relentless throbbing of his hand, and the fact that Joe's tense efforts over slippery, snowy roads toward help never seemed to end.

When they finally arrived, both a nurse and a doctor greeted them at the door of the Brandon Lake hospital. "Did you bring the finger?" the doctor asked. "Sometimes it can be re-attached."

Beth and Joe had never even thought of it.

Once inside a curtained-off cubicle, Spencer laid in the bed while the medical staff bandaged him up on one side and Joe and Beth crowded in on the other. He thought he recognized the nurse from last year when he'd stayed at the hospital after his parents were killed.

The doctor kept Spencer in the hospital for two days for observation before he would pronounce him fit to return home. He couldn't help overhearing how annoyed the doctor was to be handed the pile of forms and all the phone calls he fielded because Spencer was in state care. Susan came by and seemed more irritated than sympathetic about the accident, too.

Beth and Joe alternated staying with Spencer the entire time and were glad to be able to take him home. Joe drove, and just as they had traveled to the hospital, Beth stayed beside Spencer in the rear seat.

It was a few more days before Spencer was back into his routine. He finally felt well enough to go outside and resume a few light farm chores but first he went over to the chopping block to see if his finger was still there, but it had vanished. A cat or a fox or even Rags might have grabbed it and had taken it away. The thought made his stomach churn and he almost lost his lunch out in the dirty snow. He looked at the stub, where his left index finger used to be, and missed it. It felt as if part of his life had been taken away. First his parents and his home and everything he depended on. Now even his body was irreparably damaged too, an important part gone forever.

———

Susan Frey's boss was furious the Alexanders had exposed Spencer to harm while he was under their care.

Apparently, a newspaper had found out, allowing the critics of the Family Services department to make some political hay from the incident. Susan would have to move him to another foster home.

She felt awkward about the whole situation as it had been her personal request the Alexanders look after Spencer. She felt guilty for pushing them into a situation they might not have been ready for. Now, from Vancouver, she could give them very little support in their bid to keep Spencer after the finger incident, in spite of the fact he'd made a complete recovery and was thriving in their care.

Her supervisors had other ideas, other priorities, more concerned about how the accident made them look, than poor young Spencer's adjustment.

They ordered a "fresh start".

Clara

Susan, the social worker, took Spencer to a foster home in Williams Lake for a night.

Next day a new social worker picked him up, driving him into Vancouver, explaining they were finding a place for him. He sat quietly, clutching his possessions.

The second social worker handed him off to a third, who took him across on the car ferry headed to Victoria.

Under any other circumstances Spencer would have found the ferry ride exciting as he had never experienced such a thing before.

He said very little, spending his time gazing out the windows as the social worker read a magazine. Finally, they re-boarded the car and drove off, arriving at the front of a creepy old fence surrounding a gigantic, very old, ivy covered decrepit mansion.

"Here we are, Spencer. Home-sweet-home until we can get you a place. You'll only be here a week or two and then we will get you a nicer place."

Spencer hesitated, then asked, "Do the Munster's live here?"

She smiled, "No, but it's the original Ross Bay Orphanage and *is* over a hundred years old. It was a home for foundlings, orphans or children from single parents, usually mothers, who couldn't look after their children. The mothers would leave their kids for the orphanage to look after while they worked. When they could they would come visit them."

"Am I a foundling?" he asked, nudging his cheap oversized-glasses back up his nose before grasping his beat up suitcase tighter to his body. It felt better knowing Ed the Elephant was close to his chest. Yeah, he was ten now, and it was babyish—he didn't care.

The social worker looked back at him, and it occurred to Spencer she might be seeing him for the very first time. After a moment of silence, she murmured, "No, you're not," and placing her arm around him, another first, guided him to the main entrance.

Spencer looked at the giant old building, obviously neglected and appearing to be ready for some renovation to convert it into a school or college. The brick work was shabby, dirty with ivy barely clinging. The old window sills had not been painted for years but looked odd because big silver tubes extended down to the ground making the irritated old building look like a monstrous octopus.

The building was the size of a high school and seemed mostly empty. It reminded him of a creepy old horror show mansion on TV. Eventually he was registered, then escorted by a friendly, elderly nun who hobbled along on a cane and showed him around. His assigned room contained four bunk beds, though it seemed he would be the only occupant.

"There you go, Spencer. You have a room all to yourself," she gasped out.

"How many kids are here?" asked Spencer.

"You can call me Sister Ann, young man. We have room for five hundred but currently only have forty children. The orphanage is being phased out. The children are to go back into homes in the community."

"Have you always been here?"

She smiled, "I've been here for forty–five years…a very long time."

Spencer had no idea what it all meant but understood there were only a few kids like him in the building.

She stood there for a few moments as Spencer looked around the room, then she added, "You can just come and ask me if you need anything. There's a bell for meals, down in the main room. We do school during the weekdays, nine to three. After school you can explore the grounds but don't go outside the fence."

"What are those big tubes at the windows?" he asked.

"Those are fire escapes. You open that window and jump into the slide to escape the building. We have four of them around the upper floors."

"Can I try it sometime, Sister Ann?"

She sighed. "Not today but you can use it if there is a fire."

He looked at the window and the slide escapes for a few moments, "Where am I going from here, Sister Ann?"

She gasped and wheezed, obviously thinking, then replied, "Usually they decide where they are going to send you. That will be a foster home somewhere. In the meantime, you can stay with us. We like having you here." She smiled kindly, then clumsily tapped him on his shoulder and hobbled away.

Spencer looked around the old room. He had an old steel bunk bed and thin mattress with bedding but no pillow. The floor was covered with old, chipped linoleum and the walls were covered with old, tattered wallpaper. After looking around, he sat on the bed and opened up his suitcase, found Ed and placed him at the top of his bed as a pillow, but couldn't bring himself to unpack—not yet.

Curious, he stood to look out the window that didn't have the slide escape, through the rusty bars to the front parking lot. There were big lawns with old trees on either side, all enclosed in a high, metal fence. Over in the far-left corner was what looked like a cemetery filled with cracked head stones, reminding him he too was an orphan.

After the evening dinner in the cafeteria, a bath, and reading a bit of a Hardy Boys novel he'd found in a book bin in the library on the second floor, Spencer went back to his room and climbed into his bed. The old bed springs creaked as he settled in. It seemed sad not having Joe and Beth here. He'd come to like being around them. The image of Beth's tear-streaked face appeared in his mind unbidden and he quickly banished it. He didn't have anyone to say goodnight to, so he simply said, "Good night Ed," and was fast asleep.

The next day, his first full day at the orphanage, was uneventful, so he took his book and went out into the grassy lawn near the cemetery, sat down and leaned his back up against one of the jagged oak trees. There was an annoying squadron of geese honking at him but a few sticks and rocks tossed their way scattered them nicely. He settled down to read his book, to transport himself away from this tenuous, difficult world.

"Wha'cha readin'?"

Spencer jolted out of his reading trance. "Pardon?"

"Wha'cha reading, I said."

He looked up to see a girl about his age standing nearby. She was about his height, very thin, with long stringy hair and was wearing an old-fashioned dress, though it was shabby and patched.

"I'm reading a Hardy Boy Book."

"Oh. Do you like to read?"

"I do. Who are you?"

"I'm Clara... Clara Hutchinson. Who are you?"

"I'm Spencer Cunningham."

They stood in awkward silence. Then Clara sat down near him and asked, "Could you read your book to me, Spencer?" He looked at her as she pursed dry lips, her unblinking eyes staring down at the Hardy Boys novel.

Why not, he thought, sat down himself and started to read aloud.

She listened, as if entranced, then asked, "Who are the Hardy Boys?"

"They're a pair of boy detectives trying to solve a mystery. They call it 'a case'."

"For real?"

"Not really. This is a make-believe story. It's meant to be fun, to take you to a different world, so you can forget about your own life for a while."

She said nothing, so he started reading again. He lost all track of time, concentrating on doing the best narration he could.

The dinner bell startled him. He looked up and Clara was nowhere to be seen among the trees or buildings. Maybe he would see her at dinner.

There weren't that many other kids at the cafeteria but he couldn't see Clara. He was so busy looking for her that he dropped his tray of food on the floor with a crash. Everyone looked up and some laughed, which, to his horror, made him cry. Here he was, all alone in a strange place with nobody, and he was blubbering like a little kid in front of everyone.

Sister Ann hobbled over to help him. After stopping the laughter with a fierce glare to the other children in the hall, she ordered someone to clean the floor while she took Spencer back to the line for more food. Soon he was seated with his new supper and Sister Ann sitting next to him, with her arm on his shoulders, though he was still hiccupping and shuddering, wiping at tears that just wouldn't quit.

"It's okay Spencer. Go ahead and dig in." She dabbed up his tears with her handkerchief which made Spencer feel a bit better. Who cared what the other kids thought now? They'd already seen his melt-down. He tried a mouthful of macaroni and cheese, found that he liked it and kept going, surprised he was still hungry.

Sister Ann patiently waited with him, trying to cheer him up. "So Spencer, you had a day off school. Were you able to find your way around here? We have some books you can read, too."

Spencer spoke between mouthfuls. "I took a book and read it on the front lawn."

"What was the book about?"

"It was a Hardy Boys mystery. I liked it and so did Clara."

"Clara?"

"Yes... she came up to me and asked if I could read it to her, so I did."

"Hmm... I didn't think we had a girl named Clara here. What did she look like?"

Spencer chewed while he thought. "She was kinda my age, as tall as me, long hair, thin and had an old dress on."

Sister Ann said nothing but watched him eat.

He read until lights out; said good night to Ed. Clara was on his mind until he fell asleep. He dreamed of home, sitting at the dinner table with his dad on the right and his mom on the left, laughing and telling stories about their day.

After the church service the next day he went back to his spot on the lawn and read. It was Sunday and the sun was out in force. He looked around to see if anyone was nearby. He was alone. Before he sat, he made sure there wasn't any Canada goose poo on the grass. Opening the book he was off in the Hardy Boy world.

It wasn't long before he heard the now familiar voice of Clara. "Hello Spencer. Would you read to me again?"

Annoyed, he looked up at her, but immediately felt guilty about it. She could be lonely, just like him; besides she was nice company. "Sure."

Eventually he was thirsty and had to go to the bathroom. "Guard my book from the geese until I get back, Clara. Want a drink or something?"

"I can watch your book but no drink, thank you."

Spencer ran back to the washroom, picked up a glass of water. Walking back to the lawn he saw a goose picking at his book and Clara nowhere to be seen. He grabbed up a stick and chased the hissing bird away. Puzzled, he sat down, re-organized his disheveled book and started to read again. It wasn't long before he saw Clara's feet in the grass standing nearby.

"You left my book. The geese were pecking at it," he accused.

"I'm sorry. I wasn't sure you were coming back so I left."

She looked even sadder than usual, so Spencer relented. "It's alright Clara. Do you want me to read to you again?"

She nodded and sat down, looking at his book with sad eyes.

He read to her for an hour straight, coming to the exciting conclusion. "The End."

"Is the story over?" she asked.

"It's over. It's the end and they all lived happily ever after."

"What does that mean, Spencer?"

"It means they all got what they wanted, the bad guys got caught and Joe and Frank move on to their next case."

"Will we live happily ever after, Spencer?"

"I don't know. I'm not sure where I'm going. My parents are dead."

Clara thought, then spoke. "My daddy died in the Great War. Mommy is coming for me but I haven't seen her for a while. She loves me, you know."

"I'm sure she does."

"Do you have anyone, Spencer?"

"No. It's just me and Ed."

"Ed?"

"Ed is my stuffed elephant. I've had him for ages. Ed's family."

He turned his head when the dinner bell rang. When he turned back, Clara was gone. Weird.

He stood up, gave the geese a dirty look, pointing at them and headed off for lunch. Once again, he didn't see Clara at the cafeteria. He saw Sister Ann sitting alone at one of the tables so brought his tray to sit beside her.

"What have you been doing, Spencer?"

"I've been reading my Hardy Boys book to Clara, near the cemetery. It's sunny out.

"That sounds like fun. What's Clara's last name?"

"It's Clara… Clara… Hutchinson," he remembered.

Sister Ann smiled, and watched him as he finished his lunch. He was glad for her company.

"So where are you off to now, Spencer?" she asked.

"I'm getting another book to read to Clara."

"Good for you. I might join you, later."

Spencer put his dishes away and dashed up to the library and the book bin, retrieving another Hardy Boys book. He then battled the annoying goose for his sitting spot, cleaned off a fresh poop, totally disgusted, then sat down and started to read, hoping Clara would meet him. Soon he was lost in the world of his book.

After a while he heard footsteps. He looked up, expecting to see his new friend, Clara. "Oh. Hi, Sister Ann."

"Hello Spencer. Did Clara come to see you?"

"No. I guess she was busy."

"Come with me, Spencer. Bring your book. I want to show you something."

Puzzled, he stood up and followed Sister Ann's limping trail across the lumpy cemetery grass to the second to last headstone on the front row.

"What do you want to show me?"

Sister Ann squinted then pointed to a small, worn stone, laying on the ground and barely readable.

Clara G. Hutchinson
1910 – 1920

"Clara died forty-five years ago, Spencer."

Spencer looked up at her, bewildered.

"Clara's father was killed in the Great War and her mom struggled to raise her, leaving her at this orphanage for long periods of time. Her mother died in the great influenza epidemic and that's why Clara waited and waited for her to come but she never did. Later Clara died from the 'flu herself in 1920."

Spencer was shocked. "But I saw her—I talked to her."

"I don't know who she was, or why she'd tell you her name was

Clara. This Clara died a long time ago. I looked up the old records. It's true. I'm so sorry about your new friend." Sister Ann rested her arm on his shoulder.

He did not know what to say. For sure he wouldn't be telling Sister Ann that Clara had been real, and was maybe even a ghost. They just stood together in silence thinking about a young soul that passed away unnoticed, so long ago. It reminded Spencer yet again how alone he was.

Spooked and sad, Spencer left the lawn area and went inside. He looked around the ancient old rooms and halls, imagining all the children who had been here before him, imagining all their stories. He knew the cemetery had stories to tell and wondered if there were more ghosts.

Eventually he got his courage back and headed to the place by the tree, book in hand, Ed under his arm for comfort and reinforcement, ready to do more reading. It was a warm spring afternoon with the sun out and flowers blooming, such a contrast to the winter weather he'd seen at Brandon Lake. It was a bit chilly, so he'd worn a sweater. He wondered why Clara only wore a thin dress but supposed ghosts didn't get cold, then stopped himself.

Did he seriously believe Clara was a ghost?

Maybe he'd day-dreamed Clara? This thought was immediately troubling. He'd known her real story before Sister Ann had told him the truth.

The goose was nowhere to be seen, so he sat down, determined to forget about Clara. Soon he was solving mysteries with the Hardy Boys. He made it through thirty pages and was quite proud of himself when he heard something and looked up, right into Clara's face. Surprised, he jolted and so did Clara. He blurted, "You scared me, Clara!"

Clara gave a wan smile, "Sorry, Spencer. I thought you wouldn't mind if I sat beside you."

"I – I guess I don't mind."

"Is this Ed?" She pointed to the bedraggled elephant, this time she wore a big smile.

"Yes, this is my old buddy Ed. We've been through a lot, together. Do you want to hold him?"

"Well... I actually can't... but will you read to me?"

"Sure." Spencer settled Ed into the grass beside her, not understanding her reluctance to hold him, but glad for her company.

He read to her for an hour, feeling pleased he hardly missed any words. Sadly, when he looked up from his book Clara was gone. He stood and looked over towards the cemetery stone Sister Ann had shown him and said aloud, "You left Ed, Clara." There was no reply. He was sad, but he wasn't surprised.

It was late. Disappointed, he collected Ed and went to his room.

From that day forward, he went to that reading place every day for the remainder of his stay, but he never saw Clara again.

It was two weeks later when Sister Ann saw the social services government car pull up in the driveway as she had so many times in the past.

"I'm here to pick up Spencer Cunningham," the worker told her.

Sister Ann handed over Spencer's file as well as a transfer form to be filled out.

The Social Worker filled in the blanks until the last box on the page, "How was Spencer? He's been through a lot in the past year."

The sister smiled. "I think he's a nice boy and he works hard. That'll help him through the tough times."

A Rolling Stone

Forty years later, Spencer stood on the street corner in his postal uniform, mailbag in hand, reflecting back on those days, the Alexanders, the orphanage, and the many foster homes that followed. He remembered being forced to move again and again, the spark of human touch he extended to each new family growing dimmer and fainter with each attempt.

His bundle of belongings grew smaller and smaller with each move. Even the pajamas his parents had given him when he was nine were abandoned, at last too small and too worn. Somewhere along the way, he lost the old suitcase, too.

It was as if his soul shrank as well, finally extinguished after the twelfth home in seven years. He'd learned to depend on himself and nothing more, nothing less.

Each foster home was often busy and crowded. It seemed at least one of the other foster kids was causing trouble and commanded a great deal of attention, the home full of stress. If Spencer had his own room, he'd eagerly stay there with the door closed, reading or doing his homework, a welcome respite from the chaos. The other kids were temporary, he was temporary, the foster home was temporary. Even the Social workers, who shifted from caseload to caseload, were temporary. It became sort of a shell game. Under which shell would Spencer be this month?

Spencer quickly learned the difference between a normal home and a foster home. In a normal home, there was undoubtedly some sibling competition, but love was unconditional. There was no real threat of banishment, just hurt feelings. Things were different in a foster home. In a foster home, there existed a continuing competition for food, for shelter, and for attention. An orphan's fate could rest on a whim, or a mood. Maybe this would be the day Spencer's unkempt room or unmade bed would be the last straw and he would be sent on his way. He was an outsider, in a game of musical chairs. Sometimes the sheer coincidence of a transfer could confirm his irrational fears.

He never got used to the shock of being told he was being moved, regardless of how many times it happened. The reasons and excuses could be made with a smile and an apology. The home he was in might seem sad to see him go but the sick feeling of packing up and saying goodbye was more or less the same. This was utterly out of his hands.

He didn't bother making friends at the various schools he attended, even when tempted. He never brought artwork, or the stories he sometimes wrote to the home he was currently assigned to because nobody was going to look at it or show it, anyway. Nobody was going to put a foster kid's artwork on the fridge. He just crumpled it up and threw it away.

Sometimes he would think of Clara and wondered if she would be willing to hear his stories. Since there was no one else interested, he crumpled his stories up too and threw them away. It made him sad nobody would see them. It was the story of his life.

After a while he had a little contest with himself on his numerous family transfers to see how little he told them about himself or how much evidence would remain of him after he was gone. It was as if he was never there.

Spencer kept it all to himself like a bottle with a cork. He worked hard enough in school to pass everything, which, instead of helping, could work against him as he often would be put into a foster home that was a bit overcrowded. Because he appeared fine on the surface, he seemed to be the first one sent away to give more time to another foster child who was having trouble adjusting.

When his latest case worker seemed overworked, or claimed she was, Spencer would smile and be polite during the interview as she hustled through the paperwork and transferred him once again with barely a second thought. He never considered how there were never enough of these foster homes to go around and how much these open, caring, loving people did for kids like him. Each home did make an effort to welcome him.

Each Christmas was traumatic at the foster homes. Spencer knew the ropes—there would be a few gifts from the parents and a dinner, not bad things. The hard part was when some of the kids were expecting to be picked up by parents or relatives. They would be told by the social worker that a parent or relative would be picking them up, and this is where the trouble began—Spencer had seen it time and time again.

Danny, a boy who shared his current foster home, and who was around the same age as Spencer, had been told that his mother was coming for him today at one o'clock. Spencer watched him as he waited in a chair looking out the front window, watching for her to come. Spencer could see Danny had his hopes up and was now vulnerable and wide open. His heart waited for his mom to come, desperately needing that human connection and fearing she wouldn't appear. It seemed to Spencer that Danny would only allow himself to believe it when he saw it but still hoped upon hope as his mother's arrival time came and slowly drifted away from him. Still, he remained at the window and Spencer suspected that he was praying that the next car would stop, that he and his mother would still have Christmas together, just this once.

Eventually the foster mom came and sat beside Danny, putting her arm around him. Danny, who normally resisted any physical display of affection because he was the home tough-guy leaned his head on her shoulder and wept, quietly, the very picture of abandonment and hopelessness, stood up again, like so many years before. It was crushing to witness his belief that this year might be different being destroyed.

Once, a girl sharing one of Spencer's foster homes traveled for eight hours to High Level on a bus, only to find there was nobody there to take her in for Christmas as had been arranged. Her hopes for love and affection were rebuffed in the cruelest way. She ended up sitting on her suitcase in the gas station that served as the bus depot, until the RCMP found her early the next morning. She was devastated, and spent days sobbing in her room after her return.

Afterwards, Spencer overheard the foster parents whispering to each other, appalled and disgusted her parents could treat their child so cruelly at such a vulnerable time in her life. This girl had opened up her jaded and disappointed heart once again, hoping for any crumb of affection and had been destroyed.

Spencer told himself that would never be him because he would steel his heart from hurt forever. He took the safe route, turning himself inwards, never sharing his thoughts and feelings with anyone anymore. It was easier than making a few connections with other people only to have them torn away when he was uprooted again and sent on another journey.

Looking back, it always felt peculiar when he arrived at a new home where everyone already knew his history, his parents' demise and the fact he was an orphan. Parents and the other kids would crowd the doorway of the house to greet the new arrival, the children's faces poking through any available viewing space. It was like being a zoo exhibit. They would look at him sadly, speak to him with pity and sympathy. Spencer knew it was not meant as derision but he still didn't like it.

Spencer was always an outsider, wherever he lived, never part of the family. The foster parents' children were often suspicious of the new foster kids, fearing they were at worst trouble makers, druggies or thieves which was seldom the case. At best, these new arrivals competed for the parent's time and affection. This all made for a general feeling of insecurity. Everyone was temporary. Fear of this quiet boy with the "active imagination" sped him along to the next home, taking his suspected deeper issues safely away with him.

Spencer made himself a promise that someday he would have a stable place to live and a stable job and stay with it until he retired. He'd had enough with the day to day circus that was his life.

He had to admit his final foster family did manage to get through to his heart. The Williams family ran a little rural post office from an old bunkhouse trailer, next to their home. They were kindly and helpful people who noticed that Spencer showed an interest in what they did. They set him up sorting the mail and doing local deliveries on his bike. He found he enjoyed the work and it earned him a bit of pocket money. It was an active job, got him out of the house and was something he could control after years of being shuffled around without options. Soon the Williams were trusting Spencer to run the post office while they were away for a day or an afternoon.

The Williams family also remembered his eighteenth birthday, and planned a surprise party for him. Spencer came home from school as usual. He finished his homework in his room and then came down for supper. They had dinner as usual and were just thinking about dessert when Mrs. Williams brought out a big chocolate cake with eighteen candles burning brightly. The other five kids sang Happy Birthday. He blew out the candles and they all had as much cake as they could eat.

Later they talked, laughed, and joked around, wearing paper party hats.

The William's gave him a wallet and a shaving kit for a birthday and farewell gift. The truth was, this was a going away and birthday party combined—Spencer had finally aged out of the system.

Everyone hugged him and wished him well. Despite himself, he had a lump in his throat. The Williams had wanted to give him a heartfelt send off and they'd done it.

With his eighteenth birthday Spencer's time as a ward of the government was at long last over. It was time for him to go out on his own, to make his way in the world. The Williams put in a good word for him at the Regional Post Office and when an opening came up in the mail depot in Donvegan, nestled on the edge of the Peace River, he was offered a job as a mail delivery person starting after school ended. While thrilled about the new prospect, Spencer dreaded having to relocate to the unknown one more time. Hopefully this will be the last one, he thought.

Barney and the Hearse

Almost forty years later Spencer still loved the fact he went to sleep every day knowing where he was, where he'd be, who he'd see, year after year. Nothing ever changed.

Delivering mail was as dull as dishwater with a delicious sameness he craved. Each day was the same as the first. This job would never change or abandon him or make him feel uncomfortable, unlike his past life. Yes, it had turned him into a loner with most contact with his fellow workers minimized, or, if he could arrange it, avoided. Privately Spencer couldn't have cared less about his co-workers. It wasn't that he hated them; it was simply that he preferred to keep to himself and do his job, get paid and go home. He couldn't imagine it any other way.

Barney worked to the left of Spencer's sorting station at the post office for eighteen years. Spencer hardly knew him other than a mumbled "Morning" to him, and only if hard pressed. Barney was a friendly guy who chattered away about this and that with Spencer barely listening. He was about the same age as Spencer but after that, had little in common. He was tall and thin with a little scraggly goatee, a gregarious family man, full of stories about his wife and the antics of their seven active kids. According to Barney, all his kids were good students, avid figure skaters and hockey players.

Spencer thought all this family stuff sounded expensive, with the kids sport costs and all. Barney never took a sick day because he simply could not afford it. He worked any overtime hours he could find at the post office as well as moonlighting for the local funeral home.

"Morning Spencer! How are you?" said Barney, looking him in the eyes.

"Um...fine." Spencer looked away, ignoring him.

Barney was tenacious. "Boy, I had another tough night driving stiffs around for the funeral home. Want to hear about it?"

"Not really..."

"I'm glad you asked! They pay me to drive this huge Cadillac hearse up to Fort Mac and back and it's so quiet you could hear a heartbeat from inside a coffin... if there was a heartbeat in a coffin. That's a "Craig" joke. He's the funeral guy up there. Funny fella or at least he thinks he is."

"I can imagine..." mumbled Spencer, wishing Barney would shut up.

Clark worked on Spencer's right as he had done for twenty-five years. As far as Spencer knew or cared, he was a single guy, about three years younger. One of Clark's annoying favorite antics was to find an interesting postcard and read it to everyone in the building. He'd call out for everyone to listen while he read the private contents with batting of eyelashes, gesticulation, animation and great theatrical flourish. Today was one of those days.

"Hey, everyone! We have a postcard from Deb in Vegas. Listen up!"

"Dear Marge! Saw Tom Jones in Vegas concert so I took my panties off and threw them on to the stage. Jim was so mad at me! Well, I didn't want to

be left out. Maybe Mr. Jones will send for me or something. Oh well, what happens in Vegas, stays in Vegas, right? LOL! Deb.'"

Everyone roared their approval of Clark's selection then drifted back to their workstations. Spencer had watched the proceedings with embarrassment for the poor lady in the postcard. He grabbed another handful of letters and continued sorting.

"That Clark always cracks me up," grinned Barney as he put his crutches to one side, gracelessly slumped into his chair beside Spencer then grimaced in pain. "Aw!"

Last week Barney had slipped on a patch of ice very early into his mail route. Heavily laden with two big mailbags, he fell awkwardly, twisting and hitting the ground. He'd shared the experience with Spencer in excruciating detail—claiming to hear the bone in his thigh snap like a dry stick. Unwilling to move, he'd stayed down and called for help. Three other nearby post office delivery people came to him to offer assistance but Barney wisely declined, waiting for the ambulance. At Barney's insistence, the three postal workers split up his route mail, each claiming the mail that was nearest their route and put it in their own satchels and departed. He used his cell phone to stay in contact with the post office while he patiently waited for an ambulance to arrive. According to the doctors, he had a compound fracture of the thigh bone and would be in a huge cast for fourteen weeks. It was a bad break.

Even Spencer couldn't ignore Barney's new cast. Barney wasn't able to drive or walk normally for some time and was currently doing light duty at the post office depot. Despite Spencer's indifference, Barney insisted on keeping in touch with him during his rounds.

Barney always stood a bit too closely for Spencer's comfort. "Hey Spencer, a friend of mine owns Giebelhaus Funeral Home and she needs a driver to go to Fort Mac and return to Donvegan on the weekends. It's usually a Saturday or Sunday night. It's easy money. As you can see, I'm out of commission, but the funeral home still needs a weekend driver. Did I mention it pays real well? You could get a new computer or a big screen TV!"

Spencer's go-to answer—'NO'—stuck in his throat at the thought of his ancient computer locking up for the hundredth time. "I don't know. I'm not sure I'm a funeral home kind of person."

Barney sensed his change of heart, and jumped in. "It's an easy job. You'd be transporting someone who doesn't make any trouble while you're driving the nicest car you'll ever have the pleasure to drive while earning a few one-hundred-dollar bills. This holds the job open for me, too, so I can step back into it when I heal up. What's not to like?"

It was not like Spencer had a busy life on the weekends. His evenings were usually him and his dog snoring on the couch until it was time to go to bed. It sounded like it could be easy money. The more Spencer thought about it, the better it sounded. He gave the funeral home a call and offered to do the job for three months. They assured him it would be the odd weekend or two, mostly night drives.

After work, Spencer had a call waiting for him on his voicemail. This was unusual. A loner doesn't get many phone calls. "Hello this is Cathy Belson from the Funeral Service with a message for Spencer Cunningham. Barney told us about you and we'd like to interview you at five o'clock, tomorrow. We hope to see you then."

Next day he arrived at the funeral home still dressed in his post office uniform. Stopping at the door, he took a deep breath before walking in.

A plump, middle-aged woman greeted him with a pleasant smile. "You must be Spencer. Come and sit down in the meeting room. This won't take a minute."

Following her, he saw at once that he would be facing four inter-viewers, each seated at an elderly wooden table. Did they think he might be someone to fear, and they needed the distance for protection?

The woman indicated that he should sit on the single wooden chair set up on the opposite side of the table. He pulled it out and sat. It was covered in old vinyl and made the requisite farting sound every time he shifted on it. Good to know. He stopped moving, and glanced around. The room was overly large for its purpose, surplus, unused, old, and smell of formaldehyde.

"Thank you for coming. We found your references acceptable and helpful," the woman said, her chair screeching as she brought it closer to the table, making more farting sounds as she squirmed, seeking comfort that would never be, all echoing in the large empty space. "To my right or …sorry …I meant my *left* is Gary Jones, the local manager, then Marino Julio, office manager, Ina Smith, shipper and Hank Reynolds, chief embalmer and furnace manager."

"You mean 'Hank of the Hell Fire department? He's the cream of cremation," laughed Ina.

"People! Be professional. We are trying to have a position interview here. Head office demands a proper interview," she scolded.

"Tell him who you are, Cathy," Hank said dryly.

"Oh yes, I'm Cathy Belson, co-office manager."

Spencer immediately regretted applying for this job and considered making a run for it, but they all watched him now, like spiders on the wall, so escape was not an option. Yet.

"I guess I'll open this discussion up and ask you, Mr. Spencer. Have you ever done this line of work before?" Cathy asked, making another farting sound as she moved forward to speak. Did they not hear this?

"Mr. Cunningham. My name is Spencer Cunningham, ma'am."

The panelists all looked at each other and at their papers, bewildered for a few moments.

"Of course, you are Mr. Cunningham. I'm very sorry."

"Shit," Hank Reynolds murmured. The one named Gary tipped his water bottle. He lunged forward to rescue it, then screeched the chair back and retreated to the washroom for paper towel.

"Sorry. Let's begin again, Mr. Cunningham. Perhaps you could tell us your name and present occupation," Cathy said, flustered as Gary bumped back into his chair.

"I'm a mailman with Canada Post. I've been there for forty years."

"Married Mr. Cunningham?" asked Ina.

Hank blurted out, "Ina! You can't ask that anymore. Sorry Mr. Cunningham."

"It's alright. No, I'm not married."

"Looking for a date, Ina?" teased Hank.

Cathy ignored them. "I trust you have a clean driver's record and no criminal record?"

Hank added, "We can't have you stealing our dead people, Spencer."

Spencer fought a smile. Okay, so that was funny. "Yes, my driver's record is clean. And no criminal record." He handed over the two documents Barney had told him to bring.

"Have you ever driven a hearse before?"

"I've driven vans that are about the same length but not a hearse."

"I have a few questions our headquarters suggested...let's see...when was the last time you had a conflict with your supervisor and how did you resolve it?"

The truth was Spencer never had an issue with any of his bosses. He was as quiet as a mouse at work. They barely knew of his existence. "Well, I've never had an issue. They give me the mail, I sort it and drop it in the mailboxes.

Spencer could see the panellists leaning over towards him, anticipating some type of story. He was almost sorry he had none to tell. He added, "I suppose I do have the odd problem with a customer during a delivery of their mail."

Cathy seemed quite excited about this. "Really? Please tell us about it."

"Well, I was making my rounds when a customer's dog bit my finger when I put their mail through the slot in the door." He held up his left hand and the missing finger.

The people on the panel gasped in horror.

"Oh, sorry...he bit my baby finger, not the missing one."

The panel expelled a collective sigh of relief.

"How did you resolve this biting dog thing?" she asked eagerly.

"Well, next day, I waited for something that looked like a cheque, then held it in the slot so the dog would wrestle it out of my hand and chew it up. The next delivery day the dog was gone."

Hank laughed so hard that tears ran down his cheeks. "You're hired, Spencer!"

Spencer blinked in surprise, relieved the interview was over.

Cathy leaned across the table and gave him some keys. "There you go, Spencer, the keys to the hearse. I'll be calling you when the next delivery comes up."

"What exactly will I be delivering, Ms. Belson?"

"Why caskets, of course."

"Will there be someone in them?"

"I hope so, Spencer."

Easy Money… With a Catch

All he had to do was drive a nearly new Cadillac hearse up to Fort Mac and then drive it back again. The road was deserted. There was hardly a house or living soul on the two-hour drive. It was on an empty road with only a few deer to dodge. He did nothing but drive and daydream. The best part was four hours of solitude for four hundred bucks. It was all cash money, under the table. No taxes or T4's. Pure profit.

He'd left right after work, arriving in the early evening. The drive up was pleasant enough. The hearse was terrific to drive. It was so luxurious, quiet and smooth he hardly knew it was moving. It wasn't until he arrived at the funeral home in Fort Mac, that he began to have second thoughts.

He did as instructed, driving up the sloping hill and backing up to the second story roll doors for the pickup. Even though he'd had been told where to find the funeral home's doorway it still seemed odd it was located over the town bowling alley. Climbing from the hearse, he could hear the sounds of balls rumbling down the alley, the banging of a strike followed by yells of triumph. Yup. It was a bowling alley.

"What an awful racket," he muttered as he approached the entrance. The attendant surprised him, flinging open the door as Spencer was about to knock. The Fort Mac office was staffed by a part-timer named Craig, and this must be him. Barney had warned Spencer that Craig was a bit odd. Apparently, he fancied himself something of an amateur comedian, with emphasis on the amateur. He looked to be in his late twenties, stood about six-foot-tall, had a medium build and was missing two front teeth.

"Oh, you're here. Back up and I'll open the roll door," he commanded with a surprising and pronounced lisp–caused by the missing teeth, no doubt—then slamming the door in Spencer's face.

Surprised, Spencer did as he was told, honking his horn as a warning and backing up. The attendant rolled the garage door open, waved him in and closed it behind him.

Transferring a coffin was private business, apparently.

As Spencer got out, he found that the attendant had already opened the big rear door of the hearse. Abruptly it dawned on him what this trip was all about...bringing back a dead person! Yikes!

At first, Spencer was not sure if he was supposed to help with the loading process or not, so just stood and watched. He couldn't help but notice that this particular casket was pretty beat up and rough, not your usual gleaming affair. The smooth wood surface and ornate corner brass work had numerous scratches, chips and dents in it. This must be the traveler version for transportation.

Craig wore faded blue coveralls, red croc flip flops on his feet and a green baseball hat that simply said, "Runs like a Deere". It was a strange outfit to wear in a funeral home, even in Fort Mac. Craig got the casket in the back of the hearse, easily accomplished with the gurney. All that remained was to secure the casket to the floor of the hearse so it didn't hop around during the long drive.

Looking around the funeral home bay, Spencer couldn't help noticing how stark and unfinished it was. The open roof beams were laced with cobwebs and the walls, while insulated, were as yet unclad. The concrete floor was unpainted and puddled with water and mud. This grubby, rented garage was the sorry end of the line for someone.

Craig woke him from his thoughts, staring at him as if expecting Spencer to say something. It was an awkward moment before Spencer found his voice and spoke.

"I should introduce myself. I'm Spencer," he said, offering his hand. Craig grinned, took his hand, giving an overly firm, clammy and protracted handshake with far too much eye contact.

"Rule #1, Spencer, is don't shake hands with someone who handles dead people." Craig grinned and winked.

Spencer pulled his hand back in horror, then stood rooted in embarrassment as Craig laughed. The attendant's lisp made the word 'someone' sound like 'thumb-one' and 'rule' sound like woo-ull', like an Elmer Fudd cartoon. It was then Spencer saw his discolored teeth and a telltale sign of chewing tobacco as it dribbled down his chin and couldn't contain a shudder.

"It's okay, I'm just pulling your leg!" From Craig's mouth, "pulling" sound like "poo-ing". He handed Spencer a clipboard with papers to sign.

"What am I signing for?" Spencer asked.

"It's not so much 'what' as 'who' are you signing for," Craig replied.

"Is there a body in there?"

The attendant smiled at him and said, "I hope so. We can pop the lid and look, if you like!"

"No... No... that's okay. I'll take your word for it."

"This is Gordon Smith from Lethbridge. Gord, meet Spencer. He will be your driver for this evening," said Craig announced grandly, introducing the casket with a sweep of his arm. After a moment's pause, he added, "Apparently he's not going to shake your hand so this is as good as a greeting."

"What happened to him?" asked Spencer, compelled to know.

"Gord had no arms and legs and was a bull fighter with fatal results," the attendant deadpanned.

The lisp made it sound like "Goad had no awms and wegs ...was a boo fightah..."

Funeral guy humor? Spencer didn't get the joke.

Craig looked at him expecting a reaction and not getting any. "Gord? Gored? Get it? You don't get it? Never mind. I hate explaining jokes to people. Gord's loaded up, signed for, and you both can be on your way," he said with a lisp. A bit of tobacco spittle escaped from the corner of his mouth.

There was no turning back now, Spencer was committed. He climbed back into the hearse. Craig opened the big roll door and Spencer drove off into the night, following the deserted road without a house to be seen for miles.

The hearse was wonderful to drive. It was smooth and quiet with a terrific sound system so Spencer could play his music as loud as he wanted. It was a nice way to make a hundred dollars an hour and he didn't have to talk to a living soul. He decided he liked this job enough to help out regularly.

Life

The Alexanders enjoyed taking in foster kids. It was like a new chapter in their lives, helping out these needy children. They came in all ages and sizes. Joe put an addition onto the house so they could accommodate three at any one time. They became attached to all the kids and believed that each one truly enjoyed being there. When the kids left, it was a tearful affair, but Beth always made an effort to keep in touch, send them a birthday card or little Christmas gift. She loved them all.

On Beth's 35th birthday, she surprised Joe with an announcement that she was pregnant. They had long given up thinking about their own children but surprisingly they were to become parents after all. Kirstin was born healthy and happy and enjoyed a continuous line of foster brothers and sisters as she grew up. There was always an endless supply.

Eventually the Alexanders retired and moved from little Brandon Lake, up to the bustling town of Donvegan to be closer to their daughter. It was nice, living in a larger center with all the city amenities, yet the town was not yet big enough to lose its small-town charm. They didn't go out often, but it was nice to have the option if they wanted it. They had a bigger, newer house, all on one floor so it was not an effort to go up and down stairs. Once in a while, they would go back to Brandon Lake for a visit to see all their old friends.

Certainly, Beth and Joe were getting older. Both of them were now in their mid-seventies. They were spry and cheerful, making every effort to get out and enjoy the day with exercise or some activity. With Kirstin, her husband Jason and their two children so close now, it was easy to meet up somewhere, or have them over. Beth and Joe's network of foster kids, now adults, would drop by when they were in town to visit, the Alexanders always glad to see them—and their children. It was like a large, great extended family.

Once in a while, Joe or Beth would ask the other about that first orphaned boy, Spencer, who they'd taken in so long ago. "What do you suppose ever became of Spencer?"

Mail

After a walk to work, Spencer's day at the Donvegan Post Office started at the early hour of six o'clock in the morning. The depot itself was an old three-story stone building, situated in the middle of town. The building's stonework was old and weathered with winter-killed ivy hanging off the walls, their gnarled brown stalks like withered fingers. The windows were all filthy, covered with mud and bird excrement. Nobody was concerned about the state of the building as it was irrelevant to its function. There were only the postal workers, a few front office clerks and a supervisor. They had no time or interest to look out the windows anyway.

Coming in from the pretty Donvegan street, Spencer found the back-entrance door open and walked in. The thick steel door had big locks at the sides and a heavy cross bar to keep out prowlers who continuously tried to break in from the alley.

The workers got to work as soon as they arrived. The sooner they were done, the sooner they went home, the sooner the days, weeks, months and years went by, the sooner they got to the age of sixty-five and could retire. It was an urgent, never-ending treadmill of mundane tasks but came with a solid pay check. They started in the dark, early morning, sorted their own mail routes in an hour or two and were on their way through the streets of Donvegan.

Spencer sometimes wondered what kept him in Donvegan after all these years. Sometimes he fancied moving somewhere exciting but the move never took place. His last foster home with the Williams family had been in Fort Mac and he'd moved directly to Donvegan when the post office hired him on the William's recommendation. He didn't think much of the town, but had fallen into a routine that suited him. The people were kind enough and the town was rural enough to offer anything he needed. Houses were affordable. It was a pretty place with all the four seasons. Once he'd bought a house, Donvegan became his home.

Spencer entered the huge, cluttered mailroom filled with mail carts, sorting boxes and bustling postal workers. Both the postal boss and the postal union steward watched the proceedings closely for signs of trouble or contract interpretations. Spencer was of two minds of the postal union. While the union seemed confrontational at times, something Spencer disliked, they *did* make sure the workers were paid a healthy wage and benefits package for something the private postal contract delivery people and sorters got pennies for. Considering how simple a postal workers job was, on a technical level, they enjoyed job security and received a good wage. The postal union had looked after them very well, over the years.

Once at his station, Spencer grabbed his pile of mail from the mail cart and sorted the envelopes into the little "pigeon holes". The "pigeon holes" was a wall of wooden dividers set up in rows. The rows of slots were stacked next to each other in the order of the houses up and down a street on a mail run.

The wooden mail slot cabinets were beat up, dirty thin plywood, built decades ago. Even though Spencer spent a huge part of his working life here, it never occurred to him to request a coat of fresh paint or any kind of simple renovation from the shop steward. The man would be sure to refuse him.

Spencer was a handy guy who could fix something beat up and make it look better than new, given the opportunity. He sometimes passed his sorting time imagining how he could refurbish these mail slots into something beautiful, functional and marvelous to look at. An ordinary built-in light alone could make sorting so much easier for everyone.

Maybe he would do it on his last day before retirement. By the time the union steward spied the improvement, Spencer would be long gone.

But that would be one day. For today, he had his deliveries. He refocused his attention. Each little divider had just enough room for a few envelopes and some individually addressed junk mail. Each divider represented a mailbox. A mailbox represented the people who lived at that address. Each divider's mail was their contact with friends, family, creditors, merchants, catalogue sales and scam artists.

Lately, Spencer was hearing rumors about the new centralized sorting system the post office was trying out. All the mail would go to giant sorting stations in the major cities and was sorted by hand or machine into the street routes using the postal codes on the mail. Immigrants, contractors, out-of-country cheap labor or anyone else could get the contract to sort the tons of mail that arrived daily. There was no need for highly paid union workers to do such a simple task when it could be done by untrained cheap labor at a central location on a large scale. The public demanded the cheapest prices for every-thing including the price of a stamp, while demanding to be paid top wages for their own work, he thought wryly. These two concepts did not mesh.

It didn't take a rocket scientist to see there were going to be layoffs. They would be a well-paid dinosaur, slowly becoming irrele-vant in the age of email and the internet where the post office was transitioning into a service for junk mail, flyers and bogus winning sweepstakes applications, which in itself was considerable. It all required postage for delivery.

A few folks played pranks on the postal system, usually student-loan poor university students, if they were too poor to pay for a stamp. They'd mail the letter without a stamp, with the "return" address as the destination and the actual mailing address in the upper left corner reserved for the "return". The little "return" address was in fact their destination address where the stampless envelope was eventually sent. The mailer of the letter got a free delivery! It was a lot of work to save the cost of a stamp but it was always good for a laugh for someone.

Such were the politics of his workplace. Every job had them, each unique unto itself. Spencer would work around them just as he had for years. He just kept his head down and did his job well each and every day.

Outsider

Digging through his mailbag at the station Spencer remembered back to those first few days on the job when all he had to say was, "Nice day!" or "Sure cold, today". Nobody wanted to talk much, they just wanted their mail. His co-workers at the post office didn't say much either; they were all in a hurry to get their deliveries done. They were paid for an eight-hour day, so if they hustled and skipped lunch and breaks, they could be done in seven hours. With an early start and quick step, they could be home by one in the afternoon. It was a hard, nonstop seven-hour race, but the rest of the day was theirs.

"Spencer, what are you doing this weekend?" Barney asked.

"Oh, I don't know. I guess I'll decide when it comes along," he replied, marching out his usual evasive, non-committal answer.

"You know, there are a few of us going to Casey's, afterwards. You're welcome to join us."

"Yeah... Well, maybe. I'll think about it," was his reply. They both knew he wouldn't go.

Spencer stuffed his mail into two big sacks. He put the two registered letters in the special side pocket of his postal bag. He disliked registered letters because that meant he would have to carry on a conversation with the recipient while they signed his receipt form. The post office was sticky about getting the required signature. He made sure he had the necessary black ink pen which also meant less talk and discussion.

The post office door opened and slammed shut constantly with posties heading into the dark, damp outside world. He took his turn through the door, taking a moment to inhale a breath of the cold, morning air. As much as he enjoyed the predictability of his indoor chores, he much preferred the solitude and independence of outside. Nobody even looked his way as he trundled up and down the streets with the mail.

After years of experience, Spencer was very efficient at delivering mail. His stocky physique was well suited to the heavy trudge of carrying mail long distances—his daily route on the North West side of town. There were industrial drops, a few apartment buildings, houses old and new as well as a couple of mansions on the edge of town that bordered a big park. The route was well paved with side-walks and streetlights. The fall air was fresh as he crunched along his way.

The first house was a tiny, rundown old place, surrounded by deep, uncut grass. A very old, fragile man named Sam LaPointe lived there, although Spencer had only seen him once coming out the door as Spencer put his mail in the box. Deftly, Spencer reached into his pack for Sam's mail. Sam's mailbox was stuffed from last week so Spencer had to squeeze in a few bills, a flyer and a personal, hand addressed envelope before he was on his way down the street. Was the old guy away? He'd soon have to stop delivery.

"Quick and painless with a clean get away," he muttered grimly, and headed back to the street. As per postal regulations regarding uncollected mail, he would hand in a little card that requested a home follow-up.

Seeing Things

One extremely cold winter Saturday morning, the Giebelhaus Funeral Home sent Spencer back up to Fort Mac, in a pickup truck this time, instead of the hearse. Traveling in a pickup was a bit of a disappointment. Mind you, the pickup was nice enough, bright red, nice interior with a powerful V8 engine and stick shift on the floor. It was snappy and cool with a sound system loud enough to make his ears bleed.

The pickup's beige interior was beautiful, though cramped, with bucket seats and a wide shifter console. It was an older, non-extended cab so there was no room for Spencer's coat, boots and emergency pack which he'd had to pile in a heap on the passenger seat beside him.

Other than being very cold, the drive up was uneventful. He did see a work crew out surveying on the side of the road and pitied the poor flagman having to stand there, all day. Spencer knew what it was like to be out in the cold, but at least when he worked, he was on the move and not having to stand still all day.

When he arrived at the funeral home in Fort Mac, Craig sent him over to the government coroner's office instead. Spencer guessed there was something odd about this particular body's circumstance and shuddered.

Once there, a man wearing a grubby white smock came out and waved him around to the side of the building. Spencer hopped out, grabbing his coat and gloves, just in time to see the frozen body.

"Dead?" he blurted, recoiling in horror.

"Frozen hard as a gargoyle," the grim coroner confirmed. "The body was frozen in this sitting position. Apparently, late in the evening, he had too much to drink, became belligerent and the hotel bar bouncers threw him out into the cold. He staggered around a while, then, we think he decided to hide behind some empty crates so nobody would bother him and went to sleep at forty below. He froze to death. Nobody knew him or cared to look for him, I guess. Three days later a police officer discovered his frozen body."

Spencer was aghast. The victim was fully dressed in faded jeans, a blue lined jean coat and had a blue 'Maple Leafs' baseball cap slouched over its eyes. An ordinary guy you'd meet on the street. It looked as if he just went to sleep and never awoke.

The coroner said, "I haven't the time or the place to thaw him out and put him in a coffin. If you'll assist me, we'll secure him in the back of the pickup and he'll be fine for the short drive home."

What? Spencer couldn't believe he'd heard the request correctly and couldn't believe he was actually helping the man put the crazy plan into action. Together, he and the coroner each took an arm and a leg and loaded up the frozen corpse, placing it in the open box of the pickup with the corpse's back fit against the cab. They secured it with bungee cords until they were both satisfied it wasn't going anywhere. Weirdly, the seated body fit perfectly into the corner.

"He sort of looks like a full size garden gnome," Spencer remarked, instantly regretting his heartless choice of words.

"Yes, and still looks very life-like, sitting there," agreed the coroner, apparently not appalled at all.

Spencer stood for a minute, looking in disbelief at the frozen, seated body with its eyes frozen open. The guy looked as if he could jump up and yell 'boo!' as if this was all just a cruel joke.

After signing for the frozen man and collecting the transfer papers, Spencer got in the pickup and drove towards home with his frozen passenger in the back. Morbid fascination made him glance often in the rear-view mirror, repeatedly checking that the inert body was still there. All he could see was the back of a dirty baseball hat. Fortunately, the frozen statue never moved as long as he watched it. This distracted him so much he almost went off the road a few times, so he cursed himself and concentrated instead on the road ahead. After a half an hour of driving the lonely cold road, his music blaring, he forgot about his horrifying cargo.

Ice fog developed, making it harder to see the road ahead and taking up all of his attention. He drove on, rarely seeing another vehicle on the road, even though it was late afternoon. It was just miles and miles of desolate snow and bush. Not a moose or deer stirred; even the ravens were strangely absent. The hoar frost on the trees and brush gave the route a ghostly look.

Eventually he came to the Toad Creek Bridge crossing, slowing down after seeing construction signs on the edge of the road. Finally, a winter-clad flagman stopped him to allow a nearby work crew to squeeze into the back of a truck. They promptly drove off, forgetting their faithful flagman. He was pissed!

Alarmed, the flagman hailed Spencer, who unrolled his window, just a crack. He knew what was coming, and already didn't like it.

"Hey buddy. Could you drop me off at the camp? It's a mile on your route."

The guy was dressed well enough against this cold, with heavy boots, a thick balaclava over his head, gloves, but he was filthy with dirt and oil. Spencer couldn't let him sit inside this nice clean truck. He couldn't leave him stranded, either.

Spencer stammered, "I suppose, but..."

"Thanks, buddy!" The heavily dressed flagman thumped the side of the truck with the flat of his hand. He jumped into the back of the pickup for the short ride to camp and sought a sheltered place for the short ride beside the frozen gnome. Perhaps the fellow thought he was going to be friendly to the frozen guy in the open pickup bed. Maybe he knew him!

Spencer was horrified but it was too late to tell the flagman about the body he was seated next to. Hopefully he will think the person was drunk or asleep. In the rear-view mirror, Spencer could see the flagman was actually chatting to the dead body, trying to be friendly. The dead body ignored his conversation attempts and sat like it was made of stone.

Spencer drove as fast as he dared, hoping the flagman wouldn't notice his frozen passenger. But, just as they got to their destination and Spencer slowed down in the camp yard, the flagman suddenly spun around and put his hand over his mouth, possibly screaming, but the rush of air rendered him soundless. He jumped out without waiting for a full stop and ran to the camp entrance.

Spencer drove by him and yelled out the window, "It's okay! He was dead, already!" And he was on his way home. Spencer couldn't keep from grinning at the whole experience. Since he didn't get out much, this qualified as excitement in his world! He felt pleased with himself for getting this well-paid side job. It turned out to be a bit of harmless adventure.

Eventually winter hesitantly turned to spring and Spencer was sent to Fort Mac for another weekend's macabre delivery. Craig had his usual smart-ass remarks, one-liners and lame jokes with his Elmer Fudd lisp. *Classy.*

"Who do we have, tonight, Craig?" Spencer asked, already dreading the answer. He had to ask, unfortunately.

"Dave Manus, motorcycle driver."

"What was his problem?" asked Spencer.

"He's dead," said Craig, not his usual wealth of icky information and puns.

"How?" asked Spencer, amazed he was even asking.

"Decapitation! He was headed back to the camp in the dark and hit a tow cable strung across the road. His body got here by ambulance, his head by motorcycle. He's a head on a Honda!"

"Good one, Craig."

"Spencer, you *are* catching on in this business." Craig grinned, flashing the spaces in his tobacco-stained teeth.

Thankfully all Dave's body parts were already in the coffin, secured in the hearse and Spencer was off on the long drive home. It was another quiet night on the open road without competing house-lights to the headlights of the hearse. They were the only eerie illumination on the road.

The warm car and deathly quiet made Spencer feel a bit sleepy so he tried the car radio to see what he could pick up. It was a cool night with a brilliant dome of green and blue Northern Lights overhead, which meant he might pick up an American station to revive him. He fumbled with the dial only finding a radio evangelist on a rant. "Repent your wicked ways and find the way of the Lord or you will burn in Hell!" The radio blared, and then faded.

"Not a minute too soon!" Spencer announced with gusto.

Silence returned but not a restful one. He felt uneasy which turned to a creepy feeling in his gut, like he was being watched. The hair on the back of his neck stood out but he dared not look in the back of the hearse. He heard an unmistakable sound he had not heard since he was ten years old—the magic sound of ice that mimicked tiny wind chimes. Spencer couldn't help but wonder if this was some harbinger of things to come. Nothing came. Spencer chalked it up to the coffin driver's jitters and pushed it from his mind. By the time he saw the Donvegan city lights it was forgotten.

It was the following Fort Mac trip a few weeks later that creepy things began in earnest.

His "passenger", Les, was an older man, mid-fifties, car accident victim. He'd died a long way from home, living in a camp, sending his earnings home to his family. He'd died on a lonely road where no one cared to know him and was now going home in the proverbial "pine box".

Spencer could not imagine why these older men would choose to work endless long hours, so far away from home working in camps for months, sending money away to a house and a spouse somewhere far south. The wife would get the money and a daily routine unencumbered by his actual presence. He couldn't help wondering if this poor fellow wouldn't be missed as much as his pay cheque.

He drove on in silence, regretting he'd forgotten his music. The roadway was dark, straight and utterly deserted. He might as well be driving on a giant demented treadmill, for all he knew. It was a road from nowhere to destinations unknown. It was even hard to see the stars, it was so black. Then, he heard the sound of those tiny wind chimes, the sound he'd remember the shifting lake ice had made, all those years ago. The chime sound kept going for a few minutes until... He heard the sound of a voice coming from *inside* the coffin!

The voice asked, "Where am I?"

Spencer stiffened in his seat, the hearse swaying drunkenly on the deserted road. He gripped the steering wheel until his knuckles were white. He held his breath, his heart pounding in his chest. The car was quiet, again, except for wind noise around the hearses' extended roof line.

"I didn't hear anything. That was the wind making noises," Spencer said aloud, trying to calm himself.

"Hey!"

Spencer jumped in his seat.

"Can you hear me out there?" the insistent voice repeated, clearly coming from the coffin area of the hearse.

Spencer's grip on the steering wheel tightened, twisted. The voice was real and sounded very close. So close, it sounded like it was right behind him!

"The radio! It's the radio!" Spencer said aloud, groping for the dial and finding it already turned off.

He took his foot off the accelerator, slowing to a stop. He sat in stunned silence praying for his heartbeat to return to normal. Gradually, he could breathe normally again. More importantly, the voice had stopped. It had to have been some radio show coming in while he was driving. Maybe something was wrong with the radio so it worked even when it was shut off. He couldn't convince himself completely that it was just a radio voice. It actually sounded like it was coming from the back of the hearse.

"How would it be a voice from the coffin?" he asked aloud, daring the voice to reappear.

At the end of the trip, Spencer did his best to get out of the dead-head business but the funeral home owner was insistent.

"I need you for another two months, until Barney gets back," she pleaded. "Please..."

"I'm awfully busy these days and I just don't have time, anymore," lied Spencer. He refused to admit being haunted by ghosts.

"Come on, Spencer. You aren't that busy. You're a single guy and have lots of time. I know you don't want to let Barney down. I'll tell you what... I'll give you a fifty-dollar bonus for every trip," coaxed the funeral director.

She was right, Barney needed him to hold this job for him. How could he refuse? "Well... I suppose I could," Spencer heard himself saying.

Spencer didn't dare tell her about his experience with the voice from the coffin. Who would believe him, anyway? Maybe he was just tired or had been daydreaming on that trip or had a leaky exhaust pipe. It was probably something on the radio that he heard that night. His hearing was playing tricks on him, surely. Craig must have had some type of battery speaker in the coffin to pull a prank on him and was laughing his ass off right now. There had to be a logical explanation because there were no such things as ghosts! Yeah—that had to be it. He felt angry with Craig but relieved he wasn't going crazy.

He agreed to keep driving until Barney returned, which was only a month and a half away, barring any healing complications.

The following day, Spencer walked along the houses and delivered some flyers and a New York Times newspaper. He crossed the street, all the time mulling over the coffin runs and the possibility he might actually have met a ghost. After a few sleepless nights, he resolved to forget the whole matter.

The funeral director called him up for a Saturday pick up at Fort Mac so off he went at five p.m. after an early supper and putting Porky outside. He made sure he brought his music this time, loud, rocky, take-no-prisoners music.

"Maybe a little AC/DC music will scare away the ghosts," he chuckled.

The drive up to Fort Mac was so uneventful Spencer chided himself for believing the "voices". Craig wasn't his usual witty self, so he and Spencer simply loaded up the coffin. After Craig went into the office, Spencer had a close look at the coffin for wires or speakers, making sure he wasn't the victim of one of Craig's pranks. Confronting Craig was not his style. Satisfied all was well, he drove off into the night.

The coffin apparently contained an elderly lady named Enid Bauer. She was very old and died of natural causes, while coming through on a bus tour to Alaska. She'd taken ill and passed away, overnight.

All was quiet so Spencer just drove on, listening to his music. Eventually he tired of the music he'd brought and thought he would take a chance on the radio, instead. He picked up a few bits of radio stations but annoyingly, they kept fading in and out. The only solid signal was some crackly US talk show which was replaced by silence. There was a long pause, followed by the familiar eerie sound of ice tinkling and squeaking—and the sound of wind chimes.

Oh no.

There was a pause and a raspy voice, "Bus driver?

Spencer gave a start.

"Where are we, bus driver?" the voice continued with an edge of exhaustion. "Are we stopping, soon?"

Fighting to keep the hearse safely on the road, Spencer couldn't utter a word at first, then managed to stammer, "Go away! You are a dream or something! Craig? Are you doing this to me? Stop it!"

The irritated old woman's voice spoke again from the passenger seat. "Young man I'm right here and don't be silly. Didn't they teach you any manners at that bus driving school?" she demanded.

"Holy Shit!" Spencer shouted, barely keeping the hearse in control. "Aren't you supposed to be deceased?"

"No, I'm not deceased. Look at me! I'm sitting here beside you... and watch your language!" she scolded.

Spencer slowly stopped the hearse in the middle of the dark deserted highway. He turned his head right to see where the voice was coming from. First, he saw a hat on a head of gray hair then saw it was attached to a prim and proper eighty-year old woman! She was crinkled and old, well dressed, complete with a veil, hat and clutched a purse in her lap. And she was translucent...

Spencer's mouth fell open. "No ma'am, I think you're possibly dead and could be a ghost. Are you here to haunt me?" he managed to mumble.

"Dead? Now that you mention it, I do feel a bit queer. Land sakes, my hands look kind of pale. But I do feel better than I have in years. Do you suppose I'm dead? Are you St. Peter or something?" she asked, looking at him intently.

"My name's Spencer, not St. Peter."

"Saint Spencer? What happened to Saint Peter? Have I gone to Hell?" she demanded. "God knows that endless bus ride felt like Hell. Have I spent all those years in church for nothing? Lord, I did try to lead a good life and prayed once a day..."

Spencer interrupted her lament, "No ma'am, I think you passed away and have somehow turned into a ghost or a spirit."

The elderly ghost sat wordlessly, considering her situation, taking in all these shocking details and facts. She turned and stiffly looked towards the rear of the hearse, particularly at the big black ornate coffin. The ghost then glanced back at Spencer and settled into her seat with a sigh. She stared down the lonely highway for some minutes before speaking again.

"Now I see what you are saying, Spencer. I remember now. I wasn't feeling very well and they took me to the hospital and I must have died."

"Yes, ma'am that could be what happened. And now I am the hearse driver transporting your body...er...you to the city. I presume your relatives will have you transported back to your home in the states."

The ghost said nothing for about five minutes. She just sat quietly, staring down the bleak highway, sighing every once in a while. Spencer thought she might be considering her options, her plight, before trusting herself to speak to a total stranger. By this time Spencer realized this was a harmless apparition so released the brake and resumed the journey. Every once in a while a passing car's headlights would pass through the windshield. The sudden light made the old woman's body vanish, then reappear.

Just when Spencer hoped she had vanished for good, she was back, and in the mood to talk. "My name's Enid, Spencer. So, it finally happened after all this time. After eighty years I've gone and died. Just like that!" she declared. "And what do I have to show for eighty years of existence? I'm not sure. I have no family. I was single all my life. What do you suppose they will do with my body when I get home? I'm not sure there's anyone who would even come to my funeral," she added sadly.

Surprised at this admission, Spencer offered, "There must be someone to receive you. You must have had friends, extended family, someone."

"There's no one. I kept to myself. I just worked and lived day-to-day. I'm not much of a people person, you see. I've probably told you as much as I've told anyone in my whole life," she confessed.

Spencer was unsure how to talk to a ghost. Maybe ghosts could turn into the devil and blow flames out of their mouths or something but somehow Spencer didn't think so. The old lady just seemed lonely and needed someone to talk to. Since speaking to people wasn't Spencer's style, he sat in silence, unsure of what to say. He was a lonely, private person too. Thirty years from now Spencer could imagine himself saying these very words.

He was spared further communication efforts as she just vanished after an hour of painful silence while he agonized over how to comfort her. He couldn't help feeling he'd failed her, not knowing what to say to a helpless old woman during her last hours on Earth.

He drove into town and dropped off the hearse and "passenger". He was shaken but didn't tell anyone about the apparition. Enid's ghost had said things that hit too close to his heart.

On Monday he walked along doing his deliveries, deep in thought about that visit from Enid's ghost. Was he losing his mind? Perhaps being alone all these years was taking its toll.

The ghost of Enid got to him. He had actually carried on a conversation with her! She'd told him things he had never considered about being alone and being forgotten. He could not imagine how anyone else, let alone a spirit, could know the things he felt. Perhaps, a trained medical person might be able to help or at least look him over to see if there was something wrong with him. Maybe it was a brain tumor or some kind of slow food poisoning. Perhaps his house had lead pipes in it and it was making him crazy.

He went to the doctor for a complete examination but of course didn't mention the real reason he was there. He just said he felt a bit funny, ringing in his ears and vertigo or something. It had been ten years since he'd last had a medical.

The young doctor checked his heart, blood pressure, looked in his mouth and poked his tongue and looked in his ears. Then the doctor checked his prostate. All this time, Spencer thought a prostate gland was in his armpit.

Apparently not.

At last the doctor told him to put on his clothes. She looked at his medical records and pronounced him healthy and fit as a fiddle. He thought the physical could have qualified as one of the better dates he'd had over the years. Spencer was confident the doctor visit cleared him of any tumors or circulatory issues. He wasn't sure if he should be happy or sad.

As additional insurance he crawled under the hearse and tightened up all the exhaust system clamps and bolts to make sure exhaust fumes weren't causing hallucinations.

Spencer went back to work vowing to never tell a soul about his ghostly encounters.

Candy

The following weekend trip to Fort Mac was uneventful… going north. It was the trip south with the coffin that strange things happened on a level he couldn't have foreseen. The office had specifically instructed him to go directly to the coroner's office for the pickup, which meant there was some legal, criminal or dreadful issue with the body.

After Spencer arrived at his office, the grim coroner helped him load up the temporary coffin into the back of the hearse.

"Who do we have, tonight?" Spencer really did not want to know but was required to confirm the pick-up.

The coroner answered without a hint of emotion, "We have an American stripper murdered in the La Marie Hotel. It's still under investigation. She's going to Donvegan, then on to Edmonton for further examination."

Spencer carefully tied the coffin down so it wouldn't move if they went into the ditch. It would be too ironic if he were killed by a flying coffin.

The coroner added, "Make sure the legal seals are not broken on this coffin lid or there'll be holy hell to pay."

Spencer asked, "Do the seals hold well enough the body can't fall out?" *Or climb out, sit beside me and carry on a conversation.* He shuddered.

"Of course! These legally sealed lids are anchored down so the contents can't get out, even if you flip over the car," the coroner explained.

Apparently we're just 'contents' when we are dead. How cold was that?

Spencer did not want to think about being trapped for a night in a car with a body that had fallen out of a coffin. He could imagine frantic Emergency Responders squeezed in beside him, busily trying to revive it. *"I think I gotta heart beat over here, Vern!"*

With that cheery thought, he drove down the chilly highway. The reassuring town lights were quickly lost behind him and it was back to the blackness of the night, illuminated only by his headlights.

To fill the silence, Spencer started up the music once again, filling the vehicle with rock. He cranked it up louder.

"Wow, I hope it isn't loud enough to wake the dead!" He forced a laugh he didn't feel.

After thirty minutes of loud rock and roll music and the "Hells Bells" climax, a soothing quiet took over the car and the darkness outside. Spencer thought the silence was a nice change from steady rock and roll so didn't press replay. Perhaps rock music scares away demons, he thought.

He found himself enjoying the silence. Occasionally headlights of passing vehicles would dazzle and flash past him. The quiet power and smoothness of the car soothed him. All he could see ahead was the cone of his own headlights drifting ahead, piercing the darkness. He adjusted the seat back a little as he relaxed. The next hour went smoothly by.

Then Spencer began to get that creepy feeling. He tried his best to ignore it but soon realized it was going to happen, no matter how much he didn't want it to. Soon he heard the peculiar wind chimes sound. Not a good sign.

"Fuck me... it's starting again!" he cursed aloud, miserably, slouching in his seat, already lifting his foot off the accelerator.

"I could arrange that, honey," cooed a sweet reply.

The source of the voice was sitting right beside him. He looked down to see a ghostly hand on his right leg. The hand led to an arm and a shapely pair of bare legs all attached to a very pretty girl, early twenties, in a very pink and very short dressing gown covered with what appeared to be spattered blood.

This must have been what she was wearing on the night she was murdered.

She looked like a pinup girl from a playboy magazine, strikingly pretty with long curly brunette hair that draped her ample breasts. Spencer couldn't be sure about her height but she sat about a foot shorter on the seat than he did. He slowed then stopped the car.

The girl tucked her legs up, bringing her head to the same level as Spencer's, likely so her bare feet would not be on the cold hearse floor. Do ghosts get cold feet?

She looked at him, her eyes brown, her skin pasty white. Spencer couldn't help but notice goose bumps on the skin in her exposed cleavage, nipples straining the thin dressing gown material.

Drafty outfit, he thought wryly.

He reluctantly looked into her eyes.

"A blow for the road?" she cheerfully said, returning his gaze intently and sporting a huge grin. Her smile lit up the car, lips wide and red with perfect rows of snow-white teeth, obviously her well-practiced "show" smile.

"Well, big boy? What do you think?" she asked. "I see you have big feet! You know what they say…"

Spencer could not believe his ears or his eyes. He was being propositioned by a ghost to do unspeakable things! "Sorry Lady. You couldn't blow out a candle in your ghostly state!"

"Ghostly state?" She was obviously shocked he would turn her down. Her gaze fell to her arms, noticing something was amiss. Her translucent body and legs had to appear odd to her, unprepared as she had to be. Amazed, her mouth fell open as she studied her body for a few minutes. "Oh my… You can see right through me?" she gasped, "What's happened to me? I don't understand! Am I … Am I dead?"

"Yes, lady, you are deceased and possibly are now just a spirit."

She put her hand up to her mouth in horror. "No! I still have two more shows to do! I can't be dead. I'm talking to you so I'm alive, right?"

"Not necessarily," Spencer cautioned, "You were killed, apparently. Turn around and look in the back. See that coffin? That's you in there."

She slowly turned and looked, studying it for some minutes.

"No, I can't be in there! I'm right here!"

"Pinch yourself. Feel anything?"

She tried pinching her arms and legs. He could see she felt nothing, her fingers and flesh had no substance. Tears filled her eyes and poured down her cheeks.

Spencer gave her a Kleenex from the dashboard dispenser. Do spirits shed tears? The answer would be yes.

She dabbed her cheeks and sat quietly for a few minutes, deep in thought. Then she looked at herself again, for some minutes before finally speaking.

"Am I really a ghost?" she asked in a hushed tone. "Do I have to be dead to be a ghost?"

"Unfortunately, yes."

The stripper was quiet for a few seconds then seemed to change her mood. "Cool! Am I still pretty, even though I'm a ghost?"

Not the sharpest tool in the shed. "Yes, you are very pretty in a see-through sort of way."

She moved her left arm to rest on his shoulder. It was like she was looking for comfort from Spencer.

They sat quietly for a few moments, thinking about their situation, which was either being a ghost or talking to a ghost. Her face was close to his, which Spencer found disconcerting, being a loner. Not to mention—*alive.*

She studied his face, waiting for a response.

Spencer gave up and broke the silence, "Well, yes...you are very pretty even though you are a ghost. That is, other than the bullet hole... I mean."

"Bullet hole?" asked Candy.

"Yes, you have a bullet hole in your forehead... you know... "

She sat stunned for a few seconds. "Oh, yeah! I forgot about that!" she exclaimed, straining to look into the hearse's rear-view mirror.

She stuck her index finger in the bloody rimmed hole in her forehead and giggled, "Kyle was a coke head but he was a good shot!"

"Lucky you."

"Thanks! My mom always said I sure knew how to pick 'em!"

"I'm sure she did."

The ghost situation seemed to calm down, so Spencer put the hearse in drive and started moving on down the highway. She leaned gently against him. He sensed another change in her mood.

Shoulders slumped, her bubbly personality faded. As reality set in she asked, "What's your name?"

"Spencer Cunningham. Think of me as your driver, tonight," he said, trying to soften the fact he was her hearse driver.

"Hello Spencer."

Spencer hoped for silence but instead the girl began telling him the story of her life, tired and defeated. "My show name was Candy Kane but my real name is Barbara Stellina. My manager said men aren't going to pay to watch a "Barbara" so I had to have a name of something they could imagine licking. How lame is that?"

"Did you have a choice, Barbara?" asked Spencer, more to be polite. He did not want to know but he still wasn't sure that these ghosts didn't have some kind of power to turn him in to a goat or ornate chair.

"I guess I never thought about it. I could have got married out of high school and had a half a dozen kids by now. Heck, I could have had my own trailer in the trailer park but that was no future. I wanted excitement! I was pretty, everyone said so—so I thought I might as well cash in on my looks. It was fun for a while. I got to travel to different cities and see different men all the time. I could buy the best clothes... " She faded off with a grimace. "I just didn't get to wear them for very long."

Then she perked up. "All the money I made paid for a boob job, braces for my teeth and my coke habit. That's how I met my fiancé, Kyle. He looked after me."

"So Kyle was your pimp?" asked Spencer, already sorry for his choice of words.

"Yes, I suppose that's true, though I always referred to him as my manager, agent and bodyguard."

"No offense but he didn't do a very good job protecting you, did he?"

"He was the one that shot me! Kyle was always a jealous type with a crazy bad temper and didn't like it when other men came to visit me." She giggled.

"So, he shot you? Your own boyfriend shot you?" Spencer said in amazement.

"Right between the eyes! Right here!" Barbara said proudly, putting her face uncomfortably close to Spencer's and sticking her index finger in the hole again, as far as it would go. "See?"

He looked away, feeling nauseated.

Her excitement faded. They drove along in silence. The sad ghost of a dead girl seated close to Spencer, her arm still resting on his shoulder.

"Are there any women in your life, Spencer?" Barbara asked in a flat tone.

"No, I'm unattached at this time," Spencer replied grandly, hoping the conversation would end. It didn't.

"Are you gay?"

"No," he blurted. *Is that what people think of me?*

"Do you still live with your family at home?"

"I live alone, with my dog, and I like it that way," he declared, hoping his tone indicated he didn't want to talk about this anymore. "I don't have any family and my parents are dead!"

Rebuffed, Barbara fell silent, still leaning on his shoulder but after a few minutes quietly asked, "Have you always been lonely?"

Spencer thought about it for a bit, and then replied, "I've never felt lonely."

"Even when you were young?"

"My parents were killed when I was nine years old. They had no living relatives, so I went from foster home to foster home. I learned to be self-reliant, to live alone. It's the only way I know how. As the line in the old song says, "Alone but never lonely," he added, feeling proud of the clever "old song" line.

That statement seemed to annoy her. "Alone is lonely! Don't ever kid yourself. I've felt alone all my life. People around me had no meaning, no substance. My life, my occupation has been all about other people's fantasies. I fit into their make-believe world. I might as well have been a blow-up doll for all that I am. It's as though Barbara never existed. You want to hear how my life ended? I just finished my last dance, picked up my clothes and went to my dressing room. The hotel owner was there wanting a "freebie" because it was his hotel and was kinda feeling me up when Kyle came in. There was a fight and Kyle just looked at me funny, pulled out his gun and everything went black. Now, here I am, a ghost."

"That must have been terrible!"

"I'm alone and died alone. I'm probably going home where nobody knows me or cares, anymore. Without someone to remember me, my gravestone, if I even get one, will be just another piece of stone in a field. It will mean nothing more than a rock on a beach."

Spencer felt profoundly sad. Without reply he sat beside this depressed and lonely ghost without warmth to give her. It was cold comfort for both of them.

"So Barbara, what was life on the road like?"

Barbara looked down the road in silence for a time. She seemed content to sit close to Spencer and lean on him. "My life was awful. My job, mostly, was dealing impersonally, for the entertainment of lonely men. Some were single, ugly, awkward or an outcast. Some were older, married and far away from home or were maybe locals, frustrated with their sex life at home. They had become irrelevant. Begging or hoping for brief, predictable, infrequent, inconvenient sex with a busy and bored wife just didn't work for them, anymore. A fling with a nice looking 'pro' devoted to what and when they wanted was, to them, a breath of fresh air at a fair price. One of them even told me a night of "pro" sex with me was cheaper than an alternator he had just replaced on his wife's' SUV, but way more fun with a lot less arguing about it."

Spencer said nothing, trying to imagine what she went through.

"Do you plan to be alone, forever, Spencer?"

He hadn't thought about it before. He'd become a day-to-day guy and never considered the future—not seriously. Being alone was all he knew or thought he would ever know.

"Forever is a long time. I suppose until I die, anyway."

Barbara sharply pointed out, "So when you die nobody will remember you. No one will visit your tombstone. It will be as if you never existed. You'll be just like me. People won't forget us because it'll be as if we never existed in the first place. You have to live and be with people and have relationships to belong."

"I live with people, all day long. It's just the closeness that I avoid. Isn't that enough?" said Spencer.

"Unless you try to make connections with the people around you, meaningful ones, you'll always be alone. In a way, you and I are the same. We meet people on a superficial level, do our jobs, then move on. We miss the emotional contact and the risk it takes to get close to someone. Without closeness, it's all superficial. You're already a ghost others barely see, Spencer."

He was surprised how perceptive she was. He risked turning to her. "You know Barbara, you're much more intelligent than you ever let anyone know."

"I suppose," she said ruefully, "And I waited until I was dead to use it. Don't wait too long, yourself!" It sounded like a death sentence, especially coming from a dead person.

"Maybe I've waited too long already."

They drove along in solitude, Barbara's arm still resting on his shoulder. He could not feel it but could sense it. For once, he didn't mind offering comfort to someone, even if it *was* a ghost.

Ironically, of all the men who spent time with "Candy", he was probably the only person who took the time to actually listen to her and truly learn something about her.

Spencer couldn't say at what point she vanished. She just did. He suddenly felt badly that he hadn't said goodbye, not even offering the barest of soothing words to a ghost of a lonely person. The radio played a gentle Tom Waits song, "Closing time", triggering something, deep down in his hidden, unappreciated soul. He slowed the hearse to a stop once again, this time pulling over onto the shoulder, tears streaming down his face. He hadn't cried like that since he was a teenager, shuffled yet again to another foster home. He'd always make sure to cry only when nobody was around, fearing someone would laugh at him or tease him or worse, someone would ask him earnestly about his feelings and actually want to listen. His sense of privacy would never allow it.

All those feelings of loneliness and sadness flooded over him. It had been decades since he had felt this way. He had been successful at keeping his sorrow in a little compartment in his soul, never to be opened. Until tonight.

"Candy" and Barbara had somehow found the key to his soul and had unlocked it. His feelings were out and raging for release and would never go back into hiding.

He arrived at home feeling as empty and alone as the ghosts who had visited him. He was a shell of a person. Nobody knew if he was here or not. Normally, he wouldn't have cared if they did, but today? Today was different. Today it mattered. He was determined to never be lonely again. He would become part of a family, somehow. Maybe he would find someone to care about him and who he could care for.

He just wasn't sure how to go about it.

———

It was nine-thirty in the morning and Spencer walked along his route on the wide, paved quiet street. It was a warm, spring day. He was making good time today while thinking about his situation. Was being a loner such a good idea in the long run? It had protected him from being torn away from new people but ultimately had come at a great cost.

He'd observed many relationships from a distance over the years, and thought he understood them, but observing is not the same thing as experiencing. He did not offer any relationships and in fact had rebuffed all offers, ever since he'd left Brandon Lake. He left all his school friends and contacts there, when they moved him away and into the system. The last good relationship he'd allowed himself to experience with any warmth at all had been his brief, strange friendship with Clara.

It was depressing to realize he had told the hearse ghosts more about his feelings and thoughts than he'd ever told a living human being.

Lost in thought, Spencer continued his delivery run on automatic pilot, approaching each home and dropping off their mail bundles, barely registering the day go by.

Beth Alexander heard the mailbox lid lift then clink shut outside her front door. She walked over and opened the door just in time to see the back of the postman walking away, on his appointed rounds. Spencer did not hear her as he was lost in profound friendship thought. She had no idea their postman was that sad lonely boy they had taken in so long ago at Brandon Lake.

Approaching his own house after work, Spencer could hear Porky barking. She knew the sound of his steps and wasted no time letting him know she was excited he was home. A flood of warmth came over him.

Porky was the one exception in Spencer's private existence. She had arrived unbidden at his door step three years ago, shivering and hungry without a collar or markings. There were no notices around town about her being lost. When Spencer thought about it, he recalled seeing her on his route, as she wandered aimlessly around the area before arriving on his doorstep. His first impulse had been to push the mutt away, but something in her upturn face and pleading eyes had stopped him. He'd thought back to the days when he was an orphan and had needed help himself. This dog was reaching out to him, asking for his help—he couldn't refuse her. The dog was so grateful, and he was so touched that a bond formed between them within a week. This dog had such an amazing grunting and snuffling sound when it ate that Spencer started calling her "Porky" and the name stood.

Porky was a mixed breed of some kind. She was a medium size, built thin, but not skinny, and was mostly black with some white spots. While certainly no purebred, neither she nor Spencer cared. It appeared she was an older dog and was house broken, which sealed the deal.

Spencer's house was not big, by anyone's standards. He liked the fact it was well made, older with some character, and on the edge of town overlooking a large park. He could look out the kitchen window and see deer, moose and birds out in the wooded areas amongst the trees and in the tall grass. It had the added bonus that he could run Porky around the area to her heart's content.

It had been a big purchase, twenty years ago, but now it was worth triple the price he had paid. It had been a huge decision and he'd agonized for weeks over buying it, but he'd hated renting more, having to talk to a landlord about anything his place needed. His own house would safeguard his precious privacy and security. The settlement he'd received from his parents' estate mostly paid for the place, so it was a good deal for him.

He looked over his property as he approached from the sidewalk. His yard had an agreeable fluffy green hedge covering the tough, impenetrable old chain link fence inside it, rather like his personal feelings; outwardly benign but came with a hidden barrier.

"Hello, Richard," smiled his neighbor, busily raking his leaves.

Spencer nodded in response, though the neighbor had his name wrong and Spencer didn't know his, either.

Spencer glanced at his two-bay garage in the backyard, one containing his well-equipped workshop and the other his precious Lexus car. He was a thrifty guy most of the time, but when he did buy something, it was top quality and kept for a long time. His 1995 Lexus was in perfect shape, despite its age, purchased when it was a couple of years old and looked better than it did when he bought it. He'd fixed any little scratch or dent immediately. Mechanically, it was as good a car as any collector would expect to see.

As Spencer entered the gate, Porky excitedly circled him, wagging her tail, almost grinning. Spencer petted her as he went to the front door. It was an older, eight hundred square foot place, with a grey stucco exterior. As he unlocked the door, he reached into his own mailbox to retrieve the mail and the local newspaper.

He held Porky outside, gently, with his knee and a smile. "You can stay outside, Porky! It's a nice day," and petted her head once more.

The interior of the house was nicely finished with original hand-hewn wood floors. The old wooden window seats were refurbished to perfection. The elderly majestic stone fireplace sat there, waiting to be started. Spencer had long since converted it to natural gas. He'd had a bad experience chopping wood he wasn't eager to repeat. The house had a couple of old built-in china cabinets which he refurbished to perfection. Even the kitchen had its old-time charm but he gently brought it up to modern standards with a granite counter top and a dishwasher.

Spencer was proud of his house. He'd done almost all the work himself. It took a lot of time, but he'd carefully researched every part of the project beforehand. He'd bought the best materials and parts. Eventually, he'd built a very good workshop in his garage, complete with all the power tools he needed. As it turned out, he was a very handy guy when it came to refurbishing wood furniture. He was natu-rally gifted, and it showed.

The only labor he'd brought in was an electrician to improve the old house's electrical service panel to bring the wiring up to the latest building code. As he could afford it, he'd brought in a plumber to add more piping and drains for an improved bathroom upstairs and a new one, downstairs. It was a first-class job.

Slowly he'd added various pieces of furniture from the same time period as the house. Each piece was lovingly refinished and recovered, all matching and looked terrific. Even the kitchen table and chairs were redone to match the rest of the house. The only exception to the antiques was the big screen TV set up on the wall. That was courtesy of driving the hearse. Sadly, other than Porky and himself, nobody else had ever seen these masterpieces or had so much as sat in one of his beautifully refurbished chairs.

After letting Porky in, he headed for the kitchen, turned on the kettle then dug out some dry dog food, poured it into the dog dish and put it on the floor for Porky. Opening the fridge, he pulled out a frozen lasagna, opened it up and put it into the microwave. By that time the water was boiling for his tea. Red Rose tea was his favorite.

He walked into the bedroom he'd converted into a study and turned his new computer on, another happy benefit from his ghostly side hustle. He consulted a couple of news feeds to see what had taken place in the day, then it was back to the kitchen to dish out his supper which would be hot by now. Porky ate her dinner while Spencer sat at the kitchen table and ate his own while absentmindedly picking through his mail.

Afterwards, he brought a second cup of tea into the living room, sat down in the big chair with Porky at his feet. He turned the TV on to the news and they both slowly drifted off to sleep. At ten o'clock he awoke with a snort, sent Porky outside, showered, brought the dog back in and went to bed, ready for the same routine tomorrow.

His schedule rarely changed except for weekends. He got up a little later for a leisurely breakfast. Instead of going to work, he would take the dog for a long walk in the park. Spencer might take a thermos of coffee with him to sit on a bench and listen to the wildlife if the weather was nice. Unless it was garage sale season, then he'd get up early and would drive to the various flea markets and garage sales looking for certain types of old furniture for his house. Last month he found the perfect end table for his bedroom. It was beat up and abused but he knew how to fix it up. He was out in his workshop in the evenings and on weekends working on it. To repair the old wood, he carefully took it apart, stripped off the numerous layers of paint and dirt. The base was trued up, drawer runners fixed and the table reassembled. At last, the ancient wood was carefully sanded and re-varnished with a number of coats, to look like it was new. Admiring his handiwork, he thought, it sure could use a lamp from the same time period. He would have to consult his computer to find some type of lamp from the 1900 era that could be modified to use a modern electric bulb.

Tomorrow was Saturday. Maybe he could spy one at a garage sale. He set his alarm clock.

The Sale

Beth and Joe Alexander had accumulated a lot of old stuff from their retirement move from Brandon Lake. They were not much for throwing anything away, regardless of how old and beat up it was. They would good-naturedly accuse each other of being hoarders.

"The difference between us and a hoarder is we don't have enough storage space to hoard!"

They had an accumulation of old skiing gear, old books, furniture, shoes, clothing, china and general household flotsam and jetsam. They felt guilty about throwing stuff out and considered it wasteful. Their parents had survived the Great Depression and their thrift had been imbedded in their children. Perhaps a garage sale would be a better idea. They could give their old stuff a new home and get a little money for it along the way. They were getting older now and it was time to downsize their possessions. It would be a good Saturday project. In the meantime, they would poke through it all and sort it, with every piece while telling its story. There is a fine line between junk and treasure and a sale sounded like fun.

They wondered what fair market value was for each piece and what they should price it at. Worth is subjective. Friends told them everything needed to be priced cheap or you get to take it to the dump when the sales over and get nothing for it. They took all this under advisement and worked on the garage sale items for a few weeks until the sale was ready to go. A Saturday date was set and suitable advertising was placed in the local paper. Joe had even stapled a few posters to power poles about town.

Early in the morning of the sale they slid the table full of sale items out of the garage and into the sunshine. They added a few pieces of furniture, some old car tires, a hanger stand loaded with clothes and boxes brimming with books—all were placed along the driveway by six a.m.

Customers came in like vultures.

The Alexanders were surprised the garage sale people were so serious about it all. They drove like maniacs, some zooming past the Alexander's yard display but kept going. Many of the garage salers, noticing their mistake, would then jam on their brakes and back their cars wildly and erratically up the block, like crazed, blindfolded firemen arriving at a fire.

More and more people arrived, digging through their stuff with fierce determination, looking for specific items like jewelry, china and kid's toys. A few argued about prices. A few skinflints wanted to haggle over some cheap articles. Joe just told them with a smile, to take them, if they were that "hard up".

Both Joe and Beth enjoyed the day and made two hundred and seventy-five bucks. It was a good haul for a bunch of junk.

At about one o'clock in the afternoon an older white Lexus car drove up, parked and a man in his mid-fifties got out. He walked up to the garage sale area, obviously looking for something specific. Joe and Beth said hi to him and he shyly said hi in return. He looked around for a few more minutes then noticed an old lamp sitting on the ground. *Cool!* He picked it up, and had a good look at it.

"How much you asking for the lamp?"

"Fifteen bucks," replied Joe, "But just so you know, it doesn't work. It's pretty old."

"I may be able to fix it. I pull the insides out of it, refurbish it and put in a new lamp core. I'll take it."

He approached Beth but suddenly got a pained look on his face as he patted his pockets fruitlessly. "No wallet! Damn!" he said, "Would you mind holding this for me while I go home and get my wallet? I'm sorry about this."

"Please go ahead and take it. Come back and pay us later," Beth said, thinking his face was vaguely familiar. Did she know him from somewhere?

"Oh, I couldn't," he said. "I'll be back in a little while."

He returned to his car and drove off.

By the time Spencer got back to the house, it was after three p.m.

He went into the garage and put another coat of varnish on his latest wood project and set it down to dry. Timing of the coats was important. Being close to supper time, he went into the house so he and Porky could eat. They took a walk afterwards, then hunkered down in the chair in front of the TV falling fast asleep. When he woke up he realized he had forgotten all about the lamp.

The Lamp

Beth and Joe Alexander were at the breakfast table, early as usual. They had their favorite breakfast of eggs, toast and fried potatoes, just as they always did.

"Did you get a look at the fellow who wanted that old lamp, Joe?"

"Not really. Why?"

"I think that might have been Spencer Cunningham."

Joe stopped eating, sitting upright in surprise. "Are you sure? He'd be mid-fifties by now. You aren't getting dotty, are you?"

"No."

"The first thing I thought when I saw him on Saturday was, 'Hey, there's our mailman,'" Joe pointed out.

"I'm not a hundred percent sure, but he looks like Spencer, or at least how I imagine Spencer would look today. He said he'd come back to pick up the lamp, so we'll see. I can't get over bumping into Spencer Cunningham, at a garage sale!" said Beth.

"If he's really Spencer," Joe cautioned. "Oddly, I picked up that very lamp at Jeff and Carol's estate sale."

"I wonder if Spencer would appreciate knowing that? Should we be going slowly with this? It has been a long time. I don't know where he's at with all this. He may be shocked, or he may prefer his privacy, or he may not want to have anything to do with us," Beth said, looking at Joe.

"That's true. He may prefer to not say anything to us. It may bring up some painful memories he may not want to stir up," said Joe. "We *are* the ones who decided it was okay for a ten-year-old to chop firewood."

Beth shuddered. "Don't remind me. What we didn't know about children back then. After all these years, I'd like to think we know a lot more about how to deal with all this, certainly more than we knew when we took him in. In a way, we are all very different people."

"We're certainly older and wiser than we were. What do you suggest?"

"If he's delivering our mail, I'll leave it to Spencer to decide how he wants to approach this, if he wants to at all—if it *is* him. I can be out working on the garden when he comes by. I won't trap him."

"Sure, say hi and leave it to him to start a conversation or not."

"This might be a little like making friends with the stray cat of the neighborhood," she warned.

Discovery

"Morning, Spencer."

"Good morning, Barney," Spencer greeted him with a smile. "It's a nice day out there."

Barney's face registered surprise. "Wow, that's the most you've said to me since you started working here."

"That's because I'm relieved you've taken over driving the hearse. It was both a lucrative and very creepy experience."

"Well, I'm glad to be back. My leg's finally good to go."

"I'm glad. Oh… Ah … Did you ever see things or hear things when you were doing the "deadhead runs" from Fort Mac, Barney?"

"Not a thing. Why?"

"Oh, no reason. Hey, we'd better get sorting. Look at the time."

Standing side-by-side, as always, they sorted their mail for the daily run. After Barney was done, Spencer put on his coat, hat and thin gloves and headed for the door himself. The sun was just cresting the horizon, a pretty sight to start his daily rounds.

Monday had been a long day and Spencer was glad to be home. After supper both he and Porky were poised to drift asleep on the couch, as usual. Suddenly he snorted and sat up with a jerk. Porky jumped up in alarm.

"My lamp! Porky; I keep thinking about that old lamp from Saturday! Should we try phoning the lady to see if we can still get it?" He grinned and leaned over, petting the dog who was quite excited but didn't know why.

Spencer rarely used the phone but for some reason he was extraordinarily drawn to that old lamp. He looked up the name from the garage sale. "Alexander," he announced, then dialed their number.

"Hi. Mrs. Alexander?" He gave Porky a thumbs up. "I was at your garage sale on Saturday and was the one looking at an old lamp. Remember me, the guy without his wallet? I hope you will forgive me, but once I got home, I forgot all about it. Do you still have it?"

The answer was yes. He grinned. "When would be a good time to come by and get it?"

"It's only 7:30 now. You could come by and get it tonight, if that works for you," Mrs. Alexander offered, her voice sounding as if she was happy he'd called.

"Sure, I'll be right over."

Soon he was there and knocking on their door.

Mrs. Alexander opened the door. "Come on in!"

"I don't want to be a bother." Face to face, he felt suddenly shy, but Mrs. Alexander insisted he come in.

While she went to get the lamp, Spencer stood awkwardly in the hallway. Standing inside someone's home was a rare social event for him, one he would normally avoid, but he felt almost compelled to get that antique lamp.

She reappeared. "Here you go! I hope this is the right one."

"That's the one!" He reached into his pocket for the money. "Thank you very much!"

He handed her the fifteen dollars. Turning to leave, a framed photograph stopped him. It was of the Alexanders, much younger here, standing in front of a different house with four kids of varying ages beside a beat-up jeep wagon. Everyone was grinning.

"That looks very familiar," Spencer remarked, then surprised himself by asking, "Where was this taken?"

"Oh, that was our old house in Brandon Lake," Mrs. Alexander remarked, seeming to be watching him closely.

Spencer stood in stunned silence for a few moments, recalling the house. It—it couldn't be. After years of guarding his feelings, he hastily covered his thoughts, glanced over at Mrs. Alexander then quickly away. "Thank you," he blurted and was off to his car.

———

Beth Alexander stood in the window and watched Spencer walk to his car and drive away.

"Joe!" she called.

Joe came out of the study and asked, "What's wrong? You look spooked!"

"Almost... I'm ... I'm almost *positive* that was Spencer Cunningham! He recognized the picture of us and the house at Brandon Lake!"

"Did he say anything about it? How do you know it's him?"

"He recognized the picture but tried not to let on that he knew it. And... and he has a missing finger on his left hand!"

———

Spencer drove off, his mind swimming with memories firing at him from all sides. Was that the foster people from Brandon Lake he had first stayed with, so long ago? He was fairly sure it was, but what should he do about it?

It was a sleepless night for Spencer. Re-discovering his first foster parents, the Alexanders, from so long ago left his mind a jumble of confused thoughts and murky memories, and with them came a flood of images and incidents from all the years and all the different foster homes of his past.

He thought back to his foster home days, only this time, his memories were truer. This time, he saw some of the good things that had happened along the way. Perhaps he should not have been too hasty to condemn it all.

He remembered one family in Abbottsford. The lady used to sing while she cooked amazing meals for her foster kids. It was a delight for them to arrive at the table to see the delicious meals.

There was the father balancing a jumble of children on his knees and on the arms of his chair, reading them stories such as "Call of the Wild" and "Nancy Drew" stories, thrilling them with a deep, baritone voice making the stories come alive with tales of Mounties' dog teams and mysteries.

Another foster family would pile all of them in a big, old van and take them out for a day picnic at a lake. They all went swimming and fishing and anything else they wanted to do. Afterwards, they had a huge picnic of potato salad, cold cuts, pop and homemade buns and pickles around a campfire. In Victoria, one couple took all of them to see the museum and the Butchart Gardens. They'd explored the Harbor walkways afterwards.

Some homes made sure all the kids had bikes to ride. Others made sure skates were available if the kids went to the arena. Some had fishing gear for everyone to fish the nearby river.

In hindsight, all the foster homes were not so bad. Perhaps Spencer had been looking inward more than he should have. Personally, he seemed to have turned out alright. He was no axe murderer.

He glanced down at his hand and grimaced. He'd only been a danger to himself, all along.

In fact, he was reasonably well adjusted, other than occasionally talking to ghosts.

Eventually he fell asleep. All too soon, his alarm clock went off at 5 a.m., and he was up and ready to meet the day.

He had his coffee machine set to start on a timer, so it was ready. After sending Porky out into the yard, he cooked himself two eggs, a slice of toast and added a glass of orange juice to complete his breakfast. Then it was into his uniform and out the door and off to walk to the Post Office. Spencer felt strangely happy and optimistic, for no apparent reason.

The post office station was a busy place, as usual, full of hustle and bustle. Mail was going in all directions in the big mail carts, the union steward was crabbing at the post office supervisor. Barney and Clark were yammering on about their weekend and Spencer didn't mind. For the first time in many years, he heard it all and enjoyed it. It was the sound of life going on around him. He could choose to be a part of it, listen to it or choose to ignore it. It was his choice and he was listening!

Clark was sifting through his mail when he grabbed a post card, looked at it and called to everyone to listen:

"Dear Jane,

Having a great time at Betty's. There is a cute guy that comes to pick up her trash Monday and Thursday. I tried talking to him but he always seems too busy, so next garbage day I'll meet him wearing something revealing! That should improve my sex life! Ha Ha

Sabrina'"

The crowd laughed and cheered its approval of Clark's selection of the postcard. Even Spencer laughed, which was very unusual.

Spencer was off doing his rounds, whistling as he walked. Eventually, he made it to the Alexander's house. As he walked along, he realized he had been anticipating this particular delivery all morning and was nervous at the prospect of seeing the Alexanders in the yard. He was not sure what he would say to them or even if they were, in fact, his first foster family after all these years. Family. He thought he liked the feel of it but this was unfamiliar territory. He stepped through the gate and headed for the mailbox.

Beth Alexander was working in the garden. Spencer had to have been by their house thousands of times, delivering their mail, yet this was the first time he noticed the amazing roses the Alexanders grew. They had all types, spread all over the yard and up in trellises.

Beth stood up, her face flushed and said, "I'll take that." Then she asked, "Is that actually you, Spencer Cunningham, after all these years?"

His heart sprang up into his throat. He swallowed it away and answered, "Yes, it's me, Spencer! I had no idea it was you. I could hardly remember your names. It was a long time ago and those were such dark days for me."

"We are just so pleased to see you after all this time, Spencer. We wondered where you were and how you were doing ..."

"I've been well. I had some adjusting to do. Got kind of shuffled around a bit but here I am, healthy and happy."

"I can see you are healthy and happy," Beth replied. "Will we be seeing more of you in the future?"

"Yes, I'll be delivering the mail until I retire," Spencer said, knowing that wasn't what she meant, but powerless to react in any other way. "Must go. Duty calls."

"Of course, you have to go back to work," said Beth, patting him on the back as he turned and left. With that touch, Spencer remembered suddenly that she'd often shown affection by patting a person she liked on the back. It was gentle, informal contact, and it pleased him more than he could describe. With her touch, good memories of his time with the Alexanders flooded into his brain, into his heart.

He made his rounds and then headed home. Porky was thrilled to see him, dancing around him, wagging her tail. Spencer went in the house for his usual dinner time routine. Afterwards, he went out to his workshop to work on the old lamp he acquired from the Alexanders. Porky went in and out of the open shop door to keep him company as he worked. It was almost ten o'clock when he finally finished and went to bed.

The next day, late into his delivery run, he came to the Alexander's, again. He opened the gate and walked through, headed for the mailbox. Both Beth and Joe were at work, moving plants around their garden, but they stopped when Spencer came through the gate.

"Hello Spencer. Nice day, isn't it?" Beth asked.

"It's a very nice day," said Spencer, pleased to take a moment to talk to her.

"Spencer, I have someone here I'd like you to meet. It's my husband, Joe. Do you remember Joe?"

Spencer looked at Joe for a moment, trying to find some features to recognize. Joe was about medium height, medium build with a big nose and a face that always seemed to smile. He had less hair than

Spencer remembered, but his expressive bushy eyebrows remained. He extended his hand to Joe.

"It's been a long time, Spencer. It's good to see you after all these years! I see you never found that finger!"

"Nope. It still might grow back, though," Spencer replied with a chuckle.

They all laughed about it. For a minute or so, all three just stood in the quiet and enjoyed each other's company before Spencer saluted them both and was off on his mail run.

Discovery

Spencer worked on the antique lamp for a week. Carefully, he took it apart, noting the pieces he needed. He cleaned the shade and used steel wool to clean the rust off the metal parts. Later in the week, he went to an electrical parts supply store and picked up some internal replacement parts to make it work like a modern lamp, yet still retain its antique look.

Each day, he would go by the Alexander's on his run. He would exchange a few more pleasantries with them and then be on his way.

Finally, on Thursday night, he had the old lamp all together. He plugged it in, turned it on and it worked like a charm. It had a beautiful antique look with modern efficiency. Spencer was very excited with his project. He showed Porky the new lamp. She wagged her tail because she was easily impressed by anything Spencer did.

For some reason, Spencer was a little down, having completed this project and not having anyone to share it with. Normally, this didn't concern him but today it did. Then he had a thought he had not had for decades. He picked up the phone.

"Hello Beth? This is Spencer Cunningham. How are you?"

"I'm fine, Spencer. How about you?" She sounded excited to hear from him, sending a rush of warmth through him.

"I just wanted to tell you that I just finished that old lamp you sold me! It came out very nicely," he said, suddenly nervous. What if the Alexanders weren't interested in the old lamp—or reconnecting with him? Normally he held himself above trying to impress or make other people happy, but the Alexanders were different; they mattered.

Before he could think about it anymore, Beth answered, "Why, that's lovely, Spencer! You must be very clever. That was one beat-up lamp. In fact, I think that might even be a lamp from your parent's house, from long ago."

Spencer literally felt the blood drain from his head. He slumped back into a chair, abruptly unable to maintain his own weight. Porky cocked her head to one side, her expression puzzled. He raised a shaking hand and stroked her head unsteadily. He had not thought of his parents for decades. They had vanished from his memory. He did get a settlement with interest on his twenty-first birthday but he thought everything had been sold off.

"Spencer? Are you still there?" Beth sounded worried.

"Ah... yeah. Still here. It's just been a long time since I thought about them. So... you think this lamp was actually my parents at one time? That... that would be incredible."

"I believe it is. Spencer, what are you doing tomorrow evening? Joe and I would like to see the lamp. Why don't you come over? Better yet, how about having supper with us?"

Spencer took a moment, thinking. His first impulse was to say no, like he always did, to escape social contact but he resisted the old urge. "Sure...what time?" he answered, his voice a bit shaky.

"Come over about five-thirty. Do you still like meatloaf and mashed potatoes?" asked Beth.

"Yes, I do," he answered, scarcely believing he was doing this.

"Bring your lamp and come on over," said Beth. "We'd love to have you."

"I'll be there."

Spencer thanked her and hung up the phone. He was surprised he had the courage to say yes. He hadn't accepted a dinner invitation since he'd left the last foster home when he was eighteen years old. Leaving that home had been his birthday present. His last one.

He remembered that day, well. The Williams family had celebrated his birthday and given him a wonderful send-off while they were at it.

How had he allowed himself to forget their kindness? Despite himself, he had a lump in his throat just thinking about it. It was funny how fondly he remembered that day, after all these years.

Dinner

Spencer was nervous about the dinner with the Alexanders. He thought back to his foster home days, the years in which he'd sat and had dinner with other people. He hadn't shared a meal with anyone since.

At five-thirty he made it to the Alexander's carrying his lamp. It was a nice, warm summer evening. The moon was full. Spencer enjoyed the scent of the Alexander's rose garden as he made his way to the front door and knocked. Joe Alexander was there to let him in and take his jacket, hanging it in the closet. He invited Spencer to sit down in their living room. Spencer looked around and marveled at all the family photos displayed on the table tops.

Beth came out wearing an apron and said, "Welcome, Spencer! It's so nice to have you here! The last time we had you for dinner was when you were ten years old." Her expression was a happy one, recalling the memory.

"Wow, that's true. I didn't think of that."

"Is that the old lamp?" she asked.

"Yes, all fixed up."

"It's just like new—it's better than new! You've done a wonderful job, Spencer."

The Alexanders both marveled at his workmanship. Joe was completely impressed. He and Spencer talked about the way Spencer did the refurbishment, right down to the technical details about the transformation.

Soon, Beth had them come into the dining room to eat. Supper was wonderful. Spencer found he was enjoying their company. It had been so long since he had eaten with other people, he'd forgotten the fellowship of the foster homes. Everyone felt welcome when they ate together. It was a warm feeling, long forgotten. Afterwards, they had their coffee in the living room. Spencer sat on the big, comfy couch while Joe and Beth sat in nearby chairs.

After a bit of small talk, of Donvegan, Brandon Lake and the old days, Beth brought up the subject of Spencer's parents. He could sense she was being careful of his feelings.

"I don't know if you know this Spencer, but we were friends of your parents when you lived in Brandon Lake."

Spencer was still for a few minutes, considering this. He had not talked to anyone about his parents, other than a few social workers, in decades. It wasn't that he did not want to say anything, more that he did not know what to say or think about them anymore. As a boy he'd kept his feelings tightly under wraps while he was at a new home. The government people were the only ones who ever asked, usually just prior to a transfer interview. Beth and Joe were the first ones truly interested, outside of the social workers.

"I never knew you and my parents were friends. All the time I was at your house, I never made the connection. I was so distraught it was all just a cloud of gloom."

"Your dad and I drove the trains together. That was how we met them," said Joe.

"My dad was a train engineer?"

"Oh, yes. We both drove GM Diesel Locomotives. They were great, powerful beasts," Joe said, proudly, then added with a twinkle in his eyes, "We even got to blow the whistles at the crossings!"

"That *would* be fun."

"It *was* fun," Joe confirmed.

Spencer summoned his courage and asked, "Do … do you know what happened to my parents?"

"Well, you were in school for the day, of course. Your mom picked up your dad at the train yard and they were coming back into town. The roads were icy with blowing snow, just like the day we took you to the hospital for your finger, remember?" Beth said, "They slid across a corner in front of a logging truck. I'm pretty sure they never knew what hit them, which is merciful, at least."

Spencer was trying to imagine this happening. He had put the past in a tight fist inside his heart. The fist was never unclenched and those dreadful moments would not be relived. Here, with the Alexanders, Spencer felt safe and at home. Here, the fist in his heart opened with all the past thoughts flooding out. He remembered when his parents were killed. It was a moment he tried not to re-live. To re-live it was to have no one to shelter him, understand and console him.

It was so many years ago, yet it was absolutely clear to this day. He remembered when the grim-faced social worker and policemen came to his house with the awful news. He remembered being devastated, numb and disbelieving. The adults were so grim and white-faced that he knew they were not joking.

Who would feed his pet fish? How would he get dinner and get to school? Nobody would be waiting for him at home, ever again. It would forever be an empty, silent house. Then he just crumpled into tears. The social worker took him to the hospital for a couple of days while she looked for a place for him in the interim. The nurses were busy but kind. They sat with him at every opportunity and just held him. They had children of their own and knew what it felt like.

He remembered when the social worker picked him up from the hospital and took him over to the Alexander's. She did say they were friends of his parents but he did not know them.

"I never did hear the full story. It does make me feel better knowing that," said Spencer, finding the lump that formed in his throat made it difficult to speak.

Beth and Joe came to sit on each side of him, putting their arms around him and the three of them just stayed there.

After that day, Spencer went over to the Alexander's quite often. They soon showed him family picture albums of his parents, their own huge extended family and their daughter Kirstin and her family. It was as if Spencer had been adopted into a big friendly family he never knew he had. He was back in a circle of hearts and thoughts.

Spencer remembered all those restless years of living in a house and a city that just felt temporary and empty. After reuniting with the Alexanders, it all suddenly felt like home.

Home had been with him, all along.

Good-Bye Clara

When he was in Victoria on a retirement course, Spencer drove past the old orphanage. He parked, then strolled down the sidewalk and looked over the old place. The front of the building was thoroughly repainted and modernized. The sign in front said it was "The Ross Bay Condominium".

The grotesque old fire escape tubes were long gone. For a fleeting second he missed them, thinking how fun it would have been to slide down them just once while he was there. Oh well.

He noticed the sad little cemetery was still in the corner of the front lawn but the remainder of the area was well manicured with rows of flowers growing everywhere. Even the cemetery looked good with the lawn cut and edges trimmed. The annoying geese were still there, standing guard. He could not resist going over to see Clara Hutchinson's headstone.

He stood for a few minutes, listening to the geese gabbling and fussing, enjoying the flowers and the quiet. Clara's headstone was so weathered he could barely make out her name. After a while he saw a bench nearby and headed over to sit. Spencer thought he'd just enjoy the moment after being packed in a noisy seminar all day. Lately he'd been on a classic story binge, so opened up an old copy of "Treasure Island", enjoying its simplicity of time and antiqueness. He even enjoyed the texture of the elderly book and its musty smell. Soon he was lost in adventures of boys and pirates, wishing that could have been his childhood instead.

"Spencer. Will you read to me?" A nearby voice requested weakly.

He froze where he was sitting, still recognizing her voice after all these decades. He raised his eyes to see a nine-year-old girl with a patched old dress standing before him. "Clara?" he whispered, afraid to scare her away.

"Yes, it's me, Spencer," and she sat down beside him.

Not knowing what else to do he just started to read to her. Clara said nothing and watched the book as he read aloud, trying his best to speak perfectly as he made his way through, page after page.

"Hello young man. What are you up to on this lovely evening?"

Spencer looked up from his book, surprised to see an elderly woman tending the flowers nearby. Clara had vanished. "Oh, hello. I was just reading my book."

The elderly woman smiled and said, "I see you know Clara Hutchinson."

"Clara?"

"Yes, the little girl you were reading to. I often see her, too."

"You can see ghosts?" asked Spencer, very surprised. He hadn't been the only one to see Clara.

"I'm glad to finally meet someone else who sees ghosts. My son would say I'm dotty and put me in a home but I'm managing at ninety years old and don't plan to move. How long have you known Clara...Mr...?"

"Cunningham but please call me Spencer, Ma'am."

"And you can call me Katherine. Pleased to meet you, Spencer."

"Pleased to meet you Katherine. I first met Clara when I was ten years old, when this place was the Ross Bay Orphanage, over forty years ago. I was only here for a couple of weeks before they shipped me off to a foster home."

"Same story, here," said Katherine. "We were both orphans here, Spencer."

"Yes. I eventually moved around to about a dozen different homes until I aged out at eighteen, then got my own place. It's been something of a journey."

Katherine said, "Yes, life is a journey, isn't it? After ninety years I have to say we become the people we meet along the way. You seem like a good fellow. What kept you going, home-to-home?"

Spencer pondered her question for a minute. "I haven't thought about that. I guess I took each day, one at a time, believed in myself and became self-reliant. For a long time, I thought there was no time for tears and I hardened my heart to everyone. I had to undo all that and came to appreciate the people around me. Now I know many of them did the best they could for me, and I plan to find as many of them as I can and personally thank them for it."

"You have found a wisdom that most people miss."

"Wisdom is hard to come by. I feel sorry for those who can't move on, like Clara," said Spencer.

"What happened to Clara, so long ago?"

"A nun looked up Clara's history and apparently her father was killed in the Great War. Her mother was forced to work and left her in this place. She visited Clara when she could, which wasn't often, until the 'flu epidemic killed her. Clara waited here for her for months until the 'flu got her, as well. After ninety-six years she's still waiting for her mother to come. I wish there was something we could do."

Katherine listened, thinking before she spoke, "I might have a suggestion for Clara. Could you come back tomorrow evening and meet here? At seven? I might have something we could do."

Puzzled, next evening Spencer was waiting at the cemetery, quietly reading aloud to Clara when Katherine and another woman arrived. Clara vanished with the sound of the visitors' voices.

"Oh, hello Katherine. I was just reading to Clara," said Spencer.

"I know. Please come out to see us, Clara. It's alright, Clara," Katherine assured.

Clara appeared in front of them, looking downcast.

Katherine smiled, "Hello Clara. How are you?"

"Fine, ma'am."

"Clara, this is my friend Gladys. She's a medicine woman from the Songhees Nation and lives in the building in the next condominium to me."

Gladys smiled, "Hello Clara."

"Spencer, Gladys and I are all worried about you, Clara. Are you alright?"

"...my mom is coming for me. I'm fine, thanks."

Katherine paused, then said gently, "Gladys can help you see your mom and dad again. Is this alright with you?"

"...I suppose..."

Katherine nodded to Gladys who knelt to the earth with great respect, gently chanting, while building a tiny nest of special grasses and tobacco in her hands. As she chanted ancient words the handful of special plants of the earth started to smoke and smudge harmlessly swirling and following its own path around Clara, who watched with wide-eyed wonder. The smudge went around and around her.

Clara raised her arms, smiled and looked at Spencer. "I'm going home, too, Spencer," and she slowly faded away. Clara was gone.

They stood in stunned silence until Spencer spoke. "Thank you, Gladys and Katherine, for helping Clara finally join her parents. Everyone deserves to be with the ones they love."

Spencer hugged both of them and they went on their way, leaving him standing alone by the forlorn graveyard. He went to Clara's headstone, wrote something in the front of the book he had been reading to her and placed it on her final resting place.

To Clara,
I hope you've found Peace,
Your friend, Spencer

LARSON LOGIC

(FROM THE FUTURE...)

Jess found herself numbly walking the halls of her new school. Last night's rain must have accumulated on the roof of the ancient school draining down pools of dirty water laying everywhere awaiting someone to mop it up. What a dump, she thought. Her next class was math. What can they possibly do to math, she wondered.

As she sat at the only available seat in Mr. Larson's math class—the front row—she could see why other kids quietly laughed at old Mr. Larson. He was stooped, looked possibly seventy-five... dressed in a Harris tweed coat, nice shirt and tie... and Yogi the Bear pajama bottoms with matching Boo-boo slippers. Mr. Larson clearly stopped caring about education a long time ago. He mumbled as he wrote the days assignment on the scratchy, dusty chalk board.

Missing her laptop computer, Jess worked on the project for ten minutes. This is simple crap. Excel could do in a flash! "Mr. Larson... sir."

The old teacher turned and looked up, as if waking from a daydream. A girl sat in the front row, almost in front of him. She looked tall and confident. Her eyes were full of mischief and intelligence. "Yes... you there... new? From Canada?" he asked.

"Yes sir. I'm Jessica Reid. Can we not make a spreadsheet for these problems and then move on to the next step? I know one on the 'net. I can program a calculator which would help. This method is redundant and slow."

Mr. Larson could hardly believe what he was hearing. He hadn't heard the word "spreadsheet", "redundant" and "program" in the same sentence since his days at the university. Ah, those were the days, so long ago. We had such a good program with the brightest people... forty years ago?

"... Um Mr. Larson... " the girl in the front row persisted.

"... Sorry... that's not possible... " he replied, lifting his wild bushy eyebrows.

"Jessica... "

"Of course—Jessica. Could you stay after class so we can talk about this?"

He could see concern on the young girl's face but he moved on. *So much basic math to cover and such a waste of time. She was, of course, correct.*

The class vanished and he was all alone with this new student... was her name Jess?

Her eyes searched out his. "Mr. Larson? You wished to speak to me? Spreadsheets? Math?"

He found himself nodding in agreement then turned on an old ventilation fan he kept on a side table. Long worn out, not unlike himself, it scratched and buzzed which was precisely why he kept it. He was no fool and knew someone took the time to listen to what was being taught in this dreadful school and the old fan bedevilled their efforts. Mr. Larson smiled to himself, then turned and saw the young girl watching him with concern.

"I'm very sorry..." he asked, unsure of her name once again.

"Jess!"

"Ah... Jess... spreadsheets... computers...internet... You are no doubt mystified as to why America lacks all these things. Let me sit down and tell you a very long story."

The girl slouched down in her seat a little, maybe anticipating a rambling that would burn through her twenty-minute bathroom break? Peculiarly, he looked forward to speaking to someone untarnished by his present day world.

"No doubt you know the origins of computers from the abacus to Babbage's difference engine, Turing, Micral, Osborne, IBM, Apple and so forth? The world transformed into a computerized wonderland that changed how we lived. At the same time, the Internet came along, allowing the most scientific, most entertaining and most ridiculous within everyone's hands at any time."

The young girl looked at him as if she'd suddenly met Albert Einstein.

He continued, "The computer and the internet's scientific significance to almost telepathically combine intelligence to the nth degree was a stunning renaissance for the great minds of the world. Its unregulated intelligence was its charm and eventual undoing for America. A drop of brilliance in an ocean of drivel."

The girl quietly interrupted, "Ah... spreadsheet, sir?"

Larson smiled, "Oh? Sorry. I'm a long-winded old man. Bear with me. So, this unregulated wild frontier soon became the home of unspeakable actions, crime, vices and sins which buried its goodness. As they said at the time, we found ourselves 'living in a post-factual' world. Fear mongering, hate, lies and conspiracy overwhelmed science. History, culture and science were utterly overwhelmed by poppycock and misinformation. When the Revisionists took over after the disastrous political campaigns decades ago, made up largely of vast and harmful disinformation campaigns—largely robotic in origin—they decided to end any type of internet and home computer use. They applied a simple fix for a complex issue, labeling it 'unholy', unmentioned in the Bible, useless to all, detrimental to society, and worse than television. Lethal weapons in the hands of children, so to speak. In many ways they were correct. Thus, you won't find a computer, the internet or anything but the simplest of technologies in the American public today. What little is left is carefully screened by the government to ensure we are living in a 'simpler time' our society can more easily cope with. We are no longer free to roam, intellectually."

The girl spoke, "But guns are lethal weapons and they kept those."

"Guns are a simple technology with a purpose we think we understand, going back to the 1700's, of black powder and blunderbuss's. We've had them for hundreds of years. The threat of a gun was obvious but the internet was subtle, too new for our simple brains to understand. One hand on a gun can threaten a few where the internet controls millions."

"I think you've answered my question, Mr. Larson."

"I'm sorry for the long explanation but I get new international students from time to time, just like yourself. Anything about spreadsheets and computers inevitably become a discussion of why we have no internet. I'm saving you the trouble."

"That was very interesting, sir."

"Well Jess, sadly it's paper and pencil for you unless you know how a slide-rule works."

"Slide-rule?"

He smiled, turned off his noisy fan and said, "For another day."

REMEMBRANCE DAY

Remembrance Day in Goosefield was cold, bleak and dreary, as it should be. A somber day reflecting on a somber subject.

Erika and her piper mates had an hour to practice together at the outdoor cenotaph before they were called upon to play as a group with the ceremony. Giselle dropped off Erika at the entrance of the Goosefield Community Hall then parked her Subaru across from the nearby but deserted curling rink. She saw custodian Aleck's car parked near his curling rink. No doubt he was there to shovel the pile of snow off the curling rink walkway and scrape away the ice underneath for tomorrow.

Giselle sat by herself in the car, digging out her latest Terry Reid novel, waiting. She anticipated having to run the car occasionally to keep warm, but she was okay for now. It was too late for her coffee, long gone cold.

She read a few pages in her book then glanced up at the sound of vehicle tires. A white police truck arrived with a single constable, carefully parking beside Aleck's car. A tall, black-capped policeman stepped out of the police truck and looked over the Community Hall and adjacent curling rink, considering, it seemed. Unsure of a vantage point.

Fascinated, she watched him reach into the back of the truck cab and pull out what looked like a camo painted army rifle. He inspected it, fiddled with it a bit, then slung it over his left shoulder. Then he pulled at his cap, which suddenly became a black ski mask over his face. This was when she realized he was dressed all black from head to toe. He looked like an evil robo cop, black, menacing. It made her nervous.

Giselle had heard police snipers watched Remembrance Day gatherings, assuaging a public fear. It was Ironic that a ceremony thanking soldiers from past wars for protecting the country from nameless evil doers required a sniper to guard the ceremony. She kept such thoughts to herself.

From her car she watched him approach the nearby curling rink building, particularly the snow-capped roof. The constable pulled out a phone and called. After five minutes Aleck, the custodian came out of the curling rink and greeted the menacing black sniper. The sniper pointed at the snow-covered roof, waved his arms about, gesturing. Did he want to stand up there?

The custodian shrugged and left, returning a few minutes later with a short rickety step ladder and a snow shovel, clearly inadequate. Aleck then pointed to the roof, shaking his head, shrugging then standing awaiting a reply.

Annoyed, the sniper waved his black gloved hand up to the roof of the building again while the custodian patiently listened, persistently shaking his head. The menacing sniper in black offered a few final futile gestures, obviously giving up access to the roof.

Too much snow and very icy.

He searched through the tiny eye holes, seeking guarding place Plan B which was the entrance to the hall. He went from the sniper in the sky, Chuck Norris, A-Team style, to standing at the entrance to the curling hall, Wal-Mart greeter style.

She was amazed at how this unfolded, now seeing a ferocious looking SWAT team sniper standing on the sidewalk, watching as folks began to go past him and into the Community Hall. Some thought him 'real' while some might have thought he was an actor for some purpose,

A large, jolly man in a Scottish kilt, hat and tunic of a bag piper approached the black clad sniper with his camo weapon, making direct eye contact with him. Giselle found herself slipping forward in her seat, waiting.

Altercation? Concern?

They stood, face to face, then were suddenly laughing, talking. Perhaps the sniper in black teased the big man about a kilt on a cold day, wondering if he wore anything under it.

A woman arrived in a matching kilt and hat, new infant in her arms, also standing with the sniper and large Scottish man. The menacing sniper rolled up his face mask and now had the little babe's hand on the end of his finger, making funny faces at the giggling child as they all laughed.

Giselle felt strangely comforted and went to join the ceremony.

PARADE PONY

Old Bill, the tiny pony strained as he pulled the heavy, ornate carriage loaded with six very young Cinderella princesses, all oblivious to his suffering. His little head was low, short legs dragging the carriage ahead one step at a time, the crowd watching with a mixture of amusement and annoyance at his pitiful pace.

The summer sun beat down on the hot July parade turning the pavement into an oven.

The princesses sweated, complained, bored out of their skulls as Old Bill trudged along, barely moving the pumpkin carriage up the ever-increasing hill. The parade was forced to stop and wait, time after time, as he struggled.

At mid-point on the parade route, the miniature pony could go no further, no matter how the group of diminutive princesses shouted and cried at it. The parade of pickup trucks and fire engines following behind were forced to wait, irritated at pausing for something as silly as a tiny pony. Finally, Old Bill managed to start moving again, desperate there would be a bit of water and shade offered at the end of this torment. His tiny mouth was full of spit and foam, expelled by his effort.

Spectators watched with annoyance, sadness or indifference to this little drama. Everyone was either unwilling or unable to intercede or simply wanted the parade impediment to just get out of the way. Move on. The few who could see the pony's distress were too shy to take charge.

An older man in a cowboy hat stepped wordlessly out of the parade throng and strode up to the dying pony.

He took Bill by his halter, smiled and reassured the startled princesses, "Your pony is played out, kids. We need to get him some water and shade right away. Get off the carriage kids and follow me."

The cowboy drew the pony, the carriage and a single file of six little sweating princesses in glittering costumes through the surprised crowd on the sidewalk to the shade of a nearby tree.

The cowboy unhitched Old Bill, panhandled bottles of water from the eager and surprised spectators and poured their precious contents into his big cowboy hat.

The little pony stuck his nose in the hat and drank for a long while with the kindly cowboy watching it wasn't too much, too soon.

The water and shade were a lifesaver.

The cowboy relinquished command by handing Old Bill's halter to a parent of one of the princesses and said, "Another five minutes and this pony would have been dead in the middle of the parade," giving him a stern look. "These kids can't make a life or death decision like this. You were all lucky."

Then the cowboy vanished into the crowd like the Lone Ranger.

HER LITTLE TOWN

(A POEM-ISH...)

Erika hated her little rural town with all her heart and more with every passing year. She cursed its tiny size, isolation, weather, uniqueness, optimism, pessimism, people who moved there and hated it, people who moved there and liked it, lifers who never left, small town cheerfulness, dressing like hicks, no sophistication, taking a stand against nothingness, dim-witted blue collar workers, pretentious white collar workers, farmers, little streets, empty grass lots without hope, cheerful little dead end stores, laughing at jokes that were not funny, endless snow, blowing dirt, lack of imagination, people gossiping about her while knowing nothing, talking about her and knowing something, endless repetition of town stories, having to be courteous even though she hated them and they hated her, dressing down so she didn't stand out, windblown trash, old creaky houses almost falling down with people still living in them, self-important locals, shitty no-news newspaper, old people, bums hanging around who everyone knew and talked to, the looks she got when someone smart moved to town and thought she was like all the rest, dim-witted boys trying to pick her up, dim-witted girls getting picked up, anything utterly predictable, jacked up pick-up trucks, no creativity, her school, the way new teachers from the big city looked down on the students, ashamed at her school stupidity, complaining about everything, old-fashioned courtesy, salons selling fake-bake tans and expensive hooker finger nails for the snooty rich with third world nannies looking after their kids, ancient phone booths, potholes, nothing new ever happened, wealthy old men driving ratty old pick-ups, cowboy music, mousy poor kids, rednecks, dead town devoid of excitement, a dreary treadmill from cradle to grave and a feeling of no escape.

THE DARK SIDE

An Army survival course is three weeks of solitary subsistence on tree bark and ditch water while trying not to be eaten by bears and blood sucking mosquitoes, all meant to test a trained killer.

She was first dropped by parachute into the middle of a frigid northern lake, then had to swim to shore awkwardly, thanking and cursing her floatation vest. Soaked, tired and cold, she dragged herself and parachute up on the rocky shore.

After watching her the whole time, her yellow drop plane flew low, waggling its wings cheekily. She gave it the finger while smiling at the pilot. "Thanks for your concern, assholes!"

The plane flew away until it was a vanishing speck.

All alone.

Taking advantage of a warm, late summer day she dumped water from her boots, wrung out her socks, camo pants and waited for them all to dry, somewhat. Blistered feet this early in the march would not be good. An hour later, footwear and suit somewhat drier, she redressed and started walking, sticking to a deer trail that went around the lake. Looking at the sun, she strode off towards her destination at the base, westerly, about one hundred and twenty miles away.

The bugs had joined her on her trek and were enjoying an unanticipated feast—which she largely ignored. No bug dope allowed. Fuck. Her stomach growled, which she also ignored. Her butt itched terribly after the pee break in the nettles. That was *hard* to ignore. A hungry shitty night spent in the woods. Eighteen hours done with four-hundred and eighty hours to go.

As the sun rose on the horizon, she noticed smoke over to the left and decided to investigate. Looked like a campfire in this carefully restricted remote area, DND only. Shivering and curious, she left the trail, moving quietly through the bush to come up behind the source of the smoke.

She spied a familiar older woman in a police uniform laying on one of two chaise lounge chairs, mug in hand, beside a roaring little camp fire. *Is that coffee I smell?*

"You—in the bush! Come on over," the older woman called, obviously aware there was someone behind her in the bushes.

"Inspector Shirl?"

"Yes! I have coffee! I won't tell anyone—I even brought you this chair. We need to talk!"

"You're kidding me." Terry just shook her head, emerging from the trees and out into the clearing where the fire smoked and Shirl sat.

Soon they were drinking coffee together, looking over the serene beauty of the lake, lounging on the chairs in the sun.

"Smoky campfire, Inspector... Shirl. I could see it for miles."

Her boss snorted. "I was trying to attract snoopers and I found one."

"So I'm a snooper, am I?" she asked suspiciously, sipping the delicious, unexpected coffee. "What's up? Heard you were doing a special project thing for the cops, out east?"

"I am *and* I'm on a talent search."

Terry looked comically over her shoulder, this way and that. "You see some talent around here, do ya?"

"Possibly." Shirl sat back, considering her thoughts. "How would you feel about skipping this silly survival thing, enjoying a warm shower and a *real* dinner instead of choking down grubs and peeing in stinging nettles?"

"Might be nice. What's the catch?"

"You'll have to be 'dead'."

Her eyebrows went up, "Me? dead? Is that all?"

"Yes. A position came open for an informant. Deep cover. We need a nobody, an unknown such as yourself."

"I'm not sure I like to think of myself as a nobody, thanks."

"Let me re-word that... unattached. You don't have a hubby, six kids and a mortgage."

"That's true. I *am* 'unattached' as you put it."

"We'll arrange for you to go missing and presumed dead during this survival course. You'll get some training then you'll appear in Montreal as part of the drug trade, fit in, move up and try not to get exposed, killed or worse. Remember names, dates, times and places. Life in the fast lane. One of the God Father's minions."

"Wow. What happened to the last informant... the one I'm obviously replacing?" she asked warily.

"Beth. Ah... a running shoe washed up on the beach of the St. Lawrence River. We think it has Beth's foot in it. Can't seem to find anything else of her."

Eyebrows went way up.

Shirl glanced over at her. "We'd rather not find *your* foot. Let's plan on getting all of you back— alive," said Shirl.

Grasping the reality, she gulped. "So, I'll have to be at the top of my game, is what you're saying?"

"Best not screw up," Shirl confirmed.

"Are the Army, cops and everyone in on this new job position?"

"Only a selected few... need to know basis. Fewer is best."

Terry thought for a full minute. "Let me see... live like an animal, pee in the bush and eat dirt... or... live the high life in the Montreal drug trade but possibly be chopped up into little bits." She tilted her head toward Shirl. "You know how to make a girl an offer she can't refuse."

"So, you'll do it?"

"Why not?" Terry shrugged. "All I've been doing is cop school, special courses and Army training for three years. Time to cut bait and do something with it."

Shirl already knew Terry was hard as nails on the outside—it wasn't a secret. Her attitude was stern and ever watching. Intimidating. Shirl also knew Terry was proud of her image and achievements but knew they meant isolation. A 'rock' doesn't attract affection or soulmates—perfect informant material.

No cracks in her armour just yet.

Shirl nodded succinctly. "Perfect. I brought some clothes for you to change in to. Give me your Army duds and let's arrange something to look like your sudden death. What death do you feel like? Becoming bear poop?"

"Drowning looks better. I could lose my footing on a fast river that runs off this big lake. Freeze up's in six weeks so they'll give up. I'll leave a few bits of clothing for a trail."

"I like it. Let's do it."

"So, if I'm dead, who will I become?"

"We made someone up. We'll dye your hair, new nose, maybe a boob job. Drug pedlars like 'em busty."

"No boob job and my nose is just fine, thanks. Nothing permanent."

"Okay. Change of eye color? Some tattoos? Tats only stay on for a year and fade. Latest tech."

"Sure, as long as it doesn't hurt."

"Done deal… *Tammy Anderson.*" Shirley looked at her significantly.

"*Tammy?* Is that who I am?"

"Yeah. Tammy's your undercover name. Let's arrange for your death before it gets dark and then we can get out of here."

News of Terry's "Missing in Action" and "Presumed Dead" was of little interest to anyone. There was no Dad to call, Mom was long dead, and any contact with her older sister Gloria was a vague and ominous "Last seen in Vancouver's downtown east-side" situation.

Unattached.

"Tammy" trained intensely to look and act like a drug courier.

Police experts showed her how to walk, talk and look. She got a black hair dye job. Three sketchy tattoo artists splashed typical, garish examples on her, taking care to make them look worn.

"These tats will hopefully fade away in a couple of years or so, presuming you survive this assignment."

Wasn't that just a morale booster of a comment?

Experts trained her in habits she needed to exhibit. She also learned how to watch and observe. They videoed her performance, nagging her into acting perfection.

Her trainers gave her a few defensive tools of the trade in case she needed them. Her sneaker shoelaces had wires in them to strangle, if needed. Tammy wondered if Beth's single shoe still had the wire shoe lace in them when it washed up on the beach.

Tammy's red spike heel shoes had actual spikes in the heels. Lethal chic. A small camera and tape recorder each looked like cosmetic items. The panic button on her key fob came with tiny lock picks. Two very small switch blade knives. Her bra featured an eavesdropping "wire". Not a bad fit, either.

A handgun was an expectation in her new trade. She carefully inspected it. "Small revolver... serials filed off... keeps the brass after the shoot. Close range. Tidy and handy."

Spike

Spike, the weapons tech, watched the new recruit feel and fondle the little pistol, seeming eager to use it. New undercover cops were all the same—over-trained and under-experienced. They put too much emphasis on cool gadgets and not enough on the most dangerous weapon of all—a sharp, calculating mind. Only the smart survive this lethal game of chess.

"Anything... bigger?" Tammy asked, breaking Spike's train of thought.

"A bigger gun? Like a shotgun?" Spike asked sarcastically.

"No. A pistol with a bit longer range and penetrating power but small," Tammy replied. "This gun is okay to about ten feet."

Completely predictable. Spike slid open a nearby drawer and pulled an exotic looking hand gun out. "Here's a special pistol and a silencer."

Tammy looked at it, unimpressed. "Isn't that... small?"

"CIA liked this type enough that Gary Powers carried one." Spike looked at Tammy and wondered if she even knew who Gary Powers was. *No?* "Here are a few different loads for it—one for short range the other with high penetrating power. Comes with a silencer and a holster. You'll need a good backstory if you're caught with it, though. Hide it well."

"Cool. I'll bring it back when I'm done."

"You do that." *Kids!* Hopefully this one does come back.

———

The weeks of undercover training was difficult. Tammy lost weight, muscle, and sleep, becoming thin, tired, and sallow, with bloodshot eyes and blotchy skin. She'd always taken pride in being healthy and strong but this was awful. She felt wrung out and slightly ill all the time, even mildly depressed.

Her instructors understood her dilemma. "It's part of your temporary persona. The uniform... your armour." She learned the look and walk of the defeated. The invisible people.

She hated make-up but they showed her how to splash it on. Change your look, your health, younger and older. Be someone else if needed for penetration, investigation or escape.

They made her walk around while carefully assessing her. "Wear the look like you own it, or you're dead," they said. "We want more of you to come back than just a foot in a shoe." "No marching around like you're still in the army. Slouch!" "Look downcast... but wary."

During lunchbreaks one of the instructors would sit on various public benches with her, and together they'd watch people go by, running the gambit of the entitled strut of the rich to the hesitant shuffle of the homeless and everything in between. Everyone walked and watched differently. Tammy found it fascinating.

They showed her tips and tricks to work social media to leave subtle messages with fake profiles or find out who might be doing the same. Criminals and terrorists hang out in social media just like everyone else—it was the modern street in Dodge City—where anything goes, and nobody cares. Buy a bomb, hit man, weapon or human being of any age, no strings attached. Free range crime on any level.

She dragged herself home after what seemed like years of work. *What the fuck have I got myself in to?* After tossing and turning in bed she got up, dug around the net to find out everything she could about the drug cartels. She always did research on a sleepless night and there had been more than a few.

The Montreal cartels were evil, organized and secretive. Few arrests with zero convictions. She gave up and moved on to a few news feeds, finally stumbling over the news of her own bogus demise:

Toronto Globe and Mail newspaper: "Army Special Forces member vanishes during survival exercise in remote lake country. Despite an exhaustive search no body was found. Spokesman said they suspect the army specialist may have drowned in one of the area's large, fast rivers. With no new leads, the search is winding down after two weeks.

Tammy scoffed. *Gave up on me after only two weeks of looking! Thanks for not busting your asses.*

As she explored old news stories she came across "Operation O'Tremens", a story was about an undercover informant who stayed and made it to the top of organized crime. Another story told of an undercover informant who managed to get near the pinnacle of the Klu Klux Klan organization—despite the fact that informant was in fact a black man.

Ballsy and bold was the ticket, apparently. These guys made it to the top and didn't die. Quit while they were on top. Smart. "Wow," she muttered to herself, shutting down her computer. Enough 'net time wasting. Time for bed. Training had been physically and mentally draining. When she looked in the bedroom mirror these days, she had to admit she sounded, acted and looked perilously close to someone on drugs, living on the edge... A lot like her sister Gloria. What little she remembered of her, anyway.

A low-level criminal's bio for "Tammy Anderson" was invented and placed in all the right places. A life was built up on social media platforms. Her seedy work resume was conjured up along with a small-time crime history. "Drug mule—large quantities from source to street supplier or anywhere else. Caught twice. Did not cooperate with police."

While she was being trained in her informant role, Montreal police quietly went on a campaign to arrest all the drug couriers of the target gang they could find so the new "Tammy" would quickly become a highly sought-after commodity. They then placed their precious experienced drug courier where she would be appreciated and noticed.

Next thing she knew she was being thrown in a police drunk-tank, slipping in a puddle of puke and falling sideways on the floor as the guard shoved her, slamming the door behind her.

Uh, gross!

Three female occupants laughed as she slowly got up, splattered with vomit and whatever else is on the floor of a disgusting jail cell. She resisted her urge to crack some heads. *Patience! Don't blow your cover five minutes in.*

The laughter died as quickly as it began.

"Sorry, kid," said the oldest inmate, clearly pale and ill.

Tammy said nothing, looking for a sink or a water tap.

"Don't even *try* the shitter," warned another woman. "It hasn't flushed for days."

"Dandy."

A Friendly Jail Cell

She felt disgusted, afraid to look at her hands or her clothes. *What the Hell? I'm standing in God knows what with either crack heads, drunks, ho's, or all the above.*

"Blend in" they'd said. "It'll be fun," they'd said.

She sat on the least disgusting half of a cot, leaned her head into the back wall and tried to get some rest. First day as a deep informant for organized crime and here she was, trapped in a cell. She dozed, worried her new biography and life wouldn't hold scrutiny for the crime bosses she may work for. Her handlers said this is about a six-week job. Names, dates and incidents. Big fish.

"Tammy Anderson! Yes, Anderson! You!" repeated the irritated jailer, pointing to her. It took her a few seconds to register that her name was "Tammy".

Groggily, she stood up, took stock of her surroundings so she kept her story straight and lurched towards the guard. *Will I end up as a foot in a shoe?* Last chance to run.

"Ya made bail, Anderson." The guard pointed to a well-dressed man standing in the entrance of the jail cell hall.

Who's this? He looked like a tame crime lawyer, three-piece suit, slicked-down hair—and shifty. Crime did pay and very well. Not sure what to do, she allowed her gaze to shift to suspicious, letting him speak first.

"Tammy Anderson?"

"Yeah."

"The name's Lewis." He made no effort to shake her hand. In fact, he didn't seem to want to touch her. "A benefactor paid your bail." He then used his arm in a sweeping motion for her to walk ahead of him. Tammy turned and walked the walk for all it was worth, as requested, glad to be out. Best avoid the ears in a police station.

Two police officers backed up against the wall, giving the pair room to pass through the hallway. They looked at the lawyer as if they were disgusted but resigned to his kind. No doubt Lewis the shyster had sprung scum loose to go back on the street before... Perps the police might have spent months arresting or had a partner taking a bullet from his pals.

Tammy wondered how many of those officers would enjoy taking a shot at this man if they thought nobody would find out who did it. One less untouchable crime shyster off the street. Lewis just smiled at them, no doubt reveling in the likely fact he'd made many-times their salaries last year and would again next year—with impunity.

She strutted ahead, concentrating on her new walk, skin crawling as she imagined the creepy lawyer's eyes ogled her back, butt, her straggly, clumpy hair, dirty clothes, poorly done tattoos, skinny arms and legs with mottled skin, and sad, defeated posture. Unhealthy drug user. Perfect.

They stopped outside the police station. Tammy glanced up at the nearest sign—"Montreal Police Station #23."

"Go home. Stay sober. Someone will call you," the shifty lawyer told her as he put her number in his phone and then slunk away.

Home? Right—she knew the La Marie Hotel had been set up as "home" for Tammy. A tiny room in the bad rooming house had been rented and furnished in her name. Time to check it out.

It was a twenty-block walk for Tammy. She didn't mind as it cleared her head and she enjoyed the exercise. It was a very nice morning despite the bad night. The sun shone and birds in the few sparse trees sang, ignoring the sketchy neighborhood. Bonus, out here in the fresh air, she could barely smell whatever was smeared all over her clothes.

Soon she came to the old La Marie Hotel. The building was just a big pale blue box three stories high. It was long past its prime with barred windows, dirty glass and peeling paint, proving to anyone interested that yes, it has always been a pale blue box. The bar was at street level with two stories of rooms above. An old run-down rooming house.

It was attached to the shabby street featuring a few homeless people, one with a shopping cart filled with precious belongings. Tammy made eye contact and nodded hello to each and every one. See who's watching.

As she entered the La Marie Hotel, she politely sidestepped a hooker in the doorway. Peering through the grubby window, she saw half the lights were burnt out or pulsing on and off for an eerie effect. The front desk was to the right. A piece of plywood nailed to the sill served as the reception table. A chubby worn woman had her back to her, hunched in a battered swivel chair was stuffing papers into crude mail slots.

"Hey. Got my key?" Tammy called to her, trying to sound tough. She had no idea what her room number was.

The front desk woman turned to her. She was balding, missing teeth and wore cheap drugstore glasses with thick lenses. "What?"

It was Shirl under that disguise. Tammy hid her momentary surprise. Well done!

Shirl droned, "Key to room 524?" She winked, belying her disheartened tone. She leaned out and whispered "It's really room 201 but write Marty Balsam 524 in this ledger, always. Got it?"

"Yes, 524"

Shirl handed her a key along with a piece of paper, adding for anyone listening, "You owe rent. Pay up or we'll kick your scrawny ass out."

"You'll get the money when I do," Tammy snapped back, abruptly turning away to the stairs.

The worn-out carpet hung loose on each step, almost tripping her in the dark stairwell. She emerged in the second-floor hallway, seeking room 201. What's that smell?

Urine?

Home Sweet Home

Glancing back and forth, she explored both ends of the hallway, observing the exits that worked and weren't covered over or blocked. Next, she found the door to the roof and went out to investigate. Cigarette butts, needles and condoms. She wasn't the only one that came up here. Smoke, shoot up or sex. Maybe the works.

The neighboring buildings were almost close enough to jump over to. A bit far but a jump was always shorter when someone is chasing you with a gun. She went back down the stairs, looking for her room.

She almost laughed when she found room 201 was the only one that had no actual number posted on the door. Many layers of paint revealed the ghost of number 201. The door did feature an eye hole. Handy.

Tammy took a minute to look all around the door edges for trip wires and bugs, looking closely for bits of hair stuck on the door. It was the oldest, cheapest trick in the book to see if there was an intruder waiting or someone had been there. For a full five minutes she stood in the doorway and listened. Suspicious sounds?

Satisfied, she peeked under the door for shadows, then rose up and unlocked it. She pushed it and waited for it to bump the wall, full open. Nobody was behind the door. She stepped in, motionless, just studying the room.

It was a "bachelor suite", or so they called it—another word for closet. A bed was on the left and a minimal kitchen area on the right. A tiny simple fridge was closest to the door.

Her room had been expertly set up to give a "lived in" look. A double bed mattress was laying on the floor with sheets piled, used, nearby. There was a suitcase opened, full of clothes. There was a rough, ancient chrome kitchen table and three chairs. The sink was full of dirty dishes. Nice. Housekeeping just like her own apartment, back home.

She stepped inside, opened the fridge and saw nothing but a takeout bowl of long decayed salad. The little freezer had a miniature iceberg of something she wouldn't touch. Were those possibly blue popsicles? Eewww! She slapped it shut and moved to the window. It opened on to a fire-escape but it had not been opened for a very long time. It looked down on the parking lot, below.

She found an old burner cell phone, complete with cracked screen. It was supposed to be set up with a suitable text and call history, hidden recording functions and GPS tracking. Inside it had been juiced up so it ran very well with all the latest cloak and dagger programs. There was a beat-up laptop as well, which came with a program to pick up any nearby "bugs" tracing her, intentionally or unintentionally.

The small bathroom seemed okay. The toilet flushed and the taps in the sink ran. No toilet paper. There was a filthy and elderly plunger nearby, but she decided she wasn't going to touch it—ever. Appalling!

The rusty bathtub held water with hot water if she left the tap running for a while, going from black to rust colored, then clear-ish. The medicine cabinet was filthy and had a few empty prescription bottles. "Methadone' — Dr. Singh — Tammy Anderson".

The nearby vanity drawer was well stocked with cheap make-up, special shoes and personal kit.

It took a while, but she located the hidden stash of weapons, frozen in that popsicle box in the freezer. Thawed, she slipped the knives and gun under her blouse. Damn cold! Then she took a few minutes to insert the wire shoelaces in her sneakers.

She remembered the note Shirl at the front desk gave her. "Rent: $99 plus utilities per month. No drugs or police." Handwritten underneath: "Money at your door".

Tammy ripped it up in small pieces and flushed it, plugging the toilet. She had to use the disgusting plunger. Fuck!

After she washed her hands—twice—she looked around the room to see if everything was in order.

Time to eat and get a nap, maybe? Will I catch something from this mattress? Skip the nap.

Her phone lit up with a text message from Lewis, the shitty lawyer. "Go to Bubbles Bikini Car wash. Dress for it. Ask for Ric."

Ric

Tammy rummaged through her suitcase stash of clothes on the floor and located some short shorts, a low-cut blouse and the deadly spike heels and hastily pulled them on. She needed to look the part. She dutifully put her make-up on, employing her new skills. Part of the new uniform these days.

As Tammy prepared her stomach growled persistently. Need to eat. Food money? Then she remembered "Money at the door". Door? She considered the doors she had. Unlikely to be an outside one. She ran her fingers along the bathroom door, top and sides. Nothing. She went over to the little folding door of the wardrobe and felt all around. Aha! Hollowed-out edge. She felt a roll of bills squeezed into a slot on the top. Twenty-tens.

Feeling prepared, Tammy locked up, noting the feeble knob lock and where a much sturdier one could be installed. It once had one, safe and durable, but were long gone, no doubt removed and sold for drug money.

She grabbed a sandwich with the best before date from a Q Mart and ran for the bus stop, barely getting on in time. She crammed down the sandwich on the stinky, lurching transit bus, while sitting next to an old lady who spoke to an imaginary cat named "Pebbles" the whole time.

Best get used to the loser cruiser.

The bus dropped her off next to "Bubbles Car Wash", a grubby location in a bad part of town. As she got closer to the car wash, she couldn't help noticing—and wondering *why* so many very nice, expensive cars were coming through, complete with creepy-looking drivers. The driver's gazes were invariably riveted at the girls in bikini's scrubbing the cars. Distraction.

I don't care what anyone says, I'm not washing cars in a bikini!

It was a strange sight to see the girls bouncing around in tight "Bubbles" green uniform bikinis busily wiping off foam and rubbing the cars with great effort, bums and boobs jiggling. Nearby, a seedy looking man with red curly hair, average height, about the age of thirty barked out orders and pointed. "Ya missed a spot! There!"

He also wore a "Bubbles" work shirt with "Ric" printed on the front. When he turned to yell about another missed spot, Tammy saw the back of his shop shirt featured a caricature of a standing bathing beauty.

————

Ric Casey had worked at the car wash for about five years. He'd been a pimp until Bob decided to give him a more respectable profession. All Ric had to do was run the car wash as Bob directed and he could rent the girls out on the side. Flexible and lucrative. Bob seemed to be good to work for, though Ric kept complaints to himself.

The guy before Ric complained a lot until they found him in the river with a steel spike in his head. The only reason the police found him was "bloat and float" overcame the concrete blocks tied to his ankles. Ric always pasted on a smile whenever Bob was around, like today.

Ric glanced at his watch, waiting for the new girl to get here. Late. He saw a girl headed his way—tough and strung-out. Might be her. "Tammy?"

Her eyes flicked toward him.

"Over here!" he barked.

He looked her over as Tammy dutifully strutted toward to him. She was a bit clumsy in heels, plain with a lot of makeup, a bit tall and had small tits, so no bikini for her. Must be a new drug mule. Something about her strut, her demeanor didn't quite fit, but he wasn't about to complain to Bob about her... yet.

Ric pointed at Tammy, then jerked his thumb behind him. "Car wash office. Ask for Bob!"

———

T ammy followed Ric's orders, struggling with the spike heels while trying to maintain her "strut". She managed to get through the entrance without incident and found the door that said "Office" or rather, 'OFF E'. Behind its closed door she heard a conversation in progress. A room of killers.

Knock? Why not?

She timidly tapped on the door. Conversation ceased and the door swung open. Two men sat facing each other.

"What?" said the man behind the desk.

"I'm Tammy."

The two men looked at each other, waving her inside. It was a tiny office with barely room for the three of them. The man seated at the door slid his hand up between her legs as she squeezed by.

She thought, ignore it or break some fingers? Maybe later.

The man behind the desk stood, reached over to offer his hand to shake. "I'm Bob. Welcome aboard, Tammy. My friend with NO manners is 'Zoo'." He grimaced at his colleague, who just smiled.

She shook Bob's hand, saying nothing. What a looker Bob was. The proverbial tall, dark and handsome. Gorgeous. Seemed well-mannered. Such warm eye contact.

"Follow me, Tammy, and I'll show you what you'll do for us." Bob nodded to Zoo, who stood and vanished, taking his fat hand with him. Tammy followed Bob to the wash entrance and saw a car coming out of the completion door, getting the final rub down by a short bikini clad girl in her late teens. The girl opened the doors of the expensive sports car, wiping the sills and insides with a dry clean cloth. The pricey car sparkled in the sun. The owner lecherously watched her every move, unblinking. Ric busily worked near the passenger seat.

Bob spoke, "Tammy, watch Ric with the clipboard. What do you see?"

Tammy saw the driver spellbound by the bikini girl. Ric inspected the car, smoothly reached into his pocket, pulled out a sandwich sized bag and stowed it under the seat. Slick.

"Ric is putting a stash of coke under the car seat and the driver doesn't seem to notice."

Bob nodded. "The driver knows, alright. That's Sam. He transfers the stuff around for us. Cops never know how we move our product. Who cares about a sleazy car wash, right?"

"Smooth," Tammy said.

"Ric is the manager and runs this place, he's not here to hand out stuff. The last girl left our employ and you'll be her replacement."

Beth? The foot in the shoe?

Bob looked her over, but not in a creepy way. Assessing. "You'll hate those shoes so wear something comfy. It's a long day standing around and the pavement is slippery. Keep the short shorts. You look lovely in them. I see it has a pocket which is good. Let me get you a shop shirt. All you do is stand there, write down the inspection list so it looks like a legit car wash and slip in the stash before the car's leave. Got it?"

"Write on the form and slip in the stash. Gotcha," she confirmed.

"The main stash is in the employee change room in the locker marked, "Beth". Don't carry too much at once. Nothing goes missing or our... 'quality assurance team'... will be talking to you, understand?"

Tammy swallowed. Probably, breaking fingers and toes, first offence, then kneecaps. "Yup."

"The reason you're here is our regular girls have either been arrested in a police crack-down, or retired. You have a good resume but see that camera over there? We'll be watching. You get two hundred a day to do this. Good pay for a shit job."

"When's pay day?" Tammy bravely asked. She needed to appear interested in the pay as a person in her role would be scratching for money.

"Cash, on Fridays from Ric. He's efficient but don't piss him off. He's a mean one."

"Yup."

"Let's get you dressed up and put you to work. Call me if you have questions. Here's my card."

Bob's tasteful silver card simply said: *"Make your troubles disappear 458-522-9632."*

"Nice," she gushed with appreciation, while she inwardly shuddered.

Bob winked, "I don't give many of those cards away so treasure it."

Killer joke? Tammy laughed as best she could.

Car Wash Rules

In a half an hour Tammy stood around the washed cars, checked her inspection list, dropping the coke off in the car, warding off the frisky hands of the drivers. It was hot and humid and already she was in a sweat. She wondered if her sister Gloria ever had to do this.

Such a sad story with an unknown end.

She knew Gloria had had a child at some point. Her last contact with Gloria was at their mother's place ten years ago and it had been awful. Her mom was upset with Gloria, her situation, drug use, and being pregnant. It was a short visit. Her mom cried for days. They never saw Gloria again.

Before her mom's death she remembered seeing a drawer-full of returned birthday and Christmas cards. Her mom even had some so-called private detective look for Gloria. Likely, the P.I. had simply taken her mother's money and drank it away. She'd always thought she'd search for Gloria once she was done cop school, but other priorities took over and all was forgotten.

Tammy's first day at the wash was a long one but she didn't mind. She handed out thirty-two stashes, making note of who drove what type of car. The day was done at six. She put her shirt and clip board in her locker, slipped past Ric's sneering grope and headed to her tiny apartment.

On the way she stopped at a pawn shop to pick up a cheap TV set, multi-screwdriver and a heavy-duty lock that would fit her door. She stopped for some food, soap, toilet paper and a newspaper from a tiny corner store, as well.

At the doorway of her apartment she looked carefully all around to see if there was anything suspicious and there was none. Once inside, the first thing she did was plug in the TV and turned it on. Nothing great but not a bad picture, a bit grainy, but had a whistle in the sound, perfect to drown any listening bugs if there were any in her room.

She expertly slipped the new heavy lock into the door and noted the jamb had metal strips guarding it. Now it was as good as it was ten years ago before the old lock was removed and sold for a pitiful few dollars that had maybe bought a day's drink or a jolt of something.

She made a point of looking through her eye hole in the door, noting the stains and holes in the opposite hall wall. Surveying the battlefield, so to speak.

In for the night, she turned and surveyed what was to be her home for the foreseeable future. What a dump! Where to begin? Dishes were a good starting place. She filled the tiny sink with soapy water and dug in, leaving the scrubbed items on the little countertop on a somewhat clean dish cloth before moving on. All the while her little pawn shop TV hummed with highlight news from across the border.

Tammy found working the car wash an interesting view at how the drug trade worked. She diligently filled out the car wash form listing the wash functions that had been done, slipped the stash in the correct car and took note of the licence number.

After she'd been there a week the other girls opened up to her a little. They were vulnerable, preyed upon and often drug users. Pity. Ric knew how to pick them and keep them, with a kiss or a fist. Scumbag.

It was after one o'clock and Tammy had just finished dropping in the drug package and recording the details on a black Ford Mustang with dark-tinted windows before it was driven away, as per usual. In minutes Bob followed the mustang in a mini-van, rolled down his passenger side window and shouted to her, "Hop in Tammy! Tell Ric you're leaving for an hour."

Hopefully I'm coming back. Tammy climbed in with Bob the killer then powered her window down. "Ric! I'm with Bob!" she shouted as they sped by. Her heart was in her throat, but she kept calm. Was her cover blown?

Bob steered, braked and accelerated erratically in the traffic. He managed to say, "You weren't supposed to drop a package in that mustang."

"Uh-oh." Not as bad as she'd feared, but bad, nonetheless.

"He hasn't paid his bill for a while," said Bob grimly.

"I'm sorry Bob. I didn't know…"

"It's okay. Ric's fault. He was supposed to tell you but he fucked up. Let's go get that package. I need you to spot him for me while I drive."

"There! He just came out of the gas station!" she said excitedly, pointing ahead.

"Slide down a bit. No need for him getting a good look at you. Just watch over the dash."

"Oh. Sorry."

Bob and Tammy followed the mustang in silence.

"Lots of mustangs like that here," Bob muttered in annoyance. "Is that the one?"

"Yes. His plate said 'STUD1A.'"

Bob snorted, "Jake is such a Gomer. Let's see if he goes somewhere quiet."

Tammy watched as Bob expertly stayed far enough back to retain contact. After twenty more minutes, the mustang turned into a small community park and stopped. The driver didn't get out. Waiting for someone?

Bob put the nose of the van about a length away from the mustang. "Wait here."

Tammy watched as Bob opened the van door and strolled over to Jake's car as easily as if he wanted to gossip about hockey. No hurry. Big smile. Jake's window was rolling down. She could hear them murmuring but couldn't really tell what they were saying. They were parked oddly so she looked back in the van's mirror once and a while. She wasn't sure what was going to happen.

In her side mirror she caught sight of a figure darting out from the bushes and pausing behind the van, his eyes trained straight on the idling mustang. Now he sprinted lightly along the passenger side of the van, heading towards Bob, who was still talking to Jake, unaware. Ambush?

She timed it perfectly, popped open her door as the runner tried to run past. Instead, he smashed face-first into the corner of her door.

Wham!

Hopefully he isn't one of "our" guys. Too late now. She stepped out and kicked the stunned man in the head for insurance.

Bob glanced at Tammy and figured out she'd saved him from the secret attacker. Bob hauled Jake out of the Mustang and shoved him down on to a nearby flower bed. Quick search. He kept a knee on the man's head, yanking his arm in a direction it wasn't meant to bend. The dirt muffled most of the scream.

As he held the mangled arm, Bob lectured Jake as if they were talking about the weather. "Jake. You took our property and didn't pay your bills. Not a huge deal but then your friend there tried to jump me —now that's just disrespectful. Punishment today will be this broken arm. Next time a knee cap. Understand?"

Bob stood up, tapping his pocket, newly stuffed with Jakes confiscated stash and cash. Crying, Jake craned his head from the dirt and nodded.

"Ten G's by tomorrow at eight at the wash. Come alone. You don't want to be late."

The man in the dirt nodded again, vigorously.

Bob brushed the dirt off his knees as casually as if he just pulled a dandelion from his front lawn and hoofed over to Tammy. He gazed down at the unconscious man at Tammy's feet and smiled. "Good cover. Hop in." Bob kicked one of the fallen man's arms under the tire of his van.

Tammy was still shaking as she got in and closed the van door. Bob got in the driver's seat, started it up and put it in reverse. The van bounced hard over the stricken man's arm. Clump. He stopped the van and backed up. Clump again.

"Oops!" he grinned, shifting forward and backwards, going over the man's arm another couple of times—clump, clump—before pulling away.

He did a proper shoulder check, signaled and drove away as courteously as a senior citizen. Grinning like a man who won the lottery, Bob asked, "Lunch Tammy? It's on me."

"...sure?"

"The White Spot is my favourite," Bob continued conversationally, as if he was showing a visitor around town. "Thanks for riding shotgun, Tammy. Zoo's at his Grandmother's funeral so I needed a spotter." He winked.

Granny's funeral? Tammy's stomach flopped. Someone else's funeral came up, more likely.

She said nothing as they drove to the restaurant. Bob constantly watched around him, in the mirrors, at nearby buildings, at people on the sidewalks. He abruptly turned left on a back alley, coming to a stop and rolled his window down. A mid-sized building was being put up, starting with a huge hole in the ground laced with steel rebar everywhere. There would be concrete poured in the next few days. He said, "I love to see a new cement project happening. A sign of progress. The old history of the past covered up for another fifty years." He nodded to her as he put the van in gear, going right at the street and parking at the White Spot.

Tammy wondered why Bob's construction fascination. Pouring concrete over his victims! *Oh my God!*

Bob led her to the White Spot entrance, holding the door open for her. He asked the older man at the door for his "usual table". Tammy assumed this meant something far in the back where he could rip someone's leg off in discreet silence.

Lunch with Bob promised to be a strange experience.

———

Bob Carzoni had had his eye on Tammy ever since she'd arrived at the car wash. She was more confident than the other girls, less consumed by drugs or at least she didn't show it. She was still young enough to have a nice body before the ravages of drug use took its toll.

He saw Tammy was having difficulty keeping the menu steady. "You alright?"

Tammy looked over at him, "Sorry. It was a bit of a surprise, that's all."

"You did well. If you hadn't caught that guy with the van door it might have been curtains for me and maybe you too."

"Fuck, I didn't think about that," she blurted, quickly covering her mouth after swearing.

Bob laughed, breaking the tension. "It's all good. That's why I'm at my quiet table."

Tammy took a deep breath which seemed to settle her down.

"I'd suggest the burger-fries combo and a shake. Best diner in the city."

She closed her menu and smiled at him. "Sure, I'm in."

Bob graciously ordered for both, giving the order to a nervous server, before turning his attention back to her. "So, Tammy, where did you come from?"

"Timmins, originally. A small, boring town."

"Seeking fame and fortune?"

"Started out that way. I can sing and act, apparently not as well as everyone else in Montreal, but there's no going back," she answered, seeming to relax.

"That's true. It's hard to go back home. When we leave, we make ourselves into a different person for strangers, for better or worse. We can't take that persona back home."

Tammy smiled at that. "We built our new disguise and can't bear to take it off."

She's sharp, he thought. Not many would understand that.

The food came along, and conversation ceased for a while.

"Coffee?" the server asked when Bob and Tammy finished.

"Sure, we have time," he said, deferring to Tammy, who nodded her agreement. "Ric will be okay with it."

———

Ric was not impressed when his boss and skanky Tammy rolled back to the car wash after two. Bob cornered Ric while Tammy sauntered into the washroom like she owned the place.

"Ric! I told you the stash wasn't to go to Jake."

"That bitch Tammy screwed up, not me," Ric grumbled.

Bob looked closely at Ric. "No, *you* fucked up. I got the stash back, but you'd better listen when I give you instructions. That's fuck up Number One, Ric. Got it?"

He didn't dare say anything as Bob stalked away, furious.

Ric was angry and helpless. He went to the locker room, barged in and spotted Tammy coming from the washroom. He kicked her hard in the abdomen. She collapsed in surprise and made no move to retaliate.

"That's for putting a stash in the wrong car," he warned.

"I didn't know," Tammy gasped, rolling on the gritty cement retching and coughing.

He kicked her once more. "Around here it's *always* your fault! You're dead if you tell Bob about this—understand?"

She nodded and brought her knees up, huddling in place.

Ric stomped away, slamming the door. He always liked to feel in control.

He knew Jake would be visiting him about today's lost stash—since Ric was also on Jake's payroll and obliged to deliver every stash regardless what Bob said. Getting paid twice was good so long as he didn't get caught.

———

After the beating from Ric, Tammy slowly got to her feet, noticing the other girls avoiding her and the locker room. The other girls knew how Ric operated. Cruel and nasty, even if it wasn't their fault. The other bikini car wash girls sported cuts and bruises and now Tammy knew who dealt them. She didn't dare retaliate if she wanted to keep her informer role. Maybe later. Bastard.

———

Zoo waited for Bob in the car wash office, seated as usual across from him. The faithful lieutenant. He looked around the office, waiting, muscular arms folded over his big belly. He was almost as wide as he was short.

"Hey Zoo," said Bob as he slid by and sat down in his usual chair.

Zoo just nodded—he wasn't much of a talker.

Bob looked at his phone, then up at Zoo. "I had to chase down Jake, today."

Zoo looked surprise. "By yourself? How?"

"I took the little van with Tammy to identify the car."

Zoo laughed, "Chasing Jake's mustang in a minivan with a car wash girl as protection. Funny."

Bob was a bit embarrassed but managed a grin back. "Couldn't be helped. Ric didn't stop the stash to Jake, like I told him. I caught Jake in Gables Park. Some guy tried to jump me while I talked to him but the wash girl got him with the van door as he tried to run by."

"A set up?"

"I wasn't sure. I broke a couple of arms and gave them the pep talk."

"Do you think Ric was in on it?"

Bob sat back in his chair, his expression speculative. "Maybe."

"Want me to squeeze Ric and Jake a bit more?" asked Zoo helpfully.

"I don't have a replacement for Ric. Jake is a good customer when he pays his bills. No, let this slide just for now."

Zoo smiled in a menacing way. "Too bad. I see there's a new concrete job over by the White Spot."

"I did, too. Looked cozy. Room for two."

———

The plan was for Tammy to check in with her police handler once a week or so. This was her opportunity to show progress, evidence or that she was not dead yet. Great efforts were made to do this on the sly. She was to put a cryptic message in a particular type of soda can—Orange Fanta—and leave it in the trash in front of various locations around the city.

A messenger would watch for the pop can. Someone unknown to her, disguised as a homeless bottle collector, would pick up the empty can and shake its contents, which indicated Tammy's requested meeting times. One rock meant "Ten o'clock", two rocks meant "Eleven o'clock". A balled-up piece of foil in the can meant "No meeting this week". Three cigarette butts meant "Help me". A SWAT team was dispatched in minutes. No mercy.

Her arranged meeting place was the nearest park bench east, west, south or north of the drop off trash bin, depending on the day of the week. Cloak and dagger.

Tammy was nervous about this first meeting. She made every effort to ensure she was not followed or watched. Her ensemble for the meeting was a combination she never wore and would be unfamiliar to anyone in her new world. Every bit of clothing she had was carefully inspected for tracker bugs. She made sure her Jane Bond equipment and gun were handy before she went to the Wiki-Mart for a bubbly can of Orange Fanta.

She put one rock in the empty Fanta can—"Meet at ten"—and it went into the stinky trash bin at eight o'clock that morning. Then she headed for the park taking a careful roundabout route, eventually arriving at the bench at ten, sure she hadn't been followed.

She found the bench occupied by a scruffy old man with a walker. He was shabbily dressed but clean. One toe stuck out of his worn-out shoe because his sock was missing. About seventy years old. *Is this my contact?*

Eyeing her up, the old man said, "Working, honey?"

"Fuck you," Tammy said, looking around warily.

The old man laughed. "I got the Fanta can. How's that for the secret password?"

Tammy looked around again before perching tentatively at the far end of the bench, ready to flee, if she had to. She said nothing.

The man continued, "I'm Alfred, your contact. This area is being watched by my people right now. Don't look—you won't see them."

Tammy felt safe enough to speak. "Are you a messenger?"

"Nope. I'm your handler; supervisor so to speak."

"What do you know about this informer stuff? You're an old man."

"I'm an old man *because* I know this informer stuff." Alfred smiled. "I was hanging with biker gangs before you were born. I was sneaking around Afghanistan for five years as an intel officer in the army. Best listen to me so you don't get killed like Beth."

"The one in the shoe?"

Alfred dropped his head slightly. "She got unlucky, killed,

weighted by concrete blocks and dropped in the river. Food for the fishes... except a shoe."

Tammy said nothing, looking grim.

"How's it going so far?"

"I'm not dead yet. Their lawyer bailed me out of jail. I found the crappy little apartment you set up."

"Sorry it's a dump."

"I get that—at least it's clean now. Not long after I got set up, one of the gang messengers came to me, gave me a burner phone and told me to move a half a kilo of coke to an airport locker. He was testing me out."

"Went well?"

"Yes. Passed right through."

"Did you call in prior so security would let you go through with the package?"

"No. Just snuck it by, eezee peezee," said Tammy slyly. "Airport security is unionized Mall-cop. Not even paid these days. I could have smuggled a Zamboni through. They couldn't find their butt cheeks with both hands."

"Be careful, smart ass. Met Bob, yet?"

"Yes, a week ago."

"His buddy Zoo around?"

"Yes. Bob only calls on Zoo when they have something big happening."

"I think Zoo likes his job too much. Bob is more of a detached pro."

"I heard Zoo likes to hear them scream.

"Stories of screaming keeps everyone in line."

"Bob claims it's good marketing to their competitors," Tammy said grimly.

Alfred raised his eyebrow as a reply. "Anything for me?"

Tammy looked down and examined her nails with interest, wiggled her leg and felt the little gun in her sock and its reassurance of cold steel. She murmured, "Can you copy a phone chip?"

He nodded and held his hand out to her.

She casually stretched her hand to his.

"Pretty good." He complimented, quietly tucking the chip in a napkin he produced from his pocket, pretended to blow his nose then dropped it on the ground. In minutes a woman with a stroller and a dog on a leash came by. Her dog happily scooped the hanky without stopping.

"We'll have your chip back in a few minutes," Alfred whispered.

The mom, stroller and dog were back in five minutes, dropping the hanky. Alfred smoothly got it and slid it to Tammy.

"What's Ric's background?" Tammy asked, slipping the chip under the elastic band of her shorts.

Alfred took a breath. "Ric is a very bad man. Pimp, cruel beater. Long track record with few convictions."

"Ric has friends with money?"

"Yes. He never talks and they always come to bail him out. He's sadistic but reliable."

"I'll bet he'd talk under the right circumstances."

His eyes darkened. He warned, "Don't do anything to ruin this investigation!"

After some hesitation she nodded, then got up and strolled away.

Alfred fed pigeons for a while then glanced around with faint interest before leaving the park as well, moving slowly on his walker.

Bingo!

Tammy took the bus, transferring a couple of times to confuse any followers, then a metro trip to a thrift shop near her shabby apartment. The thrift store was a treasure of worn clothing for all ages and fashion imaginings. She knew what she was looking for.

At home, Tammy spent an hour in front of the mirror carefully putting on make-up to look seventy-ish. She then mixed and matched her thrift store cache of old clothes until she looked just right. At last she slid a narrow pillow on her shoulders to get a bit of an elderly hunch, grabbed her "best grandma" bag, a red cloche hat, thick eye glasses and earplugs that looked like hearing aids. She had one last look in the mirror, happy with what she saw. On the way out she picked up the sturdy metal cane made to look like cheap bamboo—except this was metal, heavy, and nasty, featuring a spiked base for ice and snow.

She headed out the door, carefully locking it behind her before slowly sidestepping down the steps and hobbling out into the street. Helpless and slow.

———

The neighborhood was rough and sad. Storefronts that managed to stay open sold what they could to keep alive. Their windows were covered with rusty, bent bars to keep out the smash and grabs while clerks watched nervously to see who walked through the door.

Barry Henry stood on the same sidewalk as Tammy, leaning casually against the wall of the closed-up peep shop. He'd been down on his luck for over a decade and looked it, but since this drug habit wasn't going to finance itself, he watched. Lucky for him Ric allowed him to roll a few old ladies each week to keep him in drug money. "Keeps the locals on their toes", Ric said. Barry was pleased to be one of Ric's urchins.

Barry glanced over the busy roadway, seventy-two feet wide, six lanes, traffic buzzing, beeping with roaring engines belching smoke, shifting gears, cursing. Cars, busses, cabs, and trucks made the area look prosperous, which it was not. Nobody stopped, everyone who had someplace to go simply passing through on the way to someplace better—aggressive, angry, texting. An endless freeway as relentless as army ants with inferred status from their Mercedes or Cadillac ride.

Occasionally police, ambulances, even fire trucks tried a surgical pass, sirens screaming. It never worked—they were instantly locked in crawling traffic, marooned—this asphalt conveyer never stopped; there'd be hell to pay if it did. The flow of traffic trumps life and limb.

Barry warily watched the passing Beemers, Caddies and Benz's with blackened windows and expensive shining wheels, music thumping, exquisite leather seats jabbed with holes from gun barrels stabbing out from pockets. Passenger heads with crooked hats swiveling in all directions—bobble heads, staring out for cops and gangs—on patrol.

Barry liked having a steady stream of "chickens" shuffling down his sidewalk, on the edge of the freeway of death. The cheap sidewalk concrete was poorly maintained, narrowing to barely eight feet wide in places, and was littered with trash, gum and pee. An ant trail for those who couldn't afford a vehicle. Marginalized people on the edge of a prosperous road with speeding traffic a few feet away. Priorities.

These narrow sidewalks were Barry's feeding zone. There might be fifty people on the walk, if you really counted them, including the invisible ones. There were a few relatively well-dressed young people, a few hookers and a busker playing a stolen bent trumpet very badly. A dozen people were leaning on walls or laying on the concrete, stoned or sleeping. A few elderly people struggled along, dodging beggars and being shunted aside impatiently by younger, more mobile people. Barry knew who to watch for.

Tonight was Bingo Night. Tonight, old ladies herded onto buses, purses filled with squirreled away cash hidden from drinking husbands. Push them over and snatch a purse. Don't even have to run because there's no cavalry coming.

Barry spied a stooped elderly woman coming towards him, leaning heavy on her cane. The bus was coming around the corner and time was tight. Perfect.

He stepped in front of her, shoved her backwards with his left hand, grabbed her bag with his right. As he turned, already pawing around in her purse, he was slow to wonder why he didn't hear her fall down like the other elderly ladies did.

Bam! Barry was shocked to have something hit him smartly on the side of the head. He staggered then lurched around to turn to face the old lady in time for her to strike him on the other side of his head… harder! Panicking, he scrambled to escape when the third strike smacked him. He didn't notice the fourth strike as he lost conscious-ness; his body added to the others laying on the grimy sidewalk.

The "old lady" smirked as she scooped up her purse.

———

Tammy kept going, not wanting to miss the bus, happy she'd brought the cane at the Thrift shop. One jerk down.

She made it through the doors of the worn bingo hall, past the fat, bored doorman, just as the bingo caller was getting ready, sitting in his cage. Old linoleum, dingy wallpaper, dim fluorescent lights, mildew, all stinking of cigarette smoke. Choosing a table to blend in with the other elderly ladies she sat down, quickly getting out her dauber markers, the picture of her "grandson", and signaled for the coffee cart to come over. As she waited, she called the bingo paper girl for a set. Tammy paid the girl, paid for a coffee, then glued her bingo papers together in a big square. Last, she made sure her daubers worked.

Secure in her disguise, sipping her coffee, she paid close attention as the bingo caller read out the rules, noting the schedule. This wasn't her first bingo.

"Early Bird! Under the 'I, nine'!" There was dead silence as the ladies searched for nines on all their papers. They were there to win, not talk. Sounds of daubers tapping on tables filled the hall, signaling it was time to begin. As soon as they found their nines, they all started gossiping. Tammy listened to what some said, ignoring others.

"Under the B, four!" Again, brightly colored daubers tapped the tabletops in concentrated silence, only then the ladies spoke. One shouted in a thick English accent, "My word, them busses are so slow. I barely made it here."

"Under the G, five." Silence except for the sound of daubers bumping on papers. The lady seated next to the English lady replied, "Those bus drivers are afraid to come down here. The crime is dreadful."

"Under the O, zero." Daubers tapped in sudden silence. "Where's the police down 'ere? Back in England they'd have 'ad cops walking the beat, grabbing them 'oods."

"Under the N, nine!" Daubers thumping in silence. "Cops here are afraid to go on foot. They just drive around hidin' in them cars. Can't see or 'ear."

Tammy played and listened to the local gossip for four hours. It was fun to get out of her "Bubbles" world. A few hours of invisibility in her present life of deception was a tonic.

Finally, the last games were done. There was a stampede as the elderly denizens of the bingo hall stood, tucked their daubers and good luck charms back into their bags and shuffled away amid the cleanup crew who frantically scooped used bingo cards into garbage bags before running the stuffed bags out to the dumpster in the back.

As Tammy got her cane, she spotted an unpleasantly familiar someone talking to the bingo caller. Ric! Her belly still ached where he kicked her. Bastard. He stood menacingly close to the caller who then waved the cashier over. They talked some more, then the bingo caller unhappily pushed a handful of cash over to Ric. He grinned, thrusting the wad into his front pocket.

Protection money. Probably the usual story—"Would be a shame if someone robbed and beat up the elderly women," or "A shame if the hall burned down," and such evil. This must be another of Ric's side-line while pimping his girls. Multiple incomes streams was what they called it these days. Scumbag.

Tammy had won two-hundred-twenty bucks tonight. Lucky. She made her way home in the dark, making sure nobody saw her enter room 201. Taking the make-up off took a while but it was worth it. The street gossip had been full of valuable news—parts of the bigger puzzle she was working.

Tammy worked the car wash for almost a month under Ric's watchful eyes. Girls came and went, usually because Ric fired them, or they just vanished. Rumour was he had a hand in those as well. Transient, lost people on the fringe and nobody cared. He left Tammy alone now, because she had become Bob's girl. Bothering Tammy could be hazardous to Ric's health.

She had to admit enjoying Bob's company. He was charming, good looking, polite and worldly. His slight Italian accent and attentive brown eyes were panty removers. He was willing and quite a catch, bringing her flowers and champagne. The "safest place in a gang is the captain's bed" she thought. Keep the enemy close and all that. Skin to skin. She started spending a few nights over with Bob. His apartment was expensive and tasteful. The bed was huge.

Pillow talk with Bob was strangely exhilarating. He spoke of his "trade-skills", always trying to impress her with a clever execution or way to get a "customer" to talk. It scared her how his lurid stories thrilled her, and he could see it in her eyes. He spared no details impressing her.

Bob felt something about Tammy. She seemed like a long-lost kindred spirit, not like the scared, vacuous girls he usually screwed. She was confident and capable but green in the dark arts.

Tammy benefited from Bob's experience, listened and learned the tricks of the dark world of killers. After pillow talk came wild, willing sex. Satisfying and completely weird.

———

Zoo sat with Bob as they drove across town. Usually, the only thing they spoke of was the basic plan—Zoo hated small talk—but today, Zoo was unhappy with Bob's latest dalliance. "Another wash girl, Bob? This never ends well."

Bob took a breath. He respected what Zoo said because he was usually right. "I like Tammy. She's cute, nice and doesn't take drugs. She listens to me, Zoo."

Zoo nodded. *Uh-oh. She'll be around for six weeks, three months tops, meet the family, find out too much and Bob will have a hissy fit about making her disappear. Bob's love life—Part Eight. Next.*

Bob knew what Zoo thought of his girlfriends and changed the subject. "How's your mom and dad doing?"

Surprised, Zoo said, "Pretty good."

"Still working?"

"They are but not the long hours they used to. The City Zoo hired a few more people which helped a lot. Fixed the place up, too. Bigger elephant pen and glassed monkey house. Very nice."

That was a huge conversation from Zoo. Bob smiled at him. Most people looked at Zoo's odd size and huge ears and assumed that was why he was called Zoo. Not at all. He grew up in a zoo and that was why he had the nickname. So obvious.

Bob turned left and pulled into the alley, near the back of a store. They looked around before getting out. Bob nodded while Zoo opened the passenger-side door and slid out a five-foot-long steel bar. He used it to jimmy off a big old rusty manhole cover and pushed it to one side. Bob popped open the trunk, revealing a body with arms and legs duct taped together. The victim's mouth was taped as well, his eyes bulged wide open, trying to struggle... to scream.

Together Bob and Zoo carried him over to the hole so he could hear the sewer water boiling below. Zoo carefully attached a concrete block to the man's feet.

"So long Jake. That was your last double cross," said Bob.

They slid the squirming, wriggling silver worm down the hole, hearing a satisfying "Splork" before it sunk in the thick flowing sewage. Headed to the river.

"You'd better not clog my toilet!" Zoo called down with a laugh, sliding the cover back over the hole.

Bob shook his head and grinned. Zoo was the master of the funny one-liner.

———

Tammy laid on her bed in her teeny apartment, wide awake. Bob was away on assignment. A killer conference? Mafia inner sanctum like the Godfather? Best bullet ballistics in hits? She would ask him, tomorrow night. Maybe not.

She worked her regular shift at the car wash, stopping for coffee at eleven. It was raining on and off, so car washing was slow. Only cars getting drug shipments came for a wash. Wasn't that obvious to the police or were they looking the other way for her benefit or their own?

The other girls shivered in their bikini's. Ric would never let them cover up even if it was cold, regardless. He was such an asshole.

Bob walked into the locker room. "Tammy—got something for you. Follow me."

Layoff notice and a bullet? No, she knew his manner and looks now. He was very logical.

After kissing him, she followed him to the rear of the big carwash building. All by itself sat a two-year-old white Chev pick up. Bob had a group of girls diligently waxing the exterior while another was detailing the inside seat and floor.

"All yours," he said. "Project vehicle."

She made a big deal of being thrilled with the gift. Personally, she always thought a vehicle as a means to get around and nothing more, but Bob gifting her with one was a huge deal. The detailing meant evidence of various crimes and past owners was being erased. Might have been a mass murder truck. Nice.

Bob was pleased she liked it. "We had some body work and painting done to it."

Covered the bullet holes.

The truck was a simple short cab, plain-Jane white pickup. Nothing special. So bland you'd forget what it looked like as it drove by.

"We had the box sealed up so it's easy to wash out."

For bodies and blood.

Tammy played it up, squealed and jumped with joy once more for good measure. "Can I try it?' She hated the phony jump and squeal.

"Sure. You can start right now."

"Cool!"

Bob handed her a business card. "Go to 'Reds Rental' shop at this address. Zoo has something to pick up. Ask for Brendan and he'll slide it in the back. Zoo should be there, too. Help him out with this delivery."

Gulp. "Sure." She kissed Bob again, took the instructions and bounced to the truck. Everyone was done with cleaning it, so she started it up and pulled away. Big engine. Stick shift. Fast.

She broke into a sweat as she drove. The truck was fun to drive, engine roaring, changing gears and swooping around the corners. She was soon at Red's Rental main gate, asking the gate guard for Brendan. He pointed and waved her over to a parking spot.

Tammy parked and shut the engine off, waiting. She listened to the hot engine making clicking noises as the headers cooled off. It gave her time to think and worry.

This new, phony life was consuming her. Being an informant meant she was slipping further into this evil world of crime every day. The gray area was getting murky and darker. Was there a line between good and bad or was it merely defined by the best lawyer money could buy? After risking her life she'd find out if her police bosses really did have her back or would throw her to the wolves. She'd best watch her own back.

Brendan finally appeared, waving her over to the big rental shop loading dock. She backed up to it carefully and hopped out. Zoo was already standing there like a sentinel, watching a long and narrow wooden box with concern.

Was this a coffin for her or was someone else in there?

She stepped up onto the dock and helped Zoo lift the mysterious box into the back of the pickup. Zoo tied it down, then got in the passenger side and told her to drive. Right here, left there, in this back alley, behind that small house. Isolated. Tammy shuddered as she got out and helped him put the heavy box in the little wooden shed, steeling herself for what might come next.

"Thanks." He opened the top of the box and gasped.

Tammy fought the need to step back, not sure if she should run or shoot or both, her every nerve screaming. She wished she'd peed before she left.

"Wow. He gave me the better edge trimmer than we agreed on. Mom's lawn's gonna look real nice." Zoo was clearly thrilled.

Did he just set me up to scare the shit out of me?

"Nice," he continued, oblivious to her subtle panic. "I'll come back and assemble it later."

Tammy drove him back to the car wash, heart still pounding,

neither saying a word.

Was this Zoo's old truck? If these seats could only talk, the tales they'd tell. She didn't even want to know.

It was Bingo night and Tammy busied herself with her senior's makeup. She was getting efficient at it after her third session. The 'intel' from the hall had been helpful in picking up the names of local messengers for local shitty hoods. Some had already been picked up and interrogated by police, the information added to her file.

She carefully inserted the phony hearing aid piece as her little TV blared the day's news.

The bus ride to the bingo hall was uneventful. She staked out her usual spot at a table near a group of chatty regulars. Everyone here was so hard of hearing whispers became shouts of what had happened this week in the neighborhood. Good information for the big puzzle.

The ladies all smoked like chimneys, coughing and gasping all around her between loud bursts of local news and gossip. Tammy found it disgusting but never complained.

Silence proclaimed itself over the room when the caller said, "Under the G – six!" She'd just won two hundred and fifty bucks! Tammy made her way to the front and got her cash. Nobody stole her seat and she hustled back to it, ready for another game.

The nearby elderly English lady gossiped, "Me rent's goin' up. Blimey! Where am I gonna go at my age?"

Another lady groused, "Mine too. My landlord said he has expenses to cover. I heard that rough fellow is making the rounds and shaking them for more money. Scoundrel! I wish me eldest lad was still alive. He'd catch him and break 'is fingers. Shhh...there the scoundrel is right now." She leaned in and whispered to Tammy. "Look down—'e's an evil lad."

Sure enough a rough looking man in a black hoodie arrived, pestering the bingo caller for protection money. He even collared a nearby elderly bingo winner and took some money from her winnings, giving her a rude shove in the process. Tammy's blood began to boil. It was none other than Ric!

She angrily kept up with the last game, not knowing quite what to do about Ric. He'd crossed a line in her moral code yet nothing would ever happen to him if she reported him to her handlers. Small fry. Too low on the food chain.

The games were over and it was time to go home. Tammy slowly made her way to the line-up for the crowded washroom, listening all the while, then passed by the opportunity to visit the stinking toilets herself, instead ambling past the front bingo caller's chair where the managers all stood gossiping. It was time to leave for home, such as it was.

Stepping outside, she found the sidewalk mostly deserted, the Bingo hall patrons having made quick exits to the safety of their own homes. She looked carefully ahead, groping her way along the sidewalk. It was "As dark as the inside of a cow", as her mom used to say. Very few streetlights worked in this neighborhood. She abruptly made a quick right in the alley, running nimbly around to the rear of the sad bingo hall. Hidden behind a couple of old plywood signs, she watched the rear bingo hall entrance door open and close as workers brought out bags of garbage from the evening games. The dim light turned on and off as the door opened and closed, lighting up their destination and exposing a rancid dumpster shared with a Chinese food restaurant.

She wasn't sure why she was there, but then she couldn't predict who she'd see or meet. There may be a bundle of accounting receipts that may be of interest. Gambling joints were notorious for being money laundering fronts. This fit in with her plan to scout out any money operations her mafia target might be involved with. It may help fitting the gigantic crime puzzle together. Maybe Ric's presence was no accident? After a while she realized she had to pee. Dang.

To her surprise Ric appeared in the doorway, patting a bulge of cash proprietarily before shoving it in his pocket with what he'd taken from the bingo game caller and the old lady. Grinning, he lit a cigarette in the doorway before stepping forward, the door closing, the lights winking out behind him. He strutted away like a rooster. A cane swept out of the dark, hitting his face like a home run batter. There were a few more insurance blows, after that. Sweet dreams.

Ric would come to, find himself sleeping with the rotten food and rats in this dumpster. His money bulge would be gone along with most of his teeth. Asshole.

Back home, Tammy had mixed feelings about battering Ric as she removed the last of her make-up and got ready for bed. Part of her felt guilty about meting out justice on her own but she knew with her sting operation, Ric was currently beyond the law and nothing would happen to him. Picking on the elderly lady in the Bingo hall was the line he crossed. Unforgivable. One asshole tuned up and it felt disturbingly good.

Maybe Tammy was a vicious alter ego she'd get attached to.

Dental Plan

The next morning the women's locker room at the Bubbles Car Wash was buzzing. Tammy said nothing as she changed from her red heels to loafer shoes with the killer laces. The girls from the early morning shift were whispering with excitement.

"Watch out for Ric, today. He's pissed!" said Mindy.

"Why?" asked Fay.

"Did you see his mouth?" said Mindy.

"No."

"A big gang jumped him last night, back of the Bingo hall. Busted a bunch of his teeth and a couple of fingers," Mindy made a mock sad face. "He woke up in the dumpster. Too bad they didn't slit his throat."

"Too bad, alright," Fay echoed gloomily.

"Ric said he fought off two or three of them but got overwhelmed. He was so brave," snorted Mindy with a show of mock dramatics.

Tammy smiled to herself. Ric would never find out.

———

Meeting time. She was getting used to meeting with her handler, Alfred, using the pop can signal. They made sure meeting places were rotated. Clues with her phone chip and notes were passed to him. She wasn't a foot in a shoe washed up on a beach, so it was all good. At least so far.

At this meeting Tammy saw Alfred was nervous and Al was never nervous. He fidgeted in the bench as they spoke and passed information.

"What's up, Al? Everything going alright?"

He considered, then spoke, "It's all going smoothly."

"Is that a bad thing?"

"Sometimes."

"...not following you," said Tammy, puzzled.

"Smooth sailing makes me nervous because nobody asks the hard questions about what's going on or why we're doing this. Sometimes smooth means a lot of people know what's going on down here... too many people."

"You're not a fan of spreading information?"

"I only tell a minimum that serves a purpose. Barest, need to know. I learned that in Intel. Everything you say and do can put puzzle pieces together and get you—or someone else—killed."

"Is information manageable?" asked Tammy, a bit spooked.

"Yes, if you say as little as possible."

"Even if the bosses demand it?"

"*Especially* if the bosses demand it! Higher ups have no idea what the stakes are down here. Their daughters won't end up in the river. They sleep safely in their beds every night. The less those assholes know the better."

Tammy said nothing and left their meeting place, glad to be on her way.

Bob surprised her by taking her to a nice restaurant, skipping the basic diners they usually frequented. He wore a nice suit and tie while she wore a cheap cocktail dress with the killer red high heels. Classic sketchy couple.

The owner knew Bob, guiding him to a corner booth with a wink and a nod. The place was dark with red carpets on the floor and matching red velour upholstery on the seats, the interior showing signs of a recent renovation.

"Wine?" Bob asked, clearly wanting to make a good impression.

"Of course," she replied. She dreaded drinking and saying too much. Alcohol makes for tales which makes for dead operatives, then sneakers wash up on beaches.

The waiter appeared with a bottle of "the good stuff' and opened the bubbly with a flourish, filling their glasses. Bob offered a toast, "Be brave." He smiled, clinking her glass.

Be brave? She shivered.

They ordered. Bob had a steak and spaghetti while she had the Moussaka. She'd have ordered spaghetti too, but she'd likely spray sauce all over her light-colored blouse. Maybe on Bob's white shirt, too, and he was a killer.

They sat in silence, enjoying their meal and making small talk until Bob's phone rang.

"Excuse me." He looked at the screen, concerned. His eyebrows went up. "Sorry, I have to take this." Bob stood up, walked away—and didn't come back.

———

Zoo picked up Bob at the door of the restaurant, with Bob jumping in as soon as Zoo's ugly blue sedan stopped in front. "Sorry Bob. I didn't know what else to do."

"It's okay. Let's visit them and send a message. Leave one to run so he'll tell his friends. This won't take long and I'll be back before Tammy finishes dinner."

Zoo sped off, confidently covering about six blocks, then turning right into an alley, slamming on his brakes behind the Wal-Mart. Both donned disposable gloves. Bob pulled out his revolver. Keeps the brass. Zoo pulled a bat from behind his seat. He loved this part of his job.

It was desolate here, with a high fence and poor lighting. No snoopers looking down from any nearby apartments. Zoo watched as Bob quietly approach the fence and carefully looked over, signalled with three fingers, then two fingers with a cut motion across his throat, then one finger and pointed to Zoo's bat. Zoo nodded.

Both tiptoed to an open gate, surveyed the area before stepping through. They surprised three men pushing the last of several expensive cars into a grey shipping container. One man on the left guided the car in while the other two disappeared inside, pushing the vehicle carefully.

"What are you doing?" asked Bob, as if he didn't know.

The men stopped, turned towards them menacingly, all three tattooed, full-patch bikers. Together they faced Bob and Zoo, a show of pumped-up testosterone. "What's it to ya?" This from the man still outside. His arrogance vanished when he spotted Bob's gun pointed at him.

Bob spoke in a neighborly manner. "You guys! We talked about this. Keep to yourselves and stay in your area and we'll get along just fine—yet here you *are*, stealing cars from *our* district. Tsk-tsk."

"Who are you to tell us what to do, assholes?" asked the leader.

"Shall I say I'm a spokesman from an adjacent business and we don't like your attitude?" Bob's gun popped up, shooting the two still inside the container. The leader stood quaking in his boots. Bob gestured his gun at him. "That makes you the messenger, so take this back to your gang. Stay away. Zoo has something to show your buddies."

Zoo casually walked up, his bat flashing out, striking the man's shoulder, then his left knee. He collapsed in a writhing heap. Zoo muttered, "Show and tell!"

"No! No! Enough!" the man whined. "We'll stay away."

"Has our message appealed to your sense of caution?" asked Bob.

"Yes, I'll tell them!"

"Zoo, let's let this man escape tonight. A bit of mercy might smooth over this ugly situation. Some diplomacy," said Bob, winking.

"Got a phone so you can call someone?" asked Bob, with concern.

The writhing man reached painfully into his pocket with his only useable arm, pulling out a cell phone while Zoo watched. He struggled to hold the phone up enough to push a call button. Zoo's bat immediately smashed his phone and the hand holding it.

Zoo shrugged and added, "We do have excellent medical here in Canada."

"Best run, before we change our minds," Bob advised amiably.

The man staggered away, grunting and crying, dragged himself over to what appeared to be his personal car, falling into the open door with a sob of pain. He started it up and drove away, steering uncertainly, the door still hanging open.

Zoo and Bob tucked stray arms and legs into the shipping container and closed the big doors with a thunk that reverberated in the cool night air. Entombed. Zoo used the specially marked lock the bikers had so thoughtfully left behind. All the longshoremen knew it was death to touch this one.

Bob looked down, texted someone. "Container pick up, ASAP. Old Fines Food W/H, east side."

"The usual container guys?" asked Zoo.

"Yes. Same as always. Why fix what ain't broke?" Bob looked up, "My dinner's getting cold so let's be on our way."

Zoo and Bob said nothing as they headed back to the restaurant. Wordlessly, Zoo guided the car to the right lane of the Jacques Cartier Bridge, where Bob threw both his gun and Zoo's bat into the river— no stopping. Their disposable gloves were dropped on the rough rusty bridge decking where traffic would pulverize them.

Zoo was unconcerned about anyone finding out their evenings business. Nobody had watched or would admit if they had. The police would tag this an internal struggle between low lifes. Nobody down here talked—so no need to be concerned—unless there was an informer.

———

Tammy had long since finished dinner and was idly looking at her phone over coffee. She wasn't sure if she was supposed to stay or go but Bob was very old school and she didn't have anywhere else to go. Sit and wait.

If she had only brought her pick up. So far, she had only used it a few times and really didn't know much about its history. Was it bugged? Should she be worried?

Bland white, simple looking and powerful. Solid and banal at the same time. It was very nicely detailed for her so there wasn't a speck of dust, a hair or so much as a drop of blood, finger or errant shard of spleen. Zoo's old meat wagon. She'd noticed the open box had been thoroughly cleaned down to the metal and painted over to a smooth gloss. No wood or cracks to hide incriminating blood or bone.

Sitting waiting on Bob, Tammy thought about this life of an informer. It was exciting, food was good, and she was barely accountable to anyone. It had crossed her mind she could "go across" to the dark side and live with Bob happily ever after, permanently. Would her supervisors hunt her down or always wonder what her game was and leave her alone? Deep cover or gone rogue?

What a peculiar life she led.

Finally, she spotted Bob coming out of the restaurant bathroom. Needed to wash his hands, apparently. He came up to her with a big smile and kissed her. The waiter brought out his order, placing it in front of him.

"Sorry I'm late. You didn't have to wait, you know."

"I don't mind. Go ahead and eat." She sat quietly while Bob ate, occasionally pausing to gulp from his wine glass. He was finished in record time. In full girlfriend mode, Tammy reached over to romantically dab his lips with her napkin. "Tasty?"

"Good! Worked up an appetite."

"Busy night?" she asked with wide eyes, trying to keep as bland a tone as possible.

"Yes." He paused, as if considering taking her into his confidence. "We had an issue to deal with. The competition is trying to muscle into our territory. It's never ending."

"A new crowd or always the same?" she asked, stroking the back of his hand sympathetically. Let him talk.

"Bikers! Normally we usually come to some agreement with someone new and everyone gets along," he said.

"These bikers don't work that way?"

"No. Bikers they think they own the fucking world. If they aren't fighting amongst themselves, they're bothering us. They assimilate like 'the Borg.'"

What's a Borg? "Is this a new thing?"

"No. We knew they were coming. It surprised us how they did it. They took over the area by acquiring rival gangs."

"Buying other companies like Wal-Mart?"

"Yes. They even have their own structure, running like a company —complete with supervisors, policies and procedures. If the supervisors are bumped off, they just get more."

"The heads grow back?" she asked.

"They sure do. They'll be growing a couple right now. Buggers."

Tammy watched as Bob described this altercation with no more emotion than a rabbit infestation in his backyard. Chilling.

"Does… does that mean you… *eliminated* two?"

He stared back at her meaningfully but said nothing.

"Won't the cops trace the bodies or do you and Zoo always outsmart them?" She wondered if she'd finally stepped across the girlfriend/boyfriend line and held her breath.

Bob smiled smugly, looking around the empty part of the restaurant. "The trick is disposable gloves, use the gun once and toss it and never leave a body. No corpse or weapon—no case. The biker that got away will never talk, unless he's an informer, which is highly unlikely."

She put her arm around him, leaning in. "You're so smart, Bob." *And I'm such a phony.*

Bob perked up, looking at her nervously. "What do you have happening next Tuesday evening?"

Bob nervous?

"Oh, nothing on the schedule," she replied, smiling sweetly. "Why?" *Missing Bingo and I'm on a winning streak? Damn it!*

"I'm inviting you home for dinner with my family. What do you say? Pick you up at five?"

Holy moly!

"Oh, that would be lovely." She hugged him.

"And dress like a schoolteacher," he said sternly, looking her over.

"S-sure?" School teacher?

"Ma and Papa think all my girlfriends are schoolteachers."

"Ah."

———

Nervously Bob watched the family dinner date approaching. He hated these dinners but his Papa always insisted on them, regardless if Bob had a steady or not. His mom didn't care, and his sister Eva always made a scene about something. In any case, the girls he brought were horrified at how it all went, and few would speak to him afterwards. Just as well. Bob had hoped his parents would one day like one of the girls he brought home, but they hated them all. Too this or too that. What if she found out what "the family" was really all about?

His folks worried his girls were crack heads looking for cash or plants set up by their mob competitors or the cops. The girls "knew too much and something would have to be done so don't get too attached" they'd say.

Zoo was right when he said Bob's steady dalliances never ended well... for the girlfriends.

———

Tammy was nervous about dinner with Bob's family. It was one thing to skulk around, pretending she was someone she wasn't at Bubbles or the Bingo hall but quite another to show up at a boyfriend's family home and keep the informer role going under intense family scrutiny.

She dressed as conservative and normal as she could. Minimal make-up, sensible shoes, no cleavage. She even dug out a pair of glasses to wear. She did need them on occasion to read fine print, so it wasn't technically a lie. It struck her as funny that she would be a bogus person, an informant, worried about a little lie with the glasses. The least of her issues.

What had Bob told his family about her?

She carefully locked her apartment door, made a subtle mark and passed the front desk headed out to meet Bob in front of the Sally Ann as agreed. He still didn't know where she lived and she wanted to keep it that way.

The desk clerk, AKA Shirl, pointed her finger at her as she passed and winked. Tammy paused and murmured, "Meeting Bob's family." Shirl's smile vanished, her expression screaming *Oh my God!*

Tammy waited by the door of her fake apartment building near the Sally Ann. Bob arrived just after five, pulling up in a big Ford sedan. Big trunk. *I wonder if someone's in there.*

She slid in beside him and they drove off.

"Very nice suit, Bob. You're so handsome," she gushed—like the phony she knew herself to be.

"You look very nice, too. Very… schoolteacher-ish. I like it."

"Thank you," she replied demurely.

"There's something about my family you should know. Papa ran our family business for years until his heart wouldn't take it, so I took over. He… ah… has a bit of a temper."

The head mafia guy with a bad temper. Not good.

"Ma's a sweetie, though. She's as old fashioned as it gets," Bob continued, smiling now.

"Sounds nice."

"My sister Eva is a drama queen. She's always going to move away but never does. A conversation piece."

"How old is she?"

"Twenty-eight. She claims she's a social worker, but my parents keep telling her to get a man and have a bunch of kids."

"Maybe she's not ready for a family," said Tammy, immediately regretting it. Oops.

Annoyed, Bob said nothing more.

Apparently, with Bob it was better to speak of murder methods than his family.

They arrived at a very nice big old home with a big yard and dead flowers everywhere. There was a high black steel fence, gothic with tall spikes on the tops. She noticed subtle vid-cams mounted around the corners of the yard. They looked both outwards and inwards.

Keeping someone out or the family in?

Bob parked the car in front of the high gate featuring a big remote latching mechanism. He looked around before pulling out his phone, dialing a number, and speaking to someone. "Yes. It's Bob with a date.

Tammy caught some of the conversation. "...the Carzonis expecting you? Who?"

Bob lost his cool and yelled into the phone, "I'm *Bob Carzoni!* They're my parents, you moron!"

Tammy looked pointedly away, though she strained to catch any part of this conversation.

"...we'll have to check..."

"Yes. Fine. We'll wait." Bob put his phone away with a snap and when she turned back, he was smiling at her uneasily. "Security people are such dick heads. We have a few minutes."

Tammy felt awkward, sitting in silence. She should do something. She put her arm around him. After eleven excruciating minutes they heard the gate buzz and a little LED light glowed, their signal to pull it open.

"Looks like those assholes got around to us."

They got out, went through the gate, and walked through long dead grass to the front door. It reminded Tammy of the Haunted Mansion in Disneyland, grim and dark. The yard's plants and trees had been ambitiously planted at some point, only to grow in and be forgotten. Either their gardener lost interest, or they'd lost their gardener.

The front door of the house looked severe and needed a coat of paint. For a brief moment it reminded her of the heavy, specially built doors her police instructors spoke of in cop school. Tough to batter down in a hurry. Got a tank?

A door sensor light came on, shining intensely on their upturned faces. Bob rang the doorbell and they waited. Tense. She saw a door eye hole darken as someone peered out at them.

"Open the fucking door! It's us!" Bob called impatiently.

The door finally creaked open, slowly. An old face surveyed them suspiciously. Bob barged past him with Tammy following close behind.

A big old man stood in the dark hallway, gun in a shoulder holster. He had to be at least eighty years old. She imagined an elderly version of Bob in his declining years. For a few seconds she thought he was Bob's dad but in fact the old man was the butler/bodyguard. After dumping their coats on him, Bob took her hand firmly and towed her toward the only room with lights on. It proved to be a stuffy, old-style living room. An elderly couple stood up slowly as Bob went to them. They reluctantly hugged Bob, stiff and formal. Tammy was ignored.

His mom was short, swarthy and stout, sporting a huge black eye. The long blue dress she wore was tired and old, making her look frumpy. Her hair looked like a jet-black mop plopped down like a mushroom. She didn't smile at seeing Bob or Tammy.

His papa looked like a taller version of Zoo. He was almost six-foot-tall with wide shoulders and a huge belly. Bob's father's hair was almost a clone of his mother's mop hairdo.

Got them on a two-for-one Wal-Mart sale?

Papa had a fearsome, unsmiling face. His hands were huge and hairy, like an ogre.

Bob glanced briefly in the corner of the room at a young woman, barely acknowledging her.

Was that Eva?

"Ma, Papa; I'd like you to meet…Tammy."

Just Tammy? Not my girlfriend? Date?

"Hello," she said weakly and awkwardly as they dumbly looked at her in silence. The fish look? What could she say? Hi, I'm a cop pretending to be a drug mule while informing on your son who's a serial killer. Nice to meet y'all.

The father eventually mumbled a greeting to her while the mother and sister said nothing.

Eva, the sister, leaned forward with her head lowered. She made no effort to smile. Tammy thought she looked older than her years. She had a tired face and premature graying hair. No mop top for Eva —no such effort had gone into her hairdo or her make-up. Her clothing was bland.

After introductions, a large dog got up from his bed in the corner and clumped over, wagging his tail. She thought he was a Great Dane of some kind, a huge drooling bimbo hound. First thing he did was shove his nose under her dress and snort and she had to firmly push him away. Everyone watched blankly, silently. The dog was the only one showing any interest in their guest.

Bob's dad finally grunted, "Domino! Go back to bed."

The dog didn't move until Eva sullenly got up from her chair, grabbed the dog's collar and dragged it over to the corner.

The dog situation thus solved, Papa said, "Sit."

They all sat, Tammy in a single chair and Bob beside his mother on a couch—in silence—the only sound that of Domino licking himself in inescapable noisy slurps.

Bob clutched his hands together, nervously glancing at his dad, then back at his mom's huge black eye. Finally, he blurted out, "How'd you get the black eye, Ma?"

Ma replied in Italian—Tammy guessed along the lines of "fell" or "tripped and fell".

Bob shook his head, stood and angrily pointed his finger at his father. "You did this! You son of a bitch!"

The dad jumped out of his chair and yelled at Bob in Italian. Soon they were both on their feet, nose to nose, waving their arms and pointing dramatically. The mom and Eva ignored them as the argument got more animated. Tammy understood some of what they were saying, and it sounded like an old discussion about domestic abuse. Beating Up Mom.

Eva sighed, stood up and walked over to Tammy. "Let me show you the rest of the house."

When they got out of earshot, Eva added, "This argument will go on for about a half-hour then Papa will need his blood pressure meds. Follow me."

Eva shuffled along with a limp like someone tired of life. They went down the hall, turning left into what looked like a billiard room. Eva droned, "This house was originally built by my grandfather Giorgio Carzoni. Yes, he was the original Don of the Organization in Montreal. Powerful and rich. This mansion cost him ten million dollars at that time. Nothing but the best materials and workmanship. A week before he was scheduled to move in, someone blew up his car. Ka-boom!"

Tammy jumped a little.

"Papa got the house and moved in right afterwards." Eva looked at her with a twinkle in her eye, this the first sign of life Tammy had seen in Bob's sister. "There was some rumour that Papa blew up Grandpa to get his house and the organization but that wouldn't stick."

Tammy was shocked.

"This billiard table is called a Luxury Billboard which costs about the same as a decent Ferrari. Gold leaf and ivory everything. Papa decides who plays. We never touch it. We're afraid to."

"Never?" asked Tammy.

Eva walked over to the back corner and pointed her finger at a black hole that should not be part of a pool table. "Papa and one of his buddies were playing and one of them lost their temper."

"Lost the game?"

"Yes, and lost 200 G's, then shot a hole in this fancy table. Papa left the hole as a trophy."

"Ah."

"Follow me to the conservatory."

They walked around to the back of the gigantic house. Here, Eva rounded on her and looked straight into Tammy's startled eyes. "Bob is quite taken with you, Tammy. He said you are quite bright and not a coke head." She moved on, with Tammy following.

Tammy was careful and non-committal with her reply. "…Bob and I get along very well."

They next arrived at a large, glassed-in conservatory. Unlike the rest of the gloomy house, it was well-lighted. Despite the opulent setting all the plants were brown and dead.

Tammy glanced around. "Quite a room. This must have been lovely once. What happened?"

Eva shook her head, ignoring her question, murmuring, "Did you notice the senior citizen we have at the door? Wayne's seventy-nine but works cheap. Our previous bodyguard poisoned the water supply because Papa didn't give him a raise."

"Y-your last guy *poisoned* your water supply? Seems drastic. Was he after more than a raise?"

Eva sighed, "We'll never know."

More likely Bob and Zoo took the errant bodyguard for a little ride to a funeral.

Their next stop was the library. From here, they could barely hear Bob and his dad arguing. Eva put her arm around Tammy's head and drew close to her ear, whispering, "My family is extremely violent. Nothing is sacred. Do you understand?" Wide-eyed, Tammy simply nodded. Eva continued, "All Bob's girlfriends… disappear." She let go of Tammy's head and resumed her touring voice. "This is my grandfather's library. It contains the top one hundred classic books of all time though Papa has never read even one. He just smokes his cigars in this room and sips brandy."

Tammy was still trying to digest the secret Eva told her.

Bob and Papa's arguing died down. Eva led Tammy back to a dining room. Here, Ma doled out servings of M&M frozen lasagna which was eaten in stony silence. The only sounds were clinking cutlery and a strange sucking sound, which Tammy finally deduced came from Papa's dentures.

"This lasagna's too salty," announced Eva, to no response.

Coffee and cherry pie was handed out afterward.

Eva pointed out, "This pie is still frozen, Ma."

At eight-thirty Bob stood up from the table. "Gotta go. Thanks."

He kissed his mother on the cheek and Tammy thanked his parents for dinner and said goodbye. She followed him out the front door, not daring to say a word. This abnormally calm man was furious.

It was a dead silent drive home. She simply got out of the car in front of the Sally Ann building. Wordlessly, Bob drove away. Strange.

A quick walk took her back at La Marie where Shirl was waiting at the front desk, watching for her to return. Her eyes large, she whispered, "How was supper with the Carzoni's?"

"Nobody died, especially me, so it's all good," Tammy replied, with a stiff grin.

Dinner Aftermath

Bob treated her differently after that tense family dinner. He hardly spoke to her or acknowledged her for weeks, their relationship simply evaporating overnight. He didn't explain why but she suspected Papa viewed her as a liability. And Bob the killer hurt her feelings.

She wondered if Bob's Papa suggested he get rid of her. It would have been helpful to eavesdrop on their conversation but that wasn't happening while Eva gave her a tour of the creepy mansion. Eva had warned her Bob's girlfriends disappeared. Coupling that warning with Bob's sudden absence chilled Tammy to the bone. Then Shir delivered more chilling news—she'd checked Bob's romantic history and did note a half dozen of his steadies were unaccounted for after approximately six months, which just happened to coincide with the length of time Tammy had been with him. Did they go home? OD? Become nuns?

Had Tammy reached her "best before" date in Carzoni world?

Tammy secretly arranged a meeting with Alfred. He had become a valuable guide and mentor over the months. Al had more experience than he let on and she'd come to appreciate his guidance.

She saw where he was seated and carefully sat down on the other end of his bench, dodging the bird shit. Al was on the other end of the bench feeding popcorn to pigeons and any other birds crowding in.

They swarmed him in a frenzy as if these kernels of popcorn decided life or death, as oblivious to the humans as humans were to them. Each species with their own crisis to deal with.

She said, "Hi. Gotta phone chip for you. Big fish this time."

Alfred nodded, then quietly said, "Put it in that packet of smokes beside you and throw it at your feet."

Tammy did as she was asked. In a minute a little errant noisy dog ran up, snapped at her, grabbed the package of smokes and ran away. Surprised, Tammy was ready to run after it. "That fucking dog snagged it!"

Al calmed her down. "Relax. The lady with the stroller has a sick kid, today. The dog does the work, anyway. That's my dog, Pickles."

They sat in silence. Tammy said in a low voice, "I had dinner with Bob's parents a few weeks ago. Things are different now."

"The *Carzonis?*" he gasped, hastening to cover his reaction by wiping a hand across his mouth.

It was as if she said she'd dined with Hitler and Stalin. "Yup."

He stopped throwing popcorn, turned and asked her directly, "How was it?"

"Like dinner with the Addams Family except they're killers and wife beaters."

Alfred snorted, "What did you notice?"

"I wasn't sure if they were securely guarded or being held captive. It was a huge deal for Bob and I to get in to see them."

Al tossed a few more kernels. "We suspect his folks are being kept under watch as some weird ransom deal or witness protection. Not a nice bunch."

"Apparently at some point they had a young bodyguard who didn't work out. Now they've got a low budget pensioner filling in."

Al smiled. "Funny story, sort of. Apparently, Bob's anger management Papa caught that young bodyguard screwing Eva in her room and shot him in the ass, mid-stroke, if you know what I mean. He ran around the house, screaming and bleeding and Papa couldn't catch him."

"Went out with a smile?"

"Possibly. Papa called Bob and Zoo to finish the job and get rid of the body. We never found him."

"In concrete. No body, no case, as Bob always says," she added with a grimace.

Al looked at her, surprised, "He's correct, by and large. The DNA, method used, bullets and details of the way the murder was carried out is all gone."

"Conviction is in the details."

"Correct," Al confirmed.

"Speaking of bodies, I suspect Bob and Zoo killed a couple of bikers August 21st, sometime between seven to nine p.m. I think I was his alibi, waiting in Mondo's."

Alfred glanced at her. "Fits. Interpol heard of the bodies in a steel container with some stolen cars—Logos, Nigeria. Cooked in the heat to ripe perfection."

"Yummy." Tammy stuck her tongue out. "Evidence?"

"None that we could get at. The bodies had been removed upon arrival on a container ship and dumped in a nearby river. Local cops traced them back to the container and the biker gang."

"Unusually efficient for the Nigerian police. Aren't they corrupt?"

"Yes, very much so but the Nigerian buyer who got the cars was likely pissed at the bikers for stinking up his cars with bloating corpses. Unsellable except for the ragtop. He paid to trace it all back, then threw the bodies back in the river so as not to implicate his source."

Al's dog ran back to him, dropping a slimy gray tennis ball into his hand. Al squeezed the ball, pulling out the chip and slid it over to her.

Tammy dropped it into her pocket while asking, "Eva said Bob's girlfriends tend to disappear after the visit with Mom and Dad. Shirl did some digging and agrees. True?"

"Let me check on that. We've never had someone be Bob's girl before. Let me look into it. In the meantime, sleep with one eye open."

"Comforting."

"Time to go?"

"Yes." She got up and strolled away.

She took great care getting back to her little apartment. As far as she knew her home location was still a secret from the mob. She was betting her life it was.

Tammy never brought her truck to any of these meetings as it could easily track her movements, parking it instead in front of her fake apartment building and only using it to come and go from the car wash. When she had a meeting, she used public transit, switching buses, a cab and maybe throw in a subway ride to keep anyone who may be following her confused. At the front desk, a disguised Shirl was always watching her back but shit happened all the time—and fast.

Back home, Tammy made solemn eye contact with Shirl before hustling to her apartment and changed clothes. It was time to show up for the two to eight o'clock shift at Bubbles. No time for Bingo tonight. She cleaned up, changed, ate and was in and out in thirty minutes, winking at Shirl at the front desk as she left.

———

Day after day, Shirl sat stoically at her grubby desk in the La Marie Hotel—it was a dump but not as bad as others in the neighborhood. This latest informer project had been a long one for both her and "Tammy".

Shirl's bosses had assigned her to watch over Tammy after Beth's foot washed up in a shoe on a beach. Five-star fuck up that was—a sickening bolt from the blue. Nobody could say what actually happened to Beth—no body, no story other than which brand of shoe was on sale about that time. Green nail polish on the toenails of the foot inside. Would probably match Beth's DNA, if they checked.

Shirl was getting tired of the heavy make-up she was forced to wear. It was taking its toll with parts of her skin becoming alarmingly and permanently blotchy, though long-term face paint did make her look authentic—authentically awful. Her gun chafed welts on her skin that just wouldn't go away while she sat at the stuffy hotel desk. She had zero personal life.

She had a nice house in Dorval but she was never in it.

We need to wind this investigation up before someone dies. Eventually somebody blabs, makes a mistake, or a piece of the puzzle fits in and the informer's foot turns up in a blue Nike. Bob's girlfriends lasted six months and we're at six months now. Everything about this told Shirl it was time to wind this operation down—yet here she sat, chained to this desk, waiting orders that never came.

———

T ammy was running late, barely getting to the car wash in time. Ric gave her the evil eye as she ran into the locker room to get changed. One of the girls going off shift told her, "Bob wants to see you."

Gulp.

She left the locker room, ending up at the door to Bob's office. Just as she was ready to knock she paused, listening to the loud conversation. Sounded unhappy. She looked around to make sure she wasn't being watched, then leaned an ear to the door.

"No Zoo, not yet. I'm not getting rid of her," said Bob, his voice strained.

"Why not? You know she's bad news," Zoo pressed.

Me? Tammy broke into a sweat.

"I don't care. She's manageable. Besides, what makes you think she's a stoolie?"

"I have my sources. They followed her around and found she actually lived in Dorval, not the La Marie. So why's a woman who has a fancy house in Dorval slumming at the La Marie?"

Holy! Dorval? That's Shirl! Tammy waited for more, her heart thumping now.

Bob was slow to reply. "She's a watcher at the front desk for someone?"

"I think so."

"A watcher for who?" Bob went quiet. After a minute he said, barely audibly, "Yes, let's get rid of her."

Zoo was happy now that a decision had been made. "Tomorrow after breakfast? Ten-ish? Let's do IHOP first. I have a coupon."

Bob sighed with relief that they had a plan. "Yeah, some waffles and coffee first."

Holy shit!

This was bad—this was very bad. Tammy slipped away to the back alley, hiding behind a pile of wooden pallets. With trembling hands, she pulled out her phone and texted Shirl. "Your cover's blown! Coming for you tomorrow."

Should I run, too? She sank down on an old, upturned soap bucket and took a breath. Can't leave now. Oh so close to winding this up. If I can hang in for one more week, I can really load up evidence from the latest files in Bob's office computer. She knew they had a major drug move happening and she wanted those names, dates and places. Badly.

I need to talk to someone, today.

Alfred waited for her on the park bench. A young couple slept on a blanket on the grass about two hundred meters away. No doubt they were cops watching over them.

Sleepers. Funny.

Tammy sat at the far end of the bench saying nothing. Al sat at the other end silently with a medium sized "popcorn" bag separating them but this time he didn't feed the pigeons from it. Odd.

Al murmured, "Shirl was right—all Bob's ex's are dead or missing."

Tammy let that sink in. "Dandy. So, I'd best get my carcass out of here, ASAP."

Al looked around casually. "I'd say so."

"Except I can't. I need a week. Something big is coming. I want the files from Bob's office computer to seal this operation."

Al looked over at her. "Shirl's already leaving—there's nobody to watch *your* back."

"I know. I registered under a phony name and room but it wouldn't take a scientist to figure it out—but I've spent too much time in this to run now."

He shook his head and looked at her feet. "What kind of shoe do you have, so I can identify you later? What color toenail polish?"

"Ha ha."

Al grinned, enjoying the dark humour. "Keeps you from going crazy. Take precautions. Think—how would they take you down, assuming they will at some point? Think like Bob."

"Not at the car wash, but I wouldn't bet my life on it. It's broad daylight with a lot of people nearby, all the girls milling around, delivery people, cameras. Snatching someone, getting away and disposing of a body could be hazardous—yet they have the transportation rolling up all day long, if they went that way. Bob will have to figure out my fake apartment first and when he does he'll come for a friendly visit—at night. A last visit."

"Exactly. Construction yards of full of workers during the day. Bob and Zoo like concrete to hide bodies at night."

"He mentioned there's another new Jean Coutu Drugstore going up. He like's Jean Coutu…. Big and close." *Late night folks looking for toilet paper and disposable diapers walking over my final resting place? Nice.*

Al nudged the paper bag. "Take this popcorn bag and set it up at your door."

"Am I going to scare them to death with the sound of corn popping?" Tammy asked, annoyed.

"You could try it but I have a better set up," he replied patiently. He knew she was on edge—who wouldn't be? "Try a hidden camera, tape measure and a pencil."

She broke cover and stared at him as if he had a pigeon pecking his head.

Ignoring her quizzical look, he continued, "When they learn where you live, they *will* come a calling. You say you have a solid door lock. Set up the hidden camera and watch the little screen on your computer. Set it to alarm. Mark the inside of your door where Bob and Zoo's vitals will be when they're standing there. Shoot the little pencil crosses twice each. X marks the spots."

Tammy swallowed hard.

"We'll try to warn you when they come but be ready with this if you get surprised."

She needed a much better plan than what Al offered but Bob and

Zoo both dead tied up some loose ends. She was thinking like a killer now. Was that a good or bad thing?

Al added solemnly, "One way or another this is our last meeting. You never got that bag from me. It will be as if I never existed because I don't. Take care." This time it was Al who stood first, pulled out his walker from the side of the bench and inched away. After a few minutes the "sleepers" nearby got up and went to destinations unknown.

Tammy sat, immersed in her own deadly thoughts.

Killing her killers would silence the witnesses, too. She imagined the huge deal it would be if the media got the news of her sleeping with a drug lord. Not a great resume builder. The crime family's lawyers would have a field day with this information. All those scummy bastards Tammy and Shirl risked their lives to put away all go free, gunning for her later.

———

As Tammy sat and considered her plight, Shirl quietly vacated her desk at the La Marie and never returned. A random old man took her place. At police HQ Inspector Shirl and her boss watched the laptop computer screen carefully. It watched over the old desk area in the La Marie. Nothing had happened so far. They waited impatiently.

"Oh… there they are… Bob and Zoo!"

They saw the two men enter the old La Marie Hotel and walk up to the entry desk. One of them pushed away Shirl's replacement while the other man grabbed the room ledger.

Phil, her boss said, "I'm glad you didn't remove that hidden vidcam. Handy."

Shirl grimaced. "I was pressed for time—looks like it worked out."

"Will that ledger give Tammy away?"

"Nope. She always signed in another name and room."

"What a tangled web we weave," mumbled Phil.

"I just hope it's tangled enough," Shirl answered.

Tammy drove the pickup truck back to her chateau, as she derisively referred to it, eight o'clock that night. Looking up, she spotted a parking place directly under her room window and hidden from the street. Carefully she backed into the spot. She'd give them a day to learn where she actually lived—and she'd be ready for them.

Carrying the popcorn bag Al had slipped to her, she went past the front desk of the La Marie, glancing at the spot where her watch dog Shirl used to sit, noting the hotel replacement clerk was now missing. Empty desk. Pickled or sick? She kept going.

She hesitated at her door, glancing at the right middle edge to see if a tiny bit of paper was still there, carefully planted with a lick of her spit to see if she had any snoopers while she was gone. It was still there, safe and sound. The iconic cheap and easy spy trick.

Once in, she dug through her old loaf of bread and found two slices that weren't moldy. Need to buy bread. Nah—she'd be long gone by then—or dead. She made herself a quick peanut butter sandwich with the TV on loud enough to muffle her evening labours.

She put her dish in the sink on top of the growing pile, with no plans to wash them—not anymore. She might pick the habit back up again one day, when people weren't trying to kill her.

She dumped the contents of the popcorn bag on the bed. Setting up the wireless vidcam came first. Quick download.

While she was at it she deactivated the cell phone tracer with her laptop as a precaution, texting Shirl to say the loss of signal was all right. No followers at this point.

The camera looked like a simple and disgusting used fly strip. The center of the roll housed the actual camera attached to a real sticky strip complete with dead flies on it, all hanging from the bottom. Yummy. Nobody would touch that.

She made sure a signal could be picked up in her beat-up laptop. While she was at it, she used the computer's stealth bug sniffer to sweep her apartment and pickup truck. All clean except for the one in her phone which was her emergency tracer to Shirl.

Tammy crept into the deserted hall and stuck the fly killer vid cam high on the wall with a thumb tack, as far as she could reach. Next, still out in the hall she plotted out Bob's and Zoo's heights. Leaving her door open she figured out the angle of her gun hand pointing at their heart areas, then closed the door, marking two spots with little x's on the inside.

It was a dark hallway and it was hard to see her targets. She went back out and moved the working hall lightbulbs around until the one outside her door was one that worked. This way there would be shadows at the base of her door when her visitors made their move.

Next, she confirmed the line of sight from the vidcam and her door area. She imagined Bob and Zoo standing, waiting, where they usually stood. They always worked together. Bert and Ernie.

It was a doorway killing zone, one way or another.

The deadly pistol and silencer were dug out of their snug hiding place. She filled the magazine with powerful hard nose bullets. They would get through the door damaged enough to kill without passing through the bodies. No bullets left in the walls so less evidence.

What to do with the evidence after the shooting? She'd considered burning the place down but couldn't be sure an innocent bystander wouldn't get caught up in it. Invariably, the cops smelled a rat at a fire and expected something was going on under the smouldering rubble. Besides, there's always something left to further a case after a fire. Bad idea.

Carrying out a successful murder was hard.

After Tammy's break up with Bob, Ric had taken the opportunity to be a real prick toward her. Today, she had to sidestep a punch from him. Luckily a customer came up and distracted him from their alter- cation. She considered driving one of her spiked heels deep into his forehead but decided against it. That might make the national papers. Besides she had files to snitch.

If Ric was getting bold enough to bother her that meant her time at Bubbles was drawing to a close. He'd been such a coward when he knew she was sleeping with Bob. Not now. Ric sensed she was "going away" like all the others. The car wash didn't offer a severance package unless they actually severed something—like a foot.

She needed to stick to her plans.

After stopping at a used clothing store, McDonalds and London Drugs—she just couldn't make herself go into a Jean Coutu again—she made it back to her room. She wolfed down the Mac Burger then started to put her latest used creepy costume on. It was a snug fit but here her skinny Tammy look worked in her favour.

The idea was this costume would look odd enough on skid road for people to ignore her, especially as it was nowhere near Halloween. Looking clearly nuts makes people avoid eye contact—unless they too were bonkers—then it was a conversation piece.

Tammy got to work with her makeup, painting a full face of bright, sparkly white, aiming for bizarre. This was more like clown paint. The red lips went badly with the lip stick drooling in with the white paint. The eyes were worse as mascara blended into the white for a wild-eyed look. Oh well!

When she ran out of white face paint it had to be good enough. Looking into the mirror she cringed—more "Joker" than "Tinker Bell"—shit. It'll be the loony bin if a cop spotted her.

Last she put on the long white costume gloves, more beige than white with dirt from past users. She stomped into her red killer high heels and grabbed the cane as a sub for the wand. The heels and cane didn't quite match but so what? A girl's gotta protect herself. Voila: Horror show Tinker Bell!

The real challenge was squirreling her gun and knife under the tight little outfit. Maybe "Snow White" would have been a better choice? She could have hidden a rocket launcher under *that* huge dress, and nobody would notice. She was in need of something easier to move around in. Besides, Tinker Bell outfits were on sale, were cleaner and didn't smell.

She picked up the matching purse, sad as it was. It would be handy for lock picking tools, a small flashlight, disposable gloves, shaving cream, camera and two back up sticks for computer files.

Boarding the bus was peculiar. She hobbled up the steps of the bus in her heels with a bit of difficulty which was annoying. Other riders, both intoxicated and sober, ignored her and kept far away. She made sure to turn away from the bus's vidcam. Anyone seeing her would identify her as a loopy green suited person with a Joker face, wings, cane, wearing red spike shoes. A crazed Wizard of Oz Dorothy meets Jolly Green Giant's Mini-me?

Witnesses could tell nosy cops; "So, Tinker Bell with a Joker face... kinda testy with red shoes, cane...Tinker Bell on crack?"

"I think you're the one smoking the crack, buddy!"

No identification, thanks. Case closed.

Tinker Bell got off the bus and hobbling around the side of the Bubbles Car Wash. It was dark. She chose a familiar rear door under a burned-out entrance light. This was the only door not barred on the inside so they could get in each day. After digging out her lock-picking tools she easily figured out opening door. The security system timer started beeping which she stopped with the code 4590, long before the alarm company would receive a signal. She'd watched Ric and Bob use it many times.

She moved through the wash area, heading for the office. This door easily clicked open with her pick. Sliding along the wall she dug into her purse and produced a small can of shaving cream, reaching up and spraying it over the room vid-cam. Mission impossible on a tight budget.

Sitting down at the office computer she typed in the code she'd weaseled out of Bob when they were bosom buddies. The code remained "Tammy's#1". She nodded smugly to herself. "I've still got it."

She stuck the info stick into the USB port and pulled over as many files as she could find. Impatiently she finally shut the computer down and stuck the stick down her front into her bra. Gotcha!

She cleaned the shaving cream off the vid cam and slipped out the door. With any luck nobody will know she was here.

Tammy made it home after few different bus rides to confuse any chasers. Never know. A team of drunken rugby players propositioned her but were scared off when she turned around to face them—even they weren't drunk enough to see past the paint job on her face.

She needed to get this to Alfred at the pre-arranged trash can. As per the drill, she bought a can of Fanta pop, drank it. She covered the info chip with a gum wrapper marked "Text to confirm ASAP" and dropped it inside the can.

Find this very soon, Al.

Unknown to her and Alfred, a random homeless bottle collector came by just as she left and beat them to the stash of pop cans. Ten minutes later Alfred arrived, looked in the trash for the Fanta can and saw it was not there. He hobbled north on his walker, stopped and shouted on his phone, "Fan out and find that fucking can! Some bottle collectors got it!"

Tammy snuck into the La Marie and to her door, checking her little "Has not been disturbed" door marker, then went inside, locking up behind her. After a messy clean up and shower she was on the bed, gun in hand with her laptop nearby, her attention completely focused on the door.

Was tonight the night?

Exhausted, she started to doze off, wishing she could jump into the pickup and drive off, but she had to stick around for one more day. She needed confirmation they got that info stick and it contained enough to make this whole informant effort worthwhile. Hopefully she wouldn't have to return.

No news yet about the chip from Bob's computer. Dang.

She called in sick next morning. Ric was annoyed but too bad. A breakfast sandwich run was the morning's activity. She listened to her crappy tiny TV while scooping essentials into her hockey bag. There were guns, knives, money and documents hidden all over. Some items were kept and some had to be destroyed.

Tammy first disabled her smoke detector then put paper documents in her sink and put a match to them. Stinky old hotel had a century of smoking—nobody even noticed. All she needed was a text confirmation of a successful info dump from her burglary and this gig was over. She'd run like hell and needed to be ready.

Her TV babbled in the background.

Hindered Escape

Tammy crammed her bag on the floor of the front seat of her truck, under the dash, out of sight. Her cash was stowed in one of the various hidden lockers Zoo had installed in the cab. Drug smugglers special.

Come on, Al...text me! Had Al gotten that info stick chip or not? She dared not ask them in case the mob were listening to her phone. One word of confirmation from Alfred and she was gone—her phone deposited into the toilet tank.

She couldn't know Al and his men were frantically scouring the city for her Fanta can.

The pacing back and forth in her crappy room didn't relax her. The "A" plan was to hop in the truck and vamoose as soon as Al confirmed the stick and the info. Vanished.

Come on, Al... text me!

She considered making a run for it right now, plan "B", but if the info was bad she'd need to make another run on the computer at Bubbles. All her disguise stuff was here.

Plan "C" was the apartment door shootout. The last resort. Hopefully it even works. This all made her need to go to the washroom. Sit and think.

Come on, Al...text me!

She went into the bathroom and sat down on the commode, clutching her phone, staring at it.

The sound of "knock-knock" at her door froze her in horror.

———

Bob stopped in front of Zoo's house and waited. He hated to do this to Tammy but as his Papa pointed out, "It was for the good of the company." Like all the others, Tammy got too close, too nosy, and became a liability. He liked her, which made this difficult. Zoo would be there if he chickened out... But—he never did.

Spotting her truck parked by the building had put the final nail in her coffin. La Marie—all this time...

Zoo opened the car door and got in the car. They drove to the La Marie at a safe, legal speed. No need for the cops to stop them and ask questions.

Bob said, "Go easy on her Zoo. Let's just talk to her a bit, then slip a plastic bag on her head, bit of ether in it and hold on. Clean, fast and painless for her.

"No gun?"

"No gun, Zoo. I want to do her so she never knew what happened."

"You're not bumping off the family cat, you know," said Zoo.

Bob got uncharacteristically angry, "Fuck you! Do it my way, okay? She was my girlfriend."

Zoo nodded. It was always this way with Bob's girls. Too close. "Sure. So, we're gonna all sit on the couch, have a little tea, chit chat and ..." he made a cut motion across his throat.

Bob's glare was the reply.

They parked their car beside Tammy's truck. Zoo would drive it away afterwards. He always got his truck back from Bob's girls. It was a loaner. Tammy's body would go into the new Jean Coutu Drugstore concrete floor job. Zoo's buddy had even dug a hole special for this, hidden in the corner. A few bags of concrete had been left nearby, handy to sprinkle on her after they dropped her in. Camo.

They walked into the La Marie, past the front desk. Bob smiled as he pointed to the empty chair at the desk.

"Clerk broke his hip. Tsk tsk," said Zoo. "Room 201, he said?"

"That's what I figured out." Bob stopped and frowned. "You don't think the Dorval woman and Tammy are connected, do you?"

"Doesn't matter. If they were, after tonight, it won't matter."

Bob shrugged and they went up to the door to Tammy's room. Bob stood on the left and Zoo the right, just like they always did. Zoo called it chemistry.

Bob tapped on the door politely. They heard the sounds of a TV so she must be home. They waited.

"Poor Tammy" must be so sick she can't come to the door," Bob snickered, all sympathy for his ex now gone. He watched as Zoo took his turn, politely knocking then stepping back to stand beside him. Bob wondered if they would be forced to break the door down. A hell of a way to end a relationship. He grinned at Zoo and bounced his eyebrows in anticipation.

———

K nock-knock? Annoyed, Tammy stood up from the toilet, pulled up her pants and rushed on silent sock feet to investigate the knock at the door. My drunken neighbor wanting a kiss or perhaps two local mob killers come to visit at last she wondered, her every nerve at high alert.

She consulted the computer screen which beeped. Bob and Zoo! Fuck! Her blood ran cold.

Fighting to keep her emotions in check, she grabbed her pistol and silencer lying on the bed, swiftly cocking it under a pillow. She tiptoed her door, leveled it, aiming straight at her right pencil mark cross and waited.

Knock-knock. She knew where they stood. She hesitated after the second knock and squeezed the trigger. In quick succession she shot twice through the right crosses, then twice through the left. Ping-ping... ping-ping.

To Bob's surprise a little black hole appeared in the door in front of him. Instantly he felt something poke his chest. Another hole appeared from the door, right beside it. Bob closed his eyes and never opened them again.

Her muffled shots were followed by the sound of two clumps in the hall. Holding her gun at the ready, she stepped forward, unlocked and yanked the door open, surveying the carnage, ready to shoot again.

Seeing both men were down and out with nobody else watching,

Tammy shoved the gun in her belt at the small of her back, reached down and hauled Bob through the doorway by the collar. Zoo was next—and he was no light-weight. The silencer under her belt burned her skin but she ignored it, fighting to keep her breathing quiet as she struggled with the two dead weights. After pulling the door closed, she leaned back, gasping to catch her breath, looking over her handi-work—and saw Zoo was still alive!

Well, hell. She pulled her pistol out again and dispatched him with a last killing shot. She guessed Bob had died before he even hit the floor. Bye-bye Bob. It was fun.

She looked out the door a second time, to see if the coast was clear, then darted into the hall, putting large band aids over the bullet holes in her door. The band aids had smiley faces on them. Crazy tempo-rary camo. She was back inside in a flash.

Her heart rattling inside her chest in fright, she donned disposable gloves, grabbed a rag and bottle of spray cleaner and was back out in the hallway, quickly wiped anything around the door and nearby wall. No point in doing any more than she had to. The cops knew who lived here. Inside she did the same, mopping up from the final Zoo kill shot.

Time to go. Anything incriminating had to come with her or be hidden right now. For all she knew the cops could be on their way. She went over the mental list she'd rehearsed again and again.

Get rid of this phone. Burner phones like hers were always trace-able enough to be a pain. Picking it up, she noticed a message on it. 'Info good. Run. Al'.

Finally!

After saving the phone's sim card, Tammy lifted the chipped toilet tank and dropped in the phone. Ploop...the burner phone settled to the crud in the bottom. Handful of toilet paper on top. Eww. Nobody looks in the water tank especially with floaties down there.

Stop and catch your breath. She rushed to the little kitchen table. Hands shaking, she wrote on a piece of paper: "Be warned. Angels." The clumsiest detective in the known world would find it. Red herring.

No point in giving investigators a head start. Hopefully this would look like a local spat between gangs. No danger to the public and fewer scumbags in the city, the police spokesman will say. "The city is a better place."

Tammy pushed open her window and leaned out to look down at her pickup parked below. She heaved Bob out first. He landed awkwardly in the back of the pickup box, with a huge echoing *whoop!* Zoo was heavier but she flipped him out the window as well, same *whoop!* No one came running to investigate—it was *that* kind of neighborhood. Good enough. She made a mental note to thank her army trainers who showed her how to efficiently move around the dead and dying on a battlefield.

She noticed she had some blood on her but not enough to stop for. There would be time for a change of clothes and shower much later. There was a bit on her shitty carpet but so what? The La Marie was no stranger to anonymous fights.

Tammy grabbed her computer and her pistol. After a quick peek out the doorway she locked her apartment door then hustled out to her truck, started it up and drove off to the new Jean Coutu Drugs construction site.

Bob and Zoo had been quite excited about the concrete part of the project so there must be something of interest to killers. Sure enough, she spotted a dark corner connected with a paved alley.

Guiding her truck as close as she could get to that perfect dark corner, she got out and did a quick survey. It was dark; she was alone; no one cared. Totally doable. After dropping the tailgate she got back in, moved the truck forward, then, watching the rear mirror she slapped the truck into reverse and gunned it, backed up at a fair speed towards the corner of the concrete job. At the last second, she jammed on the brakes, hitting the trio of bags of concrete serving as a temporary guard rail, launching the inert bodies from the truck bed like a Bugs Bunny cartoon. Putting the truck into park, she exited and went back to see where her load had landed. Bob and Zoo were nicely heaped in the corner.

She liberated one bag of powdered concrete and dumped the

contents over the bodies. Camouflaged and invisible. Likely one of Zoo's pals on this job was getting paid to quickly cover it all with new concrete and ask no questions. *Zoo paid him to bury himself instead of me. Ironic.*

Time to get out of town. The paved alley left no tire tracks. She smudged out her footprints. The rest would all be obliterated by construction equipment and workers before the sun rose tomorrow morning. Confuse the snoopers.

Now her heart took up hammering—time to get out of this town and never come back. She drove the truck west in the dark towards Ottawa and home. Goodbye Bubbles Car Wash; goodbye "La Marie". She drove away until her heart stopped pounding, until she saw only open road and the city lights of Montreal long gone behind her. After a time, she spotted a side road with a bridge over a river, nice and quiet.

She stopped on the deck and threw the gun and silencer far out in the inky blackness of the slow-moving river, then she dropped her disposable gloves on the rough bridge deck. Passing traffic would atomize them. Thanks for the tip, Bob.

After that it was on to an all-night car wash for the pickup, herself, and a furtive clothes change in her truck cab. She showered off the bloody clothes, then got rid of them in three different dumpsters.

Goodbye Tammy.

After a drive through burger she got a room in a sleazy motel for the night.

She was spent and exhausted but alive.

———

Inspector Shirl MacDonald was beside herself with anxiety and anger. She leaned over the computer tech's shoulder, looking at his computer screen. "So, where the hell is Tammy? I thought you had bugs everywhere?"

Sweating, he leaned close to the screen, "She should be on this map. I put tracers on her phone and on her laptop but I don't see them. Did she turn them off?"

"Yes, she texted me she was turning them off at 23:00 hours but I thought she'd turn them back on. Where is she? I *never* should have left the La Marie! I should have *scooped* that fucking ledger!"

"If she turned them off, there's nothing we can do. We need to wait until she checks in. Not my fault, Inspector."

Shirl stood up and said nothing. Apologizing wasn't her style even if he was correct. "Keep looking!" She stomped off to her office and slammed the door.

Fuming, she sat, fingers drumming on her desk. She sat up, grabbing her cell phone and dialed a long unused number. "Jean?"

The person on the other end paused, "Shirley?"

"Yes, Jean. How are you?"

Shirl was glad to hear Insp. Jean Jacques' voice. She had known him for years professionally as well as enjoyed a summer fling with the man which went well until his wife threatened to cut his balls off. The affair ended. They were confidents for each other despite the baggage.

"I am well. What's up?" he said.

"Well, long story. I'm in a jam and not sure what to do and you are the closest person to the issue I can trust."

"Issue?"

"Let me go back. I have an informant in deep cover in Montreal. Mafia sting. I was watching my informant from the front desk of where she was living but the gang was on to me and I had to run. We had tracers on her but she turned them off and texted me that it was all good. That was two days ago, and I haven't heard from her since."

Jean considered her story. "So, she went off the air but said she'd get back to you and hasn't yet, correct?"

"Yes."

"Can she look after herself?"

"Very much so but sometimes it all goes to shit," she said.

"Like Beth?"

"Poor Beth. What a fucking disaster."

"How long was Beth's tracker off?" asked Jean.

"Never. That's how we located her foot. It was beeping in her shoe!"

Jean felt ill and said nothing.

"I don't know what to do. Any ideas?" she asked.

Jean thought about it. "Can't really put this in the front page... "Lost mafia informant. Have you seen—what's her name?"

"Tammy." Shirley moaned, covering her eyes. "God help me."

"—Have you seen Tammy? Milk cartons everywhere with her picture.'"

"Yes, I get that. How do I go about searching?"

"I suggest quietly asking her handler or anyone else you can trust to watch for her."

"Done that. Asked them all."

"If she's as capable as you say she is, then trust her and wait seventy-two hours for her to surface. She's been at this for a while. Perhaps she has her reasons for disappearing."

"Good ones, I hope."

"So, you've considered she may have turned—become one of them?"

Shirl paused, reluctant to admit her fear. "Yes. Alfred, her handler, watched her like a hawk and he saw nothing to indicate that. Neither did I. Her constant stream of incriminating information against the mob also means she wasn't working for them. I'm... I'm certain she's still ours."

Jean took a deep breath, "Then give her seventy-two hours and then panic if she's a no show."

"Let's go with that."

"Excellent. Call me if you need someone to go look if you are worried about loose lips in the city police."

"I'll do that Jean, thanks."

———

Terry was covering her tracks. She first had a Denny's breakfast fit for a queen, then drove for an hour, heading north until she found a creek-side secluded picnic area she was looking for. She started a respectable size campfire. Once it was roaring hot she threw in all remaining document evidence of Tammy and any remaining bits of clothes. It felt like a healing to see her infamous alter ego, Tammy, go up in smoke.

It was time to go.

This truck was growing on her. A bland hot rod. It was handy and she hoped to keep it. She'd think on it. God knows what drugs, guns and body parts were squirreled away in all the secret hiding places. Her hand felt the wad of cash in her pocket, no uncertainty there. *Mine.*

A police car came into the park, part of a boring patrol. The driver gave a simple wave but did not stop. It was then she realized she had pockets of cash, no ID, driver's license or anything that would vouch for her. Tammy was gone and her real identity... Theresa Reid... had not been reactivated. Her truck was registered to a guy sleeping under twenty feet of fresh concrete. This would absolutely be hard to explain to the cops.

She waited until the cop car finally got bored and left. Best put this campfire out. A forest fire would bring publicity and annoy the squirrels. The computer carcass was dug out of the ashes and tossed into the creek.

She drove onto the main road and headed for the nearest little berg. It had been four hours since breakfast and she was starved. It was well after the lunch crowd rush when she stopped at a roadhouse. It looked like a little family-run operation with home cooking and it advertised a real phone!

It was almost empty inside. She ordered a tuna on rye sandwich with a salad and iced tea from the waitress. As soon as the waitress left with her order, she went to the phone kiosk.

After dialing and waiting, she heard Shirl's message on her personal phone voicemail. Must be busy. "It's *me* calling. I'm in

"Scooters" in Glenville, an hour northeast of Montreal. It seems I have no ID and suspicious plates on my truck. Can someone come and get me?" Shirl knew her voice, she'd help. Terry hung up, looked at her watch and saw it was 1:43 p.m. and hoped her message got through. How long could she risk waiting here?

Lunch arrived so she sat down, relaxing, thrilled to be eating something that wasn't a lukewarm faux-burger of some kind, eaten in a mad rush. The first bites were lovely. The fries were homemade and sizzling, the salad fresh, arriving with a peppy dressing.

She looked up seven minutes later as one ghost car slid into the parking lot. Thirty seconds later a second slid in beside it. Four serious looking detectives climbed out, looking around.

She swallowed and waited, her eyes drilling the scene, flicking to the back entrance, then back to the front.

The head guy ordered one detective to stay by the outside entrance, directed the other two to stay at either side of the restaurant door. He strode to her, reaching into his pocket.

Was he going to handcuff her? Pull his gun? Something about him was confident yet reassuring.

"Theresa Reid?" he politely asked, pulling out his credentials. "I'm Inspector Jean Jacques, Sûreté."

Did he say Theresa?

It felt strange to hear her real name. It had been so many months as Tammy. "Yes, I am Theresa Reid," she answered, her body suddenly a puddle of gratitude. Still, she made Jean wait until she was done eating her delicious lunch.

———

Jean thought back to Shirl's call to him. Twelve minutes ago, his personal phone rang, again. Unusual. A voice inquired, "Jean Jacques?"

"Yes."

"This is Shirl calling from Ottawa."

"Hello Inspector. How are you?" he said formally, for the benefit of nearby ears.

"Found our informant in Glenville, at Scooters Roadhouse! Could you pick her up as soon as you can? Her name is Theresa Reid. She's out and left a message requesting pick up. Not sure if there's a problem but you are closest to her. No searches of her, her vehicle or her stuff. Got it?"

"I will go to her right now." He hung up, stood, pointing to the three Sûreté detectives nearest him, junior detectives recently arrived from uniform, paper pushers typing reports about lost pets on computers. "You, you and you! Two cars. Glenville, Scooters Diner. Right now." He wasn't sure what to expect so would bring some muscle.

Jean needed to hustle. A female informant in the mafia who'd lived to tell the tale? Unheard of—and undoubtedly a treasure of information. He had to secure her before she vanished.

The three men jumped out of their chairs and ran to the door anticipating a shootout at the OK Corral. Outside, they broke up, choosing two unmarked cars, two officers per car, and peeled out of the Sûreté parking lot, lights flashing like lighthouse beacons and sirens howling.

Jean was in the lead car passenger seat, already shaking his head at his choice of today's help. Pedal to the metal and no detective experience, yet. He noticed the speedometer was sitting at just over two hundred kilometers an hour and climbing. These young guys never missed a chance to drive like maniacs. He double checked his seatbelt.

Finally, he barked, "No sirens, Stevens! It's an empty road and not far." The two cars, lights flashing but now without sirens, flew down the quiet road like grey rockets, trees flashing by like fence pickets. "There! Turn right! Scooters, you idiot!" He immediately regretted his order as they were going too fast for a hard right turn this late.

But Stevens was determined to try. He punched the brakes, the car shuddering as it tried to slow. He bravely turned the steering wheel at a fairly high-speed giving Jean the impression they were going to flip over but the car leaned hard into the corner, tires screaming for grip.

Next he stomped the emergency brake driving out the rear of the car to aim at Scooters then hit the gas and braked again.

Jean hung on for dear life thinking their car was destined to explode through Scooters, killing everyone inside. He imagined the headlines, "Police kill valuable informant after driving though family restaurant". Fuck!

He hung on to his seatbelt as he felt the car tires lock up and they slid in the gravel until the car barely bumped the concrete barrier in front of the roadhouse. The car engine stalled and all was momentarily silent. Jean watched over his shoulder as the other car flew by, unable to stop. Wow. He gave Stevens a dark look and jacked open his door. As he climbed out, he heard the other car arriving. He hopped over to the other side of the concrete barrier for safety. He watched in amazement as the second car also slid to a shaky stop beside the first, engine and brakes sizzling.

They officers exited the cars amid the dust and dirt which was trying to settle.

They all stood together at the entrance. Jean shook his head. "Did you all learn to drive in Montreal?"

Stevens bravely admitted, "Yes!"

Jean held his tongue. Later. "Oh, for Christ sakes! Stevens; stand at the entrance. You and you come with me."

As they came through the doorway the waitress looked at them in surprise. "Are you making a car chase movie, sir?"

Jean ignored her tease. "Non! Sûreté, Madam. I'll have coffee."

"And what will these men have?" the waitress asked, pointing to the other sheepish looking officers.

"Driving lessons and more work in the lost pet department," he growled.

"Ah." The waitress suppressed a smile.

There was only one person in the place. A harmless looking female. He strode to her table. "Theresa Reid?" He showed his credentials. "Sûreté."

"Oui," she smiled, working on a plate of food.

"I'm Chief Inspector Jean Jacques. Inspector McDonald asked me to come and give you a lift back to town."

"Yes, please."

"May I join you?" he asked.

The woman was busily eating her sandwich but waved a hand at the empty seat in front of her.

The waitress came with his coffee. He sat down and added two creams to the cup and stirred. "The Inspector must think very highly of you. She told me to come right away. Shirley Mac is an old friend of mine."

"Thanks...oops. Sorry." Jean watched the woman mumble, losing a bit of food out of the side of her mouth.

"No. My fault. We can talk when you're done," Jean said apologetically. He was happy to let his adrenalin rush pass after the panic call and wild drive to the road-house.

Jean sipped his coffee and glanced at her. She looked durable, a bit thin, taller and bigger than average. Unlike most informers, she looked like she could take care of herself. She had fading tats on her arms and legs. There was a wariness, a subtle menace about her. Fearless?

Her clothes looked like they came from a second-hand shop. They consisted of a rumpled pullover top and medium length shorts. Battered short hair. A few bruises but no cuts or visible bullet wounds. Someone in a hurry.

"Thank you for your patience, Inspector. I've been on the run for the past few days. Eating and sleeping were a low priority," Terry finally said.

"Are you in any danger, Terry?"

"I don't think so. I hid my tracks fairly well. It feels nice to be called Terry Reid again."

Jean said, "Other informants say the same thing. They became so immersed in their identity they became strangers to themselves. There is a transition back to normal life—a peculiar price to be paid."

"I can see that. All the time I was in there I had to make myself believe I was that person and not me."

"And now you can forget who you were, at least until the debrief interviews and trials."

"I'm not looking forward to that."

"They will do everything they can to protect your former and present identity."

"No doubt," she said unconvincingly. They both knew mistakes got informers outed—and killed. "Could you tow that pickup to Inspector MacDonald for me?" She pointed to a plain white truck in the parking lot. "I'm not sure of ownership or what's really in there. Zoo, as in the Montreal family, was the former owner."

"Zoo?" Jean's eyes went wide. "The contract killer?"

"Yes. I worked for Bob Carzoni and Zoo. They gave me this truck to use. It could have money, guns—even body parts hidden in it for all I know."

Jean was impressed. "Those are terrible men. We think Zoo killed at least one Montreal policemen as well as an informer. You are lucky to be alive."

No luck about it. She continued, "I also worked for a fellow at the Bubbles Car Wash named Ric."

"Another unsavoury character. We never managed to get enough on him despite his reprehensible behaviour. No one has ever been willing to testify or lived to."

Terry nodded. "They're too afraid. I met lots of folks like him, immersed in the scum of Montreal crime. I even had dinner with the Carzoni family."

Jean's poker face was taking a beating today. *"The Carzonis?"* He fought to keep his mouth from gaping.

"Mama, Papa, Eva and Bob. The whole mob... literally."

"Wow. Sometimes Papa Carzoni is the last face a person ever sees."

She continued, "It was like the Addams Family with less make up and more baseball bats."

Jean chuckled. She still seemed to have a sense of wry humour despite her incredible experience. He waited until she was done and paid the lunch bill. They headed for the door and stood in the parking lot.

The three junior detectives Jean had brought with him studied the woman they were here to pick up. He judged by their expressions all three thought she looked attractive and fierce. A lounging jaguar.

Jean spoke to them. "The three of you will follow in that car."

Stevens proceeded to bicker over who would drive and the others disagreed.

Jean stopped them. "*Listen! Call for a tow truck* to get this pick up to the covered impound at the station. *Wait for the tow truck* and follow it all the way back to the lot. Got it, *Stevens?*"

Nervously Stevens repeated the orders back to Jean. All the officers bobbed their heads like little boys being warned about being late for school in front of a girl they had a crush on.

Jean heaved a sigh and continued, "We'll take this car and go back to the office."

They all nodded again.

"And don't drive like idiots!"

The three confirmed once more.

Terry added, "I'd like to get my bag from that truck."

Stevens complied, eagerly dropping her big bag in the backseat, then rushed over to open the passenger car door for her. Jean got in the car, backed up and they left the three juniors in the dust of the parking lot.

The junior detectives would stay junior for a while longer.

When the car was up to speed and Jean checked in with his radio, he dug out his phone and passed it to her. "Go ahead and call Shirley if you wish. Her cell number is the last one called in. Encrypted phone."

She took the phone, pushed the last number "unlisted" and waited for an answer.

"Hello?" the Inspector answered tentatively.

"It's me, Terry. Jean has me and we are headed to his office."

There was a happy pause. "Terry! So good to hear from you! Oh my god... I was thinking the worst when your tracker stopped."

Terry looked at Jean. "I'm in good hands. I just have to get used to being Theresa Reid, once again. I've never had to shed my skin before."

WEATHERMAN

The ad was too good to be true. *'Wanted; Weatherman – $100g's per year – PO Box #1970'.*

If only he'd ignored the ad.

Now he lay in a car trunk, hands cuffed behind his naked, shaking body.

He was suspicious when he saw the ad to the old Weatherman group after fifty years, but the box number *did* say #1970—the year the Weathermen had declared war on the US!

A secret sign? Had to be legit.

Excited, he replied to the post office box number. Bradley was sixty years old and he was getting bald and his eyesight was nothing special, either, but he knew the Weatherman were looking for men young at heart. He started growing his hair long or at least as much as he could while awaiting a reply.

The Weathermen! A radical youth group that struck fear into the heart of President Richard Nixon and his government with bombings, war declaration and riots.

His mom disturbed his thoughts. "What's this about joining the Weatherman? Those days are gone. I told you not to go near those people. They're just trouble."

Bradley ignored her. He had been just ten years old when he'd silently joined the Weatherman, or rather, he just *told* himself he belonged to them. A silent pledge in the mirror and a homemade tattoo. Ouch. Skin infection.

Fifty years later, there he was, applying to join the protest group long forgotten but had they forgotten him? He almost gave up when an anonymous reply appeared in his email inbox. It was a cryptic message, "Wanna be a Weatherman? Go where there is always snow".

Cryptic e-mail puzzle?

He was shocked to finally receive this invitation to join the Weathermen but it was getting late and it was a hot summer. Where would he find snow? He jumped in his mother's prehistoric car and drove off looking for snow in July.

Bradley drove by the recreation complex, then slammed on his brakes, backing up a half a block, into the rec-plex back lot. Snow! The ice cleaner machine cleaned the snow every day and dumped it right here. He saw a piece of paper stuck to a nearby post, "Find a Blizzard".

A Blizzard? Hot July?

Luckily the radio was on as he roamed around town like a lost puppy, "Come to DQ for a Blizzard!" He headed for the nearest outlet and asked for a "Blizzard". His drink arrived but the straw wouldn't work. It had a note tucked inside! "Go to the dead home for the dead. One-Two-One tap".

Puzzled he drove around the area. Must be a funeral home. There were only two on the streets and were clearly open and busy. Taking a wrong turn he ended up in an alley with abandoned businesses. There it was!

…a dead home for the dead. An abandoned funeral home!

He stood on the stoop. A peephole opened and a black eye stared at him. Bradley nervously gave the man a password, "Mark Madriga." The door opened to a darkened room. A gloved hand gripped his T-shirt and jerked him inside. Armed, dangerous looking masked men grabbed him, roughly strip searched him and did unspeakable inspections in places he couldn't even see. Duct tape was slapped on his ears and a hood pulled over his head.

Dang! This was a set up!

Cuffed, bared and hooded, Bradley was shoved in the trunk of a vehicle and was driven around for what seemed like hours. He felt the exhaust rumble and the vehicle lurch left and right. It was all he could do not to throw up in his hood. Heading for an airport and Guantanamo Bay or pushed out of a helicopter over the ocean? He was glad he was naked as he quaked with fear and thought he might urinate.

The vehicle stopped and Bradley heard the sound of a garage door closing. The trunk opened and people lifted him out and walked him shivering, groggily, somewhere. Torture chamber? Back when he was a kid, his mother had told everyone he was a screamer—at the dentist or at school vaccinations. Maybe this would attract attention... or get a stinky sock in his mouth. Hopefully his captors wash their clothes periodically.

He was dragged in and plopped down in a very cold chair, hood yanked off, a bright light blazing in his face. Black gloved hands clumsily clawed off the duct tape from his ears taking the last bits of his long hair with it.

"OUCH! OUCH!"

A voice shouted, "WHO ARE YOU?"

"... um... I'm... Bradley.."

"WHO?"

"...Ah, Bradley Albert... Who... are you?"

"SHADDAP! WE ASK THE QUESTIONS!" said the voice.

Bradley sat in horror and shock.

"BRADLEY MICHAEL ALBERT?"

"...ye...yes..." All he could do was not cry.

"PHD Weather control from Ryerson's?" The voice toned down a bit.

"...um...yeah...correspondence sch...school..."

"GET A GOOD MARK?"

Bradley was frightened again. "Yes, got 95%. Mom said I was the top in the class."

"YOU LIVE WITH YOUR MOM?" the voice shouted at him.

"Yes. I don't fit in well and rent's cheap. She does my laundry, too."

The voice roared "HAHAHA..."

Suddenly the glaring light went out, his handcuffs were removed. Someone stood him up and put a bathrobe around him. As his eyes and ears adjusted he saw four people standing around him, two armed with machine guns and black balaclavas, one middle aged woman in a white lab coat and one studious looking man with thick glasses in a suit with a bow-tie. Bradley stood with his arms cemented gratefully around the robe, expecting to be shot.

Bow-Tie man lowered his bright orange Radio Shack mega-phone with a look of guilt. He spoke, "Sorry to put you through all that, Bradley, but we have to be careful. A year ago, we were tracked by an angry Mafia dad who found our branch operation in Topeka, Kansas, burned the building down and lynched half the staff after it rained on his daughters outdoor wedding."

Bradley saw the balaclava men and the woman recoil in horror at the story.

The woman added, "We can't take any chances. We must remain unknown forever. You can't breathe a word to a soul about what you do or who we are. If you do, these men will pick you up and take you for a helicopter ride."

Bradley swallowed hard, "One-way chopper ride... over the ocean?"

The man calmly said, "Why yes, to a condo we own in the Bahamas where you live your life out in luxury. What did you think we meant?"

Bradley held his hands out in wonder, "Never mind. So, is this the Weathermen? You seem kind of... nice... compared to what I expected. I thought you were a violent organization."

The Bow-Tie man, woman and balaclavas looked at each other, whispering. Bradley feared he'd stirred up something.

Dang! Now they'll kill me for sure.

The woman spoke, "Oh, you think we're 'The Weatherman', that old sixties protest group... your long hair and tats... 1970 declaration of war... just a coincidence. I'm so sorry. We're nothing like them."

Bradley wasn't sure if he should try to run or hold his breath until he died though his Mother said that never works.

The Bow-Tie said, "Sit down, please, Bradley. We are the Weatherman, a secret group that controls weather on planet earth. Weather is not a random event. We really do control it."

"You can't control the weather. That's stupid," said Bradley.

"Do you have your PhD in Weather control or not?"

"Uh...yes I do. I never thought it was legit. I thought weather was interesting and I knew I could never get a job with it. Just wanted to graduate and move to Vancouver and drive a night cab for cash like my cousin Gordie."

The Bow-Tie said, "Everything you saw and learned in that Weather Control program is true. Absolutely, positively. We run the worldwide weather."

The balaclava men and the woman all looked at each other nodding in confirmation. One of the men almost dropped his machine gun but regained his grip before it hit the ground.

"So why security for Weather Control? Why not just set up an office and have a security guy at the door?"

The Bow-Tie man said, "Listen to these statistics, Bradley; 3.7 billion rained out weddings, thirty billion ruined crops, 5595 ruined outdoor fairs and circus's...circii?" he looked uncertainly around at his colleagues before continuing. "Insurance companies with thousands of liability lawyers on the hunt for us, 8.3 thousand outdoor movie shoots scrubbed... need I go on?"

"So, they all want our... *your* heads on a plate?"

"Yes. One rich reality TV star put a hundred million bucks on our heads when we rained out his presidential inauguration."

"So weather control is not... fake?" said Bradley, finally understanding the significance.

"We control the weather each and every day, on this entire planet. Each area has a group like us suggesting future weather. These suggestions go to central coordination in Victoria, BC. They decide from there."

Bradley's mouth fell open. "I wondered why Victorians seem to be so smug and knowledgeable about the weather all the time! And their weather is always the nicest in Canada because they coordinate it! Those buggers!"

Bow-Tie man said, "You are correct."

"But hurricanes and tornadoes happen? Cyclones and typhoons? Winter?" asked Bradley.

The Bow-Tie man said, "They are huge events. We can minimize them and move them around to an extent but can you imagine if that rain fall didn't fill those regional rivers and lakes? In a few decades the world would be doomed. It's all about the big picture and the planet."

Bradley was suddenly disgusted. "And you let in rain on every one of my Mom's five weddings! You assholes!"

Bow-Tie man shook his head. "And you can see our dilemma. So, what do you say, Bradley? Work for us? Wages are crazy high but you could be burned at the stake every time you make it rain on a Shotgun Dad's little daughter's sixteenth birthday barbeque."

Bradley asked, "What about bribes for weather? Could the rich oil barons pay and ask for rain in the deserts?"

The Bow-Tie man said, "Ah, actually rumour has it they pay for it NOT to rain. The sheiks like to do outdoor stuff, parties, ride their horses in dry sand. These guys are zillionaires."

"What about Global warming?" asked Bradley, thinking this was a zinger question.

Bow-Tie said, after thinking a bit, "The world trend is less winter and more warm weather. Demand for sunny days is insatiable and has slowly increased demand for summer, inching up the global temperatures. We are reasonably sure we can stop it, anytime."

"Reasonably sure you can stop it? Uh-oh."

"Well, this weather control is new and this is new territory. When was the last time someone, other than the odd farmer or ski resort owner said to you, 'Boy I wish it would rain or snow or get cold', Bradley?"

"I guess I never heard anyone—"

"Hence, our dilemma. Could get our budget cut if we don't keep at least some people happy," said the Bow-Tie man.

Bradley considered his statement. "If people didn't know what the weather was going to do before and they still don't… why would they be angry now? It's still an unknown."

"Human nature. If they *think* someone can change it then it is someone's fault."

"Ah. Like blaming the government, Masons, or someone else's God if things don't go your way."

"Precisely!"

"Sure, sign me up. Anyone got some clothes?"

The woman handed him his confiscated clothing. As Bradley hastily pulled the clothing on, he asked, "So, don't weather forecasters suspect this weather control operation?"

The Bow-Tie man answered this one. "A few TV meteorologists get suspicious so we purposely make weather opposite of their weather prediction for a week or so. Makes them look bad and they might get fired. They get the hint it's a good idea to drop the weather control conspiracy thing."

"Devious! Who's been the closest to finding you out?"

"Remember your password?" asked the Bow-Tie man.

"Mark Madriga?" said Bradley, pausing at pulling his shirt down.

The Bow-Tie man just winked. "We're going to make it rain down there for forty days and forty-nights. See who might get fired."

THE MANNERS OF POTTED CHRYSANTHEMUMS

BY PATRICIA M. EMERY

I'm noticing people of my "sixties" generation utilizing Facebook to convey their "Thanks" to hosts of dinners, parties, and barbecues via their social media.

All the Facebook community sees their "thank you posts" and "likes", including the larger audience of those of us who weren't invited to the party or barbecue.

I wonder if people still take the time to write a thank you note, bring the host or hostess a "Bread and Butter" gift, or phone to genuinely convey their thanks; or is it somehow more genuine to have the large audience of social media?

I think back to a time before social media.

The simpler times of potted chrysanthemums.

I'm a young child riding in my parents '55 Chevy Bel- Air across town to our annual New Year's Day family dinner on the west side of Victoria.

It's always very damp and chilly so I snuggle under an old grey army blanket to warm up. No seat-belts back then. The Bel- Air's fans and defrosters were blasting some heat, but never quite enough to keep the large windows from fogging up.

We often stop at Joe's Market, the Green Grocer, at Quadra and

Hillside, so my Mom and I can run in and purchase a potted Chrysanthemum.

Joe's Market is open 24/7, and the shelves out front are loaded with colourful potted plants, large bunches of cut flowers, and wooden boxes laden with fresh vegetables and fruits protected from the drizzle of rain by a large blue and grey striped awning.

My mother always explains as we go into Joe's, that it's very important to take our hostess a potted chrysanthemum to thank her and show our appreciation. What makes the potted chrysanthemum an appropriate "bread and butter" gift is it is pretty, practical, and long-lasting, and therefore a thoughtful gift.

My education in manners includes learning from mom that "cut flowers" really aren't an appropriate "bread and butter" gift as a busy hostess is preparing for guests and does not appreciate the fuss of locating a vase, trimming the stems, and trying to arrange flowers amidst the turkey or roast carvings, pots and pans, and an over-loaded countertop of bowls of salads, trifles, and pies.

I also learn that potted Chrysanthemums are appreciated as pretty and practical gifts for birthdays, visiting the elderly or ill, or special occasions such as Thanksgiving.

There is a manner and art to selecting the appropriate colour. One could purchase a pretty pastel coloured chrysanthemum for a visit to an elderly great-aunt, but never pick that colour for a great uncle. Your selection for an elderly great uncle should be yellow or deep purple. Pastels are for spring events such as Easter and golds are for autumn events such as Thanksgiving.

My mom and aunts were such green-thumbs that they would replant their potted chrysanthemums outside in the spring, where they would thrive and flower again in late summer. As children of the depression they appreciated the value of the chrysanthemum.

I remember New Year's Day in 1960, when I got to pick-out for the first time, a potted chrysanthemum as a thank you gift.

There were over fifty chrysanthemums to choose from, in a wide variety of pastels, golds, purples, yellows; all in brightly foiled pots.

I spotted that one special potted Chrysanthemum that would

convey not only my family's appreciation to our hostess—my aunt—but also my maturity in selecting appropriately and wisely.

I picked up the most beautiful chrysanthemum with twelve pompoms of three-inch diameter formed by rows of glistening snow-white florets. The plastic plant pot is covered in shiny bright green tin foil and a tall red plastic pick declaring, "Happy New Year". Joe carefully wrapped the plant in crisp cellophane and wished us a most Happy New Year.

I am so excited when we arrive at my aunt and uncle's home, running up the stairs carrying my perfect chrysanthemum, dashing quickly past my extended family who were visiting in the living room in my haste to find my aunt in the kitchen. Aunt Clara is preparing dinner among steaming pots and pans and simmering gravy on the stove-top. The aroma of turkey and dressing wafting in the air as my Uncle precisely carves the turkey.

She stops her busy dinner preparation to receive the chrysanthemum. She gives me a huge hug, and I notice her patterned red poinsettia Christmas apron is damp and there are beads of sweat on her brow from the day spent peeling and chopping vegetables, preparing dressing, baking pies, and cooking the huge turkey.

She then carefully places the chrysanthemum in the place of honour in the center of her dining table on the white lace table cloth also adorned with the best Royal Albert china, silverware, and crystal.

Throughout dinner my relatives compliment me on my selection of the chrysanthemum.

After enjoying a fabulous dinner with much laughter and stories, we pitch in and help with dishes and clean-up.

My beloved chrysanthemum now receives a new place of honour on a white lace doily in the middle of my aunt's large walnut coffee table in the center of the living room, as our family now re-gathers to play dominoes and canasta.

Joe's Market Corner Green Grocer still exists after all these years, and is surprisingly largely as I remember it, with Joe's grandchildren carrying on the tradition. Yes, the chrysanthemums there are still a delightful variety of types and colours outside on the sidewalk shelves. It always takes me back to happy childhood memories.

I moved to the Peace almost forty years ago and have always missed having a corner green grocer. I find on my grocery trips to Overwaitea, the first area of the store I go to is the flower section hoping to find a lovely potted chrysanthemum.

I often purchase one for a friend or neighbor who could use some cheer, or as a hostess "bread and butter" gift, remembering my manners I learned as a child in Victoria.

Sometimes I buy one for myself, just because, and then I feel a little tug in my heart and I smile.

Social media or not, how could you ever go wrong with a potted chrysanthemum?

FIRST SNOWS

...WE HAVE A LOVE/ HATE RELATIONSHIP WITH THE FROZEN STUFF.

Larry took his new Caribbean bride, Giselle, through the old farm-house door and into the middle of the yard. They stood under the deceased apple tree, ankle deep in the first virgin snow of the winter season. The cold air charged their nostrils, giving them both goose bumps as a Peace country breeze gently made the wind chimes sing.

Larry lovingly put his hand on her shoulder, and launched into one of his famously overly theatrical speeches. "Giselle, We need to talk... about us... and about snow. You've were here for a couple of weeks last Christmas but you've never experienced a real, full on winter before and it can get on your nerves."

"I never thought about it, Larry. Tell me; how does snow get on ya're nerves?" she asked, a bit sarcastically but with her charming Trini accent.

Larry continued to lecture, "Well, winter can be hard. You wake up sometimes and there is snow all over the place. It has to be swept, shoveled and managed."

She stood for a few moments waiting for more of the story but apparently that was all to be said. "So? Ya farm where large tracts of dirt is plowed, rocks picked, earth smoothed and weeded. Ya fertilize, plant and grow stuff which later has ta be cut, harvested, managed and moved to market. It's what ya do."

"True, but we Canadians are profoundly annoyed about snow. Weather is a personal thing up here," he reasoned.

"The weather is the weather, Larry. In case ya haven't noticed nobody has come up with a way ta control it and can barely even predict what it will do. It is what it is."

"I know, but we tend to grow up hating the snow because it is around us, all the time," he countered.

"Doesn't it just snow for a few months in the winter? Four or five months, tops? Ya do like to make up stories about how much snow ya never got and how cold it never was," Giselle pointed out, logically.

"I know we like to make it sound harder than it is because we hate it so much. It gnaws at us and eats at our souls. People will leave friends, well-paying jobs, family and everything dearest to them to move away at huge expense and hassle, so they don't have to shovel snow."

"Ya're kiddin', right?"She said.

"I kid you not," Larry replied grimly.

"So, do they move to the desert or some place that will never see snow?" she asked.

"Well, not usually because the desert gets too hot in the summer. They just move where it only snows a few times in the winter and mostly rains."

"But it does snow, there, once in a while?"

"Yes, but they do not speak of it. As far as they are concerned it only ever rains which is fully acceptable."

"So... just as long as the rain doesn't freeze it's considered better?"

"Yes."

"So instead of shoveling snow, they rake and shovel leaves, mow grass and deal with a lot of rain instead of snow?" she quizzed.

"Yes."

"But no skiin', sleddin' and such?"

"No. They do summer stuff when it isn't raining."

"But it rains a lot?"

"Yes."

"Larry; I'm confused. How is that an improvement over snow?"

"It is a huge difference to them."

"So, if I say I moved here because I was sick of beach sand and the heat, they'd understand?"

"No. They think that is better than snow, provided it's not too hot in the summer."

"Let's go back to somethin' ya said earlier, Larry. Ya said they'd hate it if it's too hot."

"Yes, it cannot be too hot."

"So ya say it can't be too hot or cold enough ta snow?"

"Yes."

"You Canadians live in heated and air-conditioned homes all year around, don't ya, generally? Seventy degrees or whatever ya set on the thermostat?"

"Correct but they still don't like snow, even if they don't live in it, exactly."

"Ah…of course. When do these snow hatin' thoughts occur to Canadians?"

"We usually grow up hating snow or heard we've should hate snow. It's a DNA thing."

"So ya're sayin' I should not like snow? But last Christmas we came up here and did a lot of winter activities and I liked the snow. Am I weird?"

"No. You are from Trinidad and don't know that you should hate the snow yet. Maybe later."

She put her arms around him and held him close, looking into his eyes, smiling, "Ya aren't kiddin me, are ya? Water falls from the sky, everywhere but when it freezes…."

"Crystallizes, Giselle… crystallizes."

"Don't interrupt. And you Canadians take this crystallizin' transformation as a personal insult and will move away from everything and everyone you hold near and dear at great personal sacrifice to escape it?"

"Pretty much."

"And you think you have gotten away from a fate worse than death?"

"I'm afraid so."

"I thought this kinda thing was a cultural, religious or economic immigration due to severe hardship but it's just to get away from snow?"

"Correct!"

She sighed, rolled her eyes, "And here I thought ya Canadians were a logical people. Ya can imagine my surprise."

"We are not quite perfect just yet, Giselle."

She pushed him over as they both giggled and laughed—and washed his face with snow.

SPIRAL STAIRCASE

Diana sat, eyeball-to-eyeball with the big white seagull, holding her ground. She was duty bound to save this last lovely table on this noisy and crowded marina patio. Tiring of the bird's game, she leaned forward and waved her hands at the hungry bird. Unimpressed, it seemed to shrug then stutter stepped along to the rail to the next table of patrons, where it watched for *their* scraps and tidbits. It hadn't given up on Diana's table and would be watching.

Relieved the bird had moved on, Diana sat back down and relaxed. She enjoyed the sun and ignored the annoying, blustery wind. Meeting with Muriel at the marina was the highlight of her week. Muriel always paid for coffee *and* did all the leg work. Best of all, she had the best gossip in town.

————

Muriel carefully balanced the tray, gingerly approach the exit to the outside patio, performed her signature graceless pivot, and pressed the door open with one of her artificial hips—no thanks from anyone seated nearby who could have held the door open. Such poor manners and breeding, she thought.

She scanned the area, spotting Diana at a table for two near the guardrail. Knowing her destination she shuffled over, teetering the tray, slopping only a little coffee into their dainty saucers.

As she wobbled along, she kept her eye on their table. It annoyed her that Diana always seemed to forget her wallet or was "A bit short of cash", followed of course by a torrent of elegant and profuse apologies. She was such a gossip hound as well. Muriel tried avoiding her but Diana could be overwhelming and tough to brush off. It was like saying no to the Queen. It *was* nice speaking to a fellow Brit, though.

"Well done!" said Diana brightly, as Muriel arrived.

"At last, I finally got the two coffees and a bit of cake for us. Seventeen dollars and me on a pension!" Muriel groused in her distinctly British accent, teetering with the clumsy plastic tray, sliding it all off and placing the cups and plates. Out of breath, she eased her old bones into her chair. She watched her friend Diana for a moment. "Is something wrong?"

Diana discreetly leaned forward. "Watch that gull behind you. It's beside that rough couple."

"Ah."

"And I'm sure they're listening to us, especially the tall man. Nosy bugger."

Muriel glanced over then shrugged. "So? I just got here—what could we possibly say that would interest them?"

"I don't know. I'll bet they just arrived from some snowy place, looking for somewhere warm to retire to—driving up the housing prices in leaps and bounds."

"Humph. Typical." Muriel sniffed. "I just don't know. Victoria used to be such a quiet, inexpensive place. Look at it. They've driven the rents up so high we can barely afford to live in our own home. Bedford and I have been looking for a new place for months and there's very little to be had."

"I couldn't agree more. Norman and I were considering moving to somewhere cheaper... like..." Diana flushed and murmured, "Nanaimo."

Muriel gasped. "Nanaimo! Surely you aren't serious? Nanaimo is such an..." She gave a little shiver. "*Uncouth* place."

"The rents are much more reasonable than here. We would still say we're from Victoria, if anyone asks."

"That seems a bit drastic." Muriel made a face, then perched up. "Bedford and I are still looking at local options."

"Here's an option for you—have you considered buying a boat and living in it? I hear old sailboats can be inexpensive."

"We did but... you know... my family had such a bad experience with living on a boat." The seagull was back, looking over their plates with beady-eyed interest. Muriel lurched from her seat to shoo it away. "Go... shoo!"

Naturally, Diana did nothing. It seemed that now that Muriel was back and taking over the defence of their table, Diana could relax in her chair and indulge her curiosity.

Diana said, "Oh, my, what boat experience was that? Was it Ann and Fredrick?"

"Um, yes."

"But I thought they... separated after Frederick lost his position over... you know..."

Muriel took over, firmly. "Yes, Frederick was fired from the government because of his drinking." She straightened her spine and added primly, "There you go. I've said it."

They sat uneasily silent at their table, making a fuss over their quickly cooling coffee and cake.

Diana broke the ice. "I'm - I'm sorry. I just didn't know."

Muriel relented. "It's a touchy subject. First Frederick was fired, then he and Ann separated."

"Oh dear," said Diana, sipping her coffee, watching her intently. "Was that... resolved?"

"I suppose. In the end, they *had* to get back together for financial reasons. He had no position, so they sold their home and bought a sailboat to live on in Beecher Bay. Cheaper."

Diana smiled. "Lovely! They can live in their boat as they sail around the world."

"Not exactly. It barely floats. It's a large, elderly sailboat, quite luxurious in its day, but not anymore—it needs a lot of restoration work to sail anywhere. It hasn't had a refit in decades."

Diana waited politely before nudging Muriel along. "With Fredrick not working, I suppose he has time now to fix it up. He's a handy fellow with a hammer and saw, isn't he?"

Muriel shook her head. "I think he got more than he could handle. Fredrick could barely hang a picture on a wall their entire marriage. But on the boat, he *did* manage to make it stop leaking water. It took him three months. The interior is looking better. They have a lovely huge bed in the front…"

"That's called the bow, Muriel."

Muriel ignored her correction. "…and Frederick was working hard on scraping and repainting the grand spiral staircase…"

"Spiral stairs in a sailboat? I can't even imagine it."

"Yes, the original owner was a rich man and built a fantastic miniature spiral staircase to get below in the boat. Those stairs were in all the sailing magazines. Quite the sensation. You know Ann—she probably went along with it because it was famous at one time."

"Did Fredrick finish the staircase?"

Muriel's eyes grew large in surprise. "Barely. Didn't you hear about the… you know?"

Diana slid forward in her seat with interest, her eyes as beady as the seagull's had been, pinning Muriel down. "No," she breathed with anticipation. This was what Diana lived for.

"They discovered Frederick had cancer, so he stopped renovating the boat to go on treatments for three months. They left him so thin and tired."

"Cancer! Has… Has he recovered?"

"He did… except for… you know."

"Except?" Diana's eyes were wide.

"Fredrick started drinking again. Ann did everything she could think of to stop him. She thought she had him under control just before…you know… it happened."

"It?"

Muriel took in a breath. "You haven't heard? Oh, this was so dreary. He... *died*."

"Oh my god! I'm so sorry to hear that! It seems so unfair after he recovered from cancer and then the drinking to... just die."

"It *was* unfair. Ann was crushed by the ordeal."

Diana sipped her coffee, her eyes no less bright with curiosity. Buying time for her next nosy question, no doubt. She asked, "Um, what did Frederick... succumb to?"

Muriel answered reluctantly, sorry she'd even allowed herself to get into this, but knew it was too late to back out now. Diana must have her news... "It - it was terrible. Fredrick was doing alright, considering. He tired easily so he and Ann went to bed early Thursday evening and went to sleep. You know how she never sleeps so she took a couple of pills and nodded off."

Diana listened for more, looking into Muriel's eyes like a cocker spaniel seeking a snack. More?

Under her prompting gaze, Muriel continued uncomfortably, "Well, just after they both nodded off, the medics figured around eight o'clock, Fredrick had a sudden heart attack and died. Ann, of course, having taken her pills, slept right through it and didn't wake up until one o'clock in the afternoon the next day. By the time she showered and had a walk it was almost three o'clock before she tried waking him."

"Oh, my lord! That's... what... over seventeen hours of soundly sleeping with her husband's corpse?"

Muriel was silent, fighting the sudden tears. "That *wasn't* the worst of it."

"Sleeping half a day with a dead husband?" Diana challenged, shaking her head. "How could it *possibly* get worse—?" She stopped short, her expression changing from judgemental to apologetic. "Oh, I am sorry. I've got you sobbing. Here's a hanky."

Muriel accepted and dabbed at her eyes. In a thin voice, she went on. "They phoned the ambulance people who came, sirens screaming, lights flashing. Ann was hysterical, of course, but she met them on the docks to show them the way. They ran their gurney down the wharf bumping over power cables and scaring the seagulls. They had to shove two shopping carts out of the way, too. Such a commotion."

"Good heavens."

"At last they arrived at Ann's sailboat and ran in with their kits. Ann said they could barely get around that awkward spiral staircase and to Fredrick's bedside. They pronounced him dead on scene. There was nothing they could do."

"Poor, old Fredrick," Diana murmured in genuine sympathy this time. "Ann must have been devastated."

"She was... and it got much worse."

"Worse?" Diana was incredulous.

"Oh yes. After being dead all that time, Fredrick was as... er... stiff as a board. The medics had to... 'manage' his body out of the sail-boat..." Muriel swallowed with difficulty.

"Up a spiral staircase?"

"Yes! Ann said it was dreadful. You remember how tall dear Fredrick was."

"Yes, he had to be six-foot-six. The center of the basketball team in Oxford," said Diana, not sure where the conversation was leaning.

"Yes, well..." Muriel swallowed again. "The ambulance people couldn't get him past the spiral staircase. Too tall and stiff as a board. They spoke of tying a rope to his feet and shoving him out the big porthole—"

"What!"

"—and into the water—"

Diana gasped and clutched her throat.

"—then fishing him out after they towed him over to the ambulance."

"That's appalling!"

"It was. Ann would have none of it."

"So, what did they do?"

"Then he had to go around the spiral staircase."

"Was it big enough for them?"

"No, so they had… they had to *make* him fit."

Diana shuddered.

"They tried Fredrick… in the stairs and then bent him a bit, here and there like a bit of pipe, until they could wind him through the staircase. Ann said it was awful watching them measuring the stairs, measuring Frederick, then bending him a bit at the knee, arm or the ankle. There were… sounds."

Diana shivered.

"Sadly, Fredrick was now in a very funny shape at the end, but they *could* spin him up through the staircase at the last. He was… shaped like a boomerang, actually. Ann said the ambulance men were very nice about it."

Diana's shook her head in horror and gasped, "So it was finally done?"

"No. It got worse."

"No!" Diana put her hand over her mouth in amazement. "Poor Ann!"

"Well, now Frederick was bent semi-circular, kind of like a part of a broken hula hoop. They loaded him onto the gurney. Ann tried to cover him with a blanket, but he was so bent up, nothing helped. They pushed Fredrick along the dock trying not to lose him over the side. Of course, there was quite a crowd watching by this time, oohing and gasping. Somebody shouted he looked like a sex doll. Well, that really made Ann start bawling."

"Some people! What then?"

"They arrived at the ambulance with Fredrick but couldn't get him in properly because he was all bent and out of shape. While the crowd was watching… those blighters… and Ann sobbing… the medics climbed up onto the gurney, both sat on him, twisted and pushed until they squished him all straight again. Apparently, Fredrick's body made all sorts of embarrassing noises… gas you know. Perfectly natural they kept saying."

Diana looked as if she was going to be ill.

"Then they stuffed Frederick into the ambulance, slammed the doors and drove away. That's why I'll not live on a sailboat," concluded Muriel with conviction.

Diana slowly shook her head. "Neither will I...."

They both stood and leaned over the guardrail to watch over all the boats in the harbour, imagining living in the nicest one while the white Gull swooped in and cleaned off their table.

A BLUE SHOE

THOSE OF YOU WHO'VE READ 'THE DARK SIDE' WILL RECOGNIZE THE SIGNIFICANCE OF BETH AND HER SHOE. THIS WAS HER STORY.

Beth

She was a stoolie, a cop snitch, until someone in the Carzoni Gang killed her and tossed her into the river. Her waterlogged blue Nike shoe washed up on a beach a month later.

Beth's murder was no one's fault in particular and everyone's in general. She'd been thrust, cajoled and pushed into a job she wasn't ready for. At the start she was eager and competent then crumpled, limping along until she met her end. Only Inspector Shirley MacDonald, Shirley Mac as she was called by her few friends, knew enough to be horrified.

Shirley recruited Beth, a young woman she judged to be a good fit, fresh face and a good enough actor. Beth knew Montreal well because she grew up there, but she'd never see anyone she knew in the seedy part of Montreal she was assigned to. The experts said Beth would travel under the radar, a grain of sand in a region of millions. Satisfied, Shirley Mac handed her over to "the experts" to train and look after. Beth jumped through all the hoops with ease.

At first Beth looked like a success story. Smooth, smart, fitting in easily. Evidence from her operation trickled in steadily, promising to become a flood. There were handshakes and backslaps up and down the Head Office chain of command. When Beth was brilliant, they all stood in her reflected glory. Promotions and medals would come later.

When Beth struggled, they watched her flounder from a distance, turning away, hoping everything would work out for the girl. It was only when her shoe turned up they knew it had become a fucking disaster. Bring in damage control to tamp down the story and make it go away.

Maybe it was business as usual for everyone else. They shrugged her off as cannon fodder... targeted...nothing to see here, but Beth's murder appalled and shamed Shirley Mac.

When Shirley Mac asked her bosses for a full investigation, they forbid it as it could jeopardize the "bigger fish" they were seeking, arguing Beth knew what she signed up for. More likely they were afraid Head Office would look bad. No questions were to be asked until at least her replacement, Terry Reid's evidence had run its course in court and sent the gang members to jail. Some but not all.

Terry Reid had followed in Beth's footsteps, or footstep, completing Beth's failed mission. Shirley Mac didn't make the same mistake twice, choosing a complete unknown this time around. Terry was a stranger to Quebec and Montreal with no family or connections to trip her up. A bolt from the blue. And this time Shirley Mac watched her back, in person, gun handy, every passing day.

This young new informer was as ruthless as Beth was kind, silently lashing out as she saw fit against those who forever seemed to escape conviction. Shirley Mac, deep down in her soul, agreed with Terry's actions, but didn't have the guts them carry it out—to decide to kill a killer; to go rogue. But Terry was made of different stuff and was secretive. But there was that look in her eyes and those persistent rumours about her...

The top brass was kept out of Terry's story as much as possible. They could gloat and backslap when this operation was completely over.

When it was over, Terry and Shirley Mac both barely survived death by the Carzoni Gang, making it out scared, scarred but lucky to be alive, loaded with incriminating evidence. All the baddies would supposedly do prison time. No mercy but don't get your hopes up. A few got out on appeal from scared judges, bored government prosecutors and unsavoury, expensive lawyers.

Now finishing her time as an informer, Terry had a long road back through endless debriefings while trying to live a normal life again. No more of her "Tammy" persona and the dark secrets she carried. She turned a page in her life.

Shirley Mac also turned a page from being Terry Reid's guardian to being back to living a normal life in Montreal. She transitioned to special projects work from home with a monthly pilgrimage to visit the minions in Ottawa Head Office. She didn't have to face her irritating boss each and every workday. Her boss probably suggested it as an opportunity to get Shirley Mac out of the office, anyway.

A call interrupted Shirley's thoughts. "M.E.'s office. Dr. May speaking. I did as you requested. Best come down here, Inspector. You'll need to witness this."

"I'll be there in an hour. Does that work?"

"Yes. Are you sure you want to open this case?"

"No doubt about it."

This called for a drive to the morgue to see the opening of Pandora's Box or shoe in this case.

Dr. May Hall had become Shirley's go-to M.E. or medical examiner, running rings around anyone else the Head Office had to offer. Her boss, Smythe, either scared good ME's away or attracted ass kissers with the exception of Dr. Hall. He steered clear of her after she'd once frightened him severely during an autopsy. May intentionally popped an eye ball into his face. He screamed and ran. She still laughed about it to this day.

Shirley Mac arrived an hour later, parking in the lot in front of the nondescript, dirty and neglected unmarked building front. Her ID card opened this door to the disquieting horrors that must be kept from searing her soul. She pushed the main door open and headed down the stairs to the dreary basement dungeon and a door marked

"Forensics". The building was dedicated to refrigeration for people, long dead and a collection of their bits and parts. The archeology of the recently deceased and dismembered or at least until they incinerate them.

What a hell hole.

Creepy old Dr. May Hall greeted her, standing in a gown and gloves, stiff white hair untamed, her face untouched by makeup except for bright purple lipstick. Crazy smart or just crazy?

Shirley sometimes suspected Dr. Hall enjoyed her job far too much. Did this job ever get to her after twenty-years and counting, or was it her way of holding off madness? Ignoring the unwashable stench of sad forgotten victims? Winnowing the story their stone-cold bodies told? Dr. Hall reminded Shirley Mac of a cross between Betty White and Albert Einstein. She was tall and birdlike with glasses in a 1950's style with lenses as thick as coke bottles. She rarely blinked. Her manner was sharp and automatic. She was old, possibly mid-to-late sixties. Shirley suspected that Dr. Hall would never retire without a fight and her supervisors were afraid to try.

Dr. Hall motioned for Shirley to follow her to a well-lit steel table. Shirley followed reluctantly shuddering in uneasy anticipation.

Reluctantly, Shirley Mac looked at the bright metal table in front of Dr. Hall. A lone shoe perched in the middle, the center of their world today. Nothing else. A blue shoe on a shiny mirrored surface. She relaxed a little—not a lot—she knew Dr. Hall too well to lower her guard completely.

Dr. May Hall looked to her, gravely. "This shoe's been in the fridge for six months, untouched. The upper brass is afraid to open the case, but since you ordered me to examine it, I thought you should be the first to know my findings."

Shirley grumbled, "Head office is scared shitless of calling any attention to the case of Bethany. They whispered the bare minimum about the shoe when it was found then hid it as fast as they could."

"Unusual," said Dr. Hall.

You have no idea. "What did you find, Dr. Hall?" Shirley Mac had never gotten friendly enough to call her May.

Dr. Hall pulled out the lace of the lone shoe. It was unbroken. "What do you notice about the lace?"

"Like new—why?" asked Shirley Mac, moving closer, still unsure where this conversation was going.

"After approximately a month underwater you'd think it would show some deterioration but it doesn't." Dr. Hall looked up at her and shrugged. "These are different. With this carbon fiber lace you could still tie someone up... or strangle them." Dr. Hall snapped the lace taunt, her sharp eyes bulging, as if she could step over and pop the laces around Shirley Mac's neck.

Despite herself, Shirley lurched backwards, her mouth dropping open, realizing for the first time she had harboured the distant hope that somehow Beth was still alive. "Is that a cop-issued lace—the ones informants have?"

"Yes." Dr. Hall slowly pulled the shoe open and slid out an emaciated woman's foot with green toenail polish. "A brief local investigation decided it probably belonged to a lost police officer but nothing definitive. Of course, you know they put a halt to actually identifying the foot, right? Why did everyone get so shy all of a sudden, I can't help wondering. We've all known this was Beth for months. At your request we finally did a DNA test on this foot."

Shirley Mac's heart shot into her throat as she braced herself against an immovable force.

"This is confirmation... it's Constable Bethany Drew's left foot."

Shirley covered her mouth with both hands as tears poured down her cheeks, tears she'd denied herself for too long. In a muffled cry, she managed to say, "It was to protect her replacement —ensure the sting continued. They couldn't afford a bright public light on what we were doing in Montreal. Beth was all but forgotten."

"Until now." Dr. Hall nodded concisely and continued, "I've had this test done by three different labs and they all came back the same."

Shirley watched Dr Hall's mouth moving like the TV with the sound turned off as she carefully pointed out various particular technical details. She could only cry more.

"Can I write this up and send this to you?" Dr. Hall asked, looking at Shirley Mac with those big magnified eyes.

Shirley nodded clumsily and rushed out, barely halting outside the building's front door to throw up in the flower bed. Then she wove unsteadily to her car, shut herself inside bawling her eyes out, incapable of driving.

She cried in her car quite often but made a point to never show emotion in front of the ME's or families. Internalized, personal grief. She was an old-school officer.

———

D r. Hall heard the door boom closed as Shirley Mac fled. Very unusual.

She was disturbed by the Inspector's reaction to the official foot ID. She had known Shirley Mac for decades as a solid and impervious person. It could be a lurid child murder, rape or horrific accident but Shirley never wrinkled an eyebrow. Ice water in her veins. Block of granite. Nothing ever fazed her... until today. She'd been crushed!

Shrugging away the thought, Dr. Hall looked up at the clock and saw it was lunch hour. Time for some fresh air. She made a point of going outside and eating her cheese sandwiches on the edge of the big stone fountain by the parking lot. Quiet. The cherry trees were in bloom with their own sweet smell, a break from the stench of bleach, formaldehyde and alcohol. A pleasant change.

The fuzzy bumble bees would buzz in agreement.

It didn't bother her that everyone gave her a wide berth. Her husband Bert, bless his heart, said her thick old school glasses made her look cerebral and severe. What about contacts? He'd passed away two years ago, rendering the discussion moot.

These days Dr. Hall knew her old lunch bag had two simple cheese sandwiches and nothing more. It made her sad to think about it. She hoped the trees and bees would cheer her up.

She walked out to her usual spot and was surprised to see Shirley Mac still there in her ghost car, grief stricken, slumped forward on the steering wheel. The poor woman was taking Beth's ID very badly. Perhaps she'd hoped on hopes Beth was still alive by some miracle. Irrational.

Dr. Hall walked to the passenger side of the car and tapped on the glass. With a surprised expression, Shirley powered down the window.

"Sorry to intrude, Inspector, but I saw you were still here. Can I sit and eat my lunch? Your car has the best view of the cherry trees."

Shirley Mac nodded, her eyes puffy and red. She unlocked the door. "I... I'm not good company, Dr. Hall."

"Call me May." Dr. Hall opened the passenger door and slid onto the cheap vinyl cop car seat.

Shirley pulled herself together. "Call me... call me Shirley Mac."

"Ah, Shirley Mac! You use Shirley Mac so you don't get confused with Shirley O'Doole in Regional coordination."

"Shirley O... yes."

May offered her one of her two sandwiches. "Hungry?"

Shirley hesitated, eyeing the sandwich suspiciously.

May added, "Our lunches are sealed in a separate food fridge. It's all good. I am a doctor."

"I – I have been accused of having a cast iron stomach from too much old cold coffee and takeout food. Sure, why not?"

They both munched on the sandwiches. May liked a good long silence but felt an icebreaker was needed. "If you roll all the windows down, we can smell the cherry trees and hear the bees."

Shirley powered them all down. They sat in silence for five minutes. A bumble bee flew through the car but didn't stop.

May thought another icebreaker was required. "You are probably wondering why I still use this beat up old lunch bag."

Shirley shrugged, and made a face that said, *Not really.*

Undeterred, May continued, "This lunch bag reminds me of my husband, Bert."

Shirley expression went from blank to embarrassed.

So, she didn't know who Bert was. Well—almost no one knew, to be fair. May let her off the hook. "Bert passed away two years ago, and

I think of him every day, especially at lunch. He always made me a sandwich or two and added in a bit of fruit, yogurt and sometimes a piece of candy. Once and a while he'd add a little poem or a note saying how dear I was to him. Such a lovely man."

Shirley's expression softened.

May turned the old lunch bag towards her. "I can't bring myself to throw this bag away. It still has one of his poems on it. 'Roses are red and violets are blue. Come home early 'cuz I have something for you;-)'."

Shirley's eyes looked brighter. "What did he have for you, May?"

"It seems he needed my pickup to haul an old fridge to the city dump." May chuckled. "Bert made a big deal of touring me around, afterwards. He took a selfie photo of us both standing in front of a big old broken Zellers sign, way in the back. Bert placed it in a frame for an anniversary present."

"La dump grand tour?" asked Shirley with a gentle laugh, clearly enjoying the story.

"Yes. Then he had a sudden heart infarction and died a week later."

"That's terrible, May."

"He didn't suffer but it was hard." May nodded, taking a breath. "I cried my tears and moved on, but I remember him every day."

Shirley considered her story and murmured, "Moving on is hard."

"It is—but you do it."

Shirley ate the last of her sandwich. "Thank you, May. I... I should be off."

"You are welcome," May smiled, getting out of the passenger's seat. Last thing she did was lean in towards Shirley. "Cry your tears, then get the evil son-of-a-bitch who killed Beth."

———

It was two days after Shirley notified the parents that she received a cardboard box from Dr. May Hall marked, "Case: Bethany Drew. Confidential".

Shirley opened the box and found Dr. Hall's thorough report on

Beth, including some tidbits of evidence unseen at the time, such as the shoe was contaminated with lime residue from concrete. The heel was damaged from being dragged a distance. Part of a story of a mystery.

And in the box was Beth's shoe, enclosed in a plastic bag, numbered and catalogued.

Shirley cuddled the box like it was the most important item on earth. Time to grab the commuter train to Head Office in Ottawa. She might get fired today, but she was on a mission.

She always found it weird to have to run her special ID card through the entrance, then to be frisked by a junior officer once inside. It was embarrassing when it was an officer she had trained. "Gotta check your boobs and crotch for weapons, Inspector. Regulations." Head Office experienced this at CIA head office and immediately aped it to prove they were just as security conscious. Bullshit.

They'd never frisk Constable Reid like that and live to tell the tale, not that she'd ever come through the front doors, anyway. Old Alfred, Terry's handler, once smuggled in six loaded sniper rifles for the ballistics department. The stuff of legends. Heads rolled while he laughed in their faces.

Cheeky behavior like that got him sent to Afghanistan.

The security officer flipped the lid of the box up and looked in. "A box with a shoe in it?" she asked.

"Informant Constable Bethany Drew."

The officer jumped back like she'd been given thirty thousand volts. "Shit... er... sorry Inspector."

Shirley Mac glowered at the officer's impertinence and slammed the lid down and stomped over to the elevator, fumbled with the box, swiped her ID card and pushed the eighth-floor button for Inspector Smythe. He was an incompetent creep, but she needed his okay to go further with Beth's investigation. She'd already stuck her neck out by notifying the family, officially, though they already knew unofficially through the media. That wasn't how it was supposed to work.

Typical Smythe malarkey.

Constable Clark typed on his desk computer watching for the ten o'clock for Inspector Smythe. Clark wasn't happy about this receptionist assignment, but he'd been told if he could endure Inspector Smythe for a year it was "gold" for a transfer anywhere he wanted to go. His first choice would be the Washington DC consulate. Easy touch and rubbing elbows with the new American people running the world. So cool! An inspector carrying an awkward box arrived, awaking him from his thoughts.

"Inspector MacDonald to see Inspector Smythe at ten," she said tersely.

"Thanks, take a seat. It's nine fifty-eight." Inspector Shirley MacDonald? Clark and everyone else in the head office had heard of her. Tough, pushy and no B.S. Smythe cringed when Shirley Mac came to visit.

"Inspector Smythe is expecting me at ten and it's now ten thirty-five. What's the hold up, Constable Clark?"

"Um, he's busy at the moment... "

"Busy doing what? Clipping his fucking toenails?" she barked.

Probably. At the moment Clark feared the wrath of Shirley Mac sitting near him more than Smythe's temper. "Let me check." He pushed the intercom "Inspector MacDonald to see you at ten, sir?"

Smythe irritably said, "Yeah, I suppose you can send her in."

Shirley stood with her box and stomped past Clark into Smythe's office. The door slammed closed behind her. Clark dug out his earbuds and started to type dictated notes. Might be a screaming match in there.

Without a hello or a salute Shirley dropped the evidence box unceremoniously on Inspector Smythe's desk. "We need to look into the case of Bethany Drew's murder. She paid the ultimate price."

Smythe sniffed at the box with little interest and shook his head. "There'll be no official investigation—you know this. You could jeopardize the case against the people residing in prison or waiting on appeal."

Or cause an internal shit storm of investigations why it all went wrong.

Shirley despised Smythe on a good day. An incompetent groper. She barely kept it civil. "I can do this case quietly. I've run hundreds of investigations. I know what I'm doing." *And I'm ten times more qualified than you!*

"You'll do nothing."

"I notified her next of kin. It's long overdue."

He reddened, "You had no authorization!"

"I'm the supervisory officer on this operation—I *have* authority!"

They both knew Smythe had claimed the operation as his when Beth was doing well and left it in limbo when everything started to go wrong. The case had been buried for months now, with Smythe undoubtedly wanting it to stay that way.

His face twisted, Smythe spat, "So, do nothing else—drop it. Constable Drew is long gone. There will be *no* official investigation. Get over it and get rid of that box of evidence while you're at it! I'm busy here with important work. Dismissed!"

Shirley was unmoved. "I have a sixty-day vacation coming and it starts tomorrow." She grabbed the box and stormed out of Smythe's office. This wasn't over.

Constable Clark bent lower at his computer avoiding eye contact as Smythe's door crashed open and Shirley shot out. Someday Smythe would push someone too far and Clark wanted to be here when it happened.

In defiance, Shirley Mac took the evidence home, plunked it on her kitchen table and removed the lid. Inside, she was disappointed to find only a few newspaper clippings and a basic report from the officer who'd arrived at the scene where the running shoe was reported. Is that it? She removed the shoe, closed the box up and placed the running shoe on top to keep herself focused.

Shaking her head, she reached into her upper cupboard, retrieved a bottle of rum and one somewhat clean glass. Lambs Navy. Good enough for her military dad; good enough for her. Sinking onto a kitchen chair, she a poured a stiff one. It was late and she was tired. Time to go through the meagre evidence, such as it was, with a fine-tooth comb. She'd see what was on the cop internal personnel files, if Smythe hadn't had them deleted by now.

Picking fly shit from pepper.

It was two a.m. and she was half a bottle in when she finally put the sparse evidence back in the box and stored it up in her bedroom closet shelf. She was struggling with this case. It was so personal to her, which clouded logic and objectivity. Where to start? There was so very little to go on. A pro hit, for sure. Smythe would banish her forever if he caught her getting outside help. Terry was tied up with the informant debrief so she was unavailable. Who to call? Who could she trust?

She finally got to bed, exhausted but sleep didn't come easily. Her mind was alive with possibilities based on too few facts. It was just before three when she fell into an uneasy night of dreams, demons and defragging memories.

"Hey Inspector. Remember me?" asked a nearby voice.

Shirley bolted upright, grabbing for any weapon and finding nothing better than a pillow. "W-who's there?"

"Going to smother me with that pillow, inspector? I'm already dead."

Shirley struggled to focus in the low light, barely making out a face and a body sitting nearby. Too much rum? "Beth? Can't be!"

"It is!" said the pale face. "I see you found my other shoe… and my foot."

Shirley gaze trailed down Beth's pale body, barely making out one blue shoe alongside an empty pant leg. Oh God.

"Sorry to surprise you but I'm glad to see you're on the case."

Shirley shook her head. "Case? Not much of a case… Beth. I don't know where to start. I have your shoe and a few newspaper clippings. Officially your story ends when you disappeared. That's it. Very little evidence."

"Was there none to begin with or did someone snitch it?"

Good question. "Could be either. The net result is the same."

Beth's apparition smiled. "As you used to tell me in cop school; start at the beginning and don't miss the funeral which is Tuesday, now that they've released a bit of me to bury."

"No, I said start at the beginning of a case, be methodical. Lurk around the funerals to see who shows up and question them later. Watch to see who really cries and who cries fake tears."

"Whatever…"

"Tuesday?"

"Tuesday at two. Don't be late."

Shirley found herself sitting up in bed, soaked with sweat. "What the…?" Beth was gone. Rum, stress, lack of food and sleep…had to be!

A Funeral

Beth's distraught parents requested a simple, low key funeral service with no police attendance. They deliberately kept the funeral date and time a secret from the cops and media but Shirley Mac found out.

Beth's childhood wish to be a cop had killed her and they had no wish to be reminded of it. The late official notification of her death and the *very* late release of her remains hadn't help. Shirley Mac persisted, insisting she was a friend and not just a policeman. They finally relented and gave her permission with the proviso she stay in the back.

How the hell did she find out?

Beth's funeral was held on a dreary, rainy day in Montreal. The dark clouds and chilly breeze ensured only the committed would come. Shirley estimated about twenty-five people did. In the church it was hard to define who was who. The urn was front and center complete with a big Stetson hat, the only grudging concession to Beth's career.

A large photo stood to the left of the urn. It was Beth when she'd graduated from University, in her grad gown. Her expression was confident, expectant. Solid, plain and adaptable.

The organ droned on. The preacher spoke of Beth's courage, her choice to join the police and her undetermined demise, at least for the hurting ears of the attendees. All heads were bowed so Shirley couldn't identify anyone. Outside would be better.

Standing around the outdoor internment on the Columbarium, or "putting the ash pot in the shelf" Shirley Mac was able to take in the pecking order of attendees and slyly snap a few pictures for identification later. Family members were closest, friends a few steps back, with strangers on the periphery where Shirley stood vigilantly studying every face.

Shirley Mac felt badly for the family who obviously were crushed by this event. They knew Beth was quietly doing something important and weren't prepared for her untimely, unexplained death. "Found her foot in a shoe". They were told nothing about what it meant or why it took so long for official word of the case advancing from a missing person to be confirmed deceased.

Beth's friends weren't numerous. Maybe childhood pals or family friends? They seemed out of touch with events but supportive. She watched closely to see who was family, who was a friend and who were merely looky-loos. The ones on the fringe, out here braving the rain were the ones she found particularly interesting.

There weren't many on the edge. Shirley Mac counted five. Nobody familiar to her. One male was dressed cheaply but perfect for this rainy day. Their mailman? An old flame?

There were a couple of little old ladies under the tree, nearby, standing under a grey umbrella. Was Dr. May Hall one of the old ladies? They both wore the old school plastic disposable head scarves to keep their hair dry. Do they still make those?

On the other side of the funeral group, detached, were two men in Armani suits, lurking in the rain. Tall, big, good looking but out of place. She made a note to herself to find them later.

The preacher declared the service over, inviting the soggy chilled people to come for tea and little sandwiches. Shirley decided holding a cup of tea while balancing a sweet would make the best fly-on-the-wall disguise. On the way over to the tea house she snapped images of the two men's licence plate. A Porsche. Might have to do a bit of stalking, later.

The tea was uneventful, not counting the evil eye she got from the family, imagining their thoughts flying at her like spears—"You got our Bethany murdered! That tea and cupcake cost us $5!" Apparently they now regretted softening and allowing her to attend.

While she circulated, she bumped into Dr. Hall... er... *May* in the corner, complete with purple lipstick. Everyone else had given May a wide berth, assuming, Shirley guessed, that May was merely a funeral groupie.

Shirley glanced around to assure privacy before murmuring, "Hi May. Nice day for a funeral."

May shrugged. "I don't usually come to these, but I've been wondering who would show up. I heard Smythe wanted this case abandoned. You don't seem the type to walk away from something like this. I might spot something to help."

"That would be great. Who's your friend with the umbrella?"

"She's a funeral lurker pal of mine. She was coming already, so we came as a pair of loopy ladies. I need to get out of the house more."

Shirley barely suppressed a smile. "Good cover, May."

With that, May's "partner" joined them, and the trio stood silently, observing the funeral tea. Lots of hugging, tears and condolences. A few didn't hug anyone. Cold or very angry?

May spoke quietly to Shirley Mac, "See the boys in the Armani suits?"

"I did. Got their car license number. A Porsche. Not cheap."

"Recognize them?"

"Um... should I?"

"They're pro sports players. Probably hockey by their lanky builds. They're dressed like their fairly successful. Team Laval logos on their left sides. Some type of pro's," May pointed out.

"Wow—good catch! I'll have a chat with those lads and see where they fit in."

When the funeral tea came to an end, they all went home, Shirley feeling glum, damp and depressed. It had been a difficult first day of the first vacation she'd had in nine years. To celebrate, Shirley had a dinner of Lambs Navy rum, stewed in front of the TV for a few hours, skipped a shower and went straight to bed, where she tossed and turned in her sleep, looking at the funeral from every angle. Then heard a voice...

"So, how was my funeral?"

Shirley bolted upright, "What?" The Beth dream was happening again! "How did you get in here?"

"I don't know. Haunting your dreams?"

"A 'Lambs' ghost?"

"No idea. I asked how was my funeral, today? Huge crowd?"

Shirley thought before speaking. "Hey, this is my dream, so your funeral went alright. Twenty-five-ish people. Damp and cold."

"Twenty-five? That's it? I have more relatives out in Toronto, alone!"

"Raining and cold. You know..."

Beth slouched, sulking. "Gone and forgotten already. What a crock. Were the triplets from Hamilton there?"

"Didn't see any triplets."

"Shit."

This is my dream so why not ask? "But two big hunks in Armani's and a Porsche came. Know them?"

Beth smiled at hearing this which looked completely weird. "Marcel and Adam? They remembered me! Wow, they almost made it to the pro's!"

"Pro's?"

"Yes, almost the NHL. They're minor pro's in Laval right now. I went out with them back in their junior A team days. Nice guys."

"Double teaming?"

Beth looked hurt. "No! Just hanging out. University."

"Ah. Why were they there?"

"I don't know. It's been four years since I've seen them. You're the experienced detective."

Beth vanished before Shirley could answer, finding herself talking to her closet. She shook her head, went to the bathroom and back to bed. No more late-night drinking!

The next day she was up early, made some calls and learned an Adam Noble owned the Porsche that was at Beth's funeral, just as

Beth's ghost said. She drove to his listed address and hunkered down to watch the place for a few hours, debating if she should or would make contact.

What to say? She could open with "Hi, Beth the ghost told me in my drunken dream that you two were friends in university". Probably not. Shit. Shirley sat outside the Noble residence... not a huge house really... and saw he was living with his parents. All grown up and mom's still cooking and doing his laundry? Maybe hockey players don't get paid that much. She noticed his folks were home. After two hours she had to pee and was thirsty so got ready to drive away when the Porsche arrived with two young men. They parked on the curb and went inside.

Shirley considered her options, all of which included going inside herself, to talk. "Do you give autographs you young studs?" or "I've been stalking you since the funeral..." Oh hell! She got out of her car and went to the door. As she was ready to ring the doorbell, she heard a huge argument taking place inside. Sounded like it was the whole family.

A man shouted—the father, she assumed, while the Mother chimed in. "You went to the God damned funeral? What the hell for? What if someone recognized you? You're trying to make the NHL!"

Shirley jumped at the chance. "Open up in there! Police!" she shouted, hammering the door.

There was sudden silence in the house. After some murmuring, the mother opened the door looking worried and sheepish. "Um, yes?"

Shirley put on her annoyed beat cop face, flashing her badge so fast it was unlikely the lady could get her name. "We've had reports of a domestic dispute going on in here. Open up!"

The woman stepped back, opening the door without complaint and Shirley waltzed in like she owned the place. She noted the two men from the funeral, Adam and Marcel seated closely together on a couch with an older man standing in front of them, red faced and angry.

She demanded, irritably, "What's going on here? Do I have to take names—and you all go down town?" She hoped they wouldn't want that. Totally not going to happen.

The older man pleaded, "No, please, officer. We were just having a discussion, that's all. My son Adam and his... er... friend Marcel play top shelf hockey you see..."

"Ah. So, nothing to see here, is that what you're saying sir?"

The mother piped in, "That's correct. It's all good. You look tired."

Shirley frowned in confusion. What was this woman attempting?

"Would you like some coffee officer? A homemade muffin perhaps?" The father shot the mother an angry glance, which she ignored, focused completely on Shirley's welfare for some reason. "How about it, officer?"

It occurred to Shirley the woman wanted someone in the house so the argument didn't restart. She could do that. Win/win. "Sure. May I borrow your bathroom. It's been a long day."

"Yes, it's on the left."

"Thank you." Shirley headed for the washroom and heard the urgent mumbling crackle back to life in the background. *I've seemed to have stumbled on to something.* She finished up, flushed, washed her hands and had a quick peek through their medicine cabinet in record time, finding nothing of interest. Coffee and a muffin were waiting. Homemade? "Wonderful," she murmured to her reflection.

Everyone was seated on the edge of their seats watching her like she was the only worm on the chicken house floor.

She opened the conversation. "So, who am I speaking to?"

The father hesitated, then pointed, "Adam, Glynnis and I'm Gord Noble. Adam's buddy here is Marcel Hefner."

"I see." She sat down in an easy chair and made a quick scribbled note inside her note pad—like it mattered—before she sipped her "fresh coffee" which was seriously luke-warm instant, and the stale as stone muffin. Blah. Nevertheless, she sent Glynnis a phony appreciative glance before continuing. "I hope everything is alright here. Sounded like quite an argument going. What was it all about, sir?"

Gord Noble broke into a bit of a sweat under Shirley's watchful eye. "Well, I...er...was just making sure the boys didn't miss hockey practice, that's all. It's almost the pro's, you know."

"They had attended a funeral instead of a practice?"

"Yes, indeed but it was an important practice and they went drinking afterwards."

Shirley hoped they didn't recognize her from the day before. "And was it a big funeral, sir? A family member perhaps?"

Glynnis tactlessly blurted out, "Just some girl cop they used to hang out with."

"Oh Mom! Don't! Oh no..." Adam protested.

Shirley looked at the Glynnis and slowly repeated, "Just some "girl cop"?"

This time Gord protested, "No offense, please. The cops... um... police are very important to us all... bless 'em."

"Good to hear it," Shirley added, nonplussed. "And how did they know this... police person?" She looked at Adam.

"We went to school with her—Bethany Drew—at McGill together. We played co-ed Ultimate Frizbee."

"Anything else? Did either or both of you... develop a 'close relationship' with Bethany?"

"No!" Marcel protested, maybe too much, actually. He flushed and added, "Just friends."

Then Gord said between clenched teeth. "Marcel and Adam were... already going out."

Shirley looked at him, slow to understand what he meant. Finally, the penny dropped. "Ah, I see." They'd been seen together at the funeral and the Gord obviously wanted to keep their relationship from their hockey team. It should be none of the father's, or team's business but it was a nosy world. This was probably the real subject of the argument.

"Will this be kept quiet, officer?" asked Glynnis, very concerned.

She seriously thought Shirley would be reporting these boys' true relationship down at the cop shop? Paranoid or what?

"At this point, yes. Just following up on a concerned neighbor's report. Thank you for the coffee and the muffin. I must go. Please, here's my card if you should need help."

The older woman stared at the card as if it would explode before handing it off to Marcel, who, in turn, glanced at it briefly and stuck it in his pocket.

"Can I wrap the muffin so you can take it with you?" Glynnis offered a bit breathlessly, standing suddenly, obviously anxious for the police officer to leave her home.

"Sure, that'd be lovely." Good doorstop.

Shirley said her goodbyes and climbed into her car wondering how the hell a dream with Beth managed to tell her the correct date and time of her funeral and the names of Adam and Marcel. Beth knew them, she didn't, yet she'd learned this in a dream? Strangely they had both turned up at the funeral after not seeing Beth for years. Guilt, fear or neglect? Some mutual pact?

At home, Shirley found herself eating the stale muffin as she picked through official information and general internet stories about Beth. Not many facts at this stage. Start at the beginning, she heard herself telling her own trainees, and followed her own advice. Beth completed high school in Montreal, average marks, went to McGill and got a Bachelor of fine arts in Languages, worked at Starbucks and a bike shop for two years.

Then Beth had abruptly quit working at the bike shop, applied to the Police Force and was accepted. She did well in "Training Depot" earning top marks. After two years as a beat cop in St. Johns she applied for an informant job.

She'd seemed to have the qualifications—no attachments, was relatively unknown herself, passed all the courses designed to stress her under those conditions, had a superb memory, was bilingual, and had the ability to be an entirely different person. This new persona could easily transform into a law-breaking insider, eagerly following the crime boss's instructions while keeping track of the details for later prosecutions. Beth would dance around a fine line of good and evil. She would be their Kim Philby the splendid soviet spy who duped MI5 for decades.

Shirley took a breath and marveled how well Beth's replacement did in the same role. Terry Reid survived, thrived and learned under those dreadful conditions, had possibly enjoyed every minute of it. That reaction could never be discovered on a form or an interview. They only learned if the informer could handle the pressure when they were thrown to the wolves—and their handlers waited and watched them blend into the pack or perish.

It was midnight before Shirley finally sifted through Beth's preliminary program and training for the Montreal job. It all passed muster to her, at least for now.

Bedtime, a shower and no Lambs Navy and the crazy dreams it caused.

The Hockey Players

Adam Noble drove Marcel home. Between the funeral, Adam's dad screaming at them, and the cop showing up, it had been a harrowing couple of days.

Marcel clutched Shirley Mac's card. "Why the huge deal about Beth's funeral? I don't get it," he complained.

Adam paused before he spoke. "I don't either. We were pals with Beth for years at McGill, she joins the police and vanishes for what... four years? We see her at the Bubbles Car Wash, she's listed in the obituaries as dead. No explanation—just dead. Then a cop "happens by" and asks about it?" He shook his head disbelieving.

"This is crazy. No more funerals unless it's me!"

They both laughed, then stopped when they really thought about it.

"Have you got the stash from the wash?" asked Marcel.

"Yep. Under the seat. We should be able to get rid of it on this next road trip. Money in the bank. Another car payment."

Marcel laughed. "Nobody questions a good Canadian hockey player."

———

S hirley Mac had a shower and snuggled into her big bed. Big, for all the good it was. She hadn't had anyone here since Jean, two years ago. Two years! This must be what a camel feels like on the desert. Thinking of the nights with Jean settled her into sleep in no time.

A voice awoke her.

"Hey, how were Adam and Marcel?"

Shirley cracked one eye open and wearily propped herself against the headboard. She croaked, "I thought I had to be drunk to see you?"

Beth sat on the edge of the bed and looked at her, "No—why? Have you been drinking?"

"Uh... that would be a no."

"And you see me, right?"

"Yes."

"Then you are talking to me, Bethany Drew!"

Shirley Mac looked confused. "Why do I see you, here?"

Beth pointed at the closet. "You have my shoe which is more than anyone else has at this time."

"Like Cinderella's shoe or Dorothy's?"

"Don't overwork this, Shirley."

"Why don't you haunt the morgue? Isn't your foot *there?*"

Beth shook her head. "The morgue already has a hundred ghosts. Besides, it's you I need to see."

"Ah. Dandy."

"I gave you the tip about Adam and Marcel. How'd it work out?"

"I talked to them. All they would say is they knew you from McGill. Nothing more."

"Hmm. Sounds legit. Are they still... a couple?"

"Seems so. The parents were furious."

"Adam's folks must have finally figured it out. So, what's next, Sherlock?"

"Not sure," confessed Shirley. "I might get my head examined to see if I'm going nuts."

"You do that."

"So why don't you just tell me who killed you? Seems obvious."

"I would if I could, but I don't know who did it. I was working at the car wash and I woke up here, with you, dead as a door nail," said Beth with a sigh.

"Was it Bob, Zoo or Ric?"

"Could have been anybody. That's why I need you to find out who did it."

"Can't you just go back in time…some ghostly thing and see who did it?"

"I'm a ghost in the here and now, not Captain Kirk."

And she was gone. *Maybe I really need to talk to someone about this dead spirit stuff.*

———

D r. May Hall carefully examined the latest corpse that arrived. This was a busy place for crime. Sometimes she wished she was an actual police officer but her family had insisted she become a physician instead. A Psychology speciality became boring, so she'd slid into the forensics. It was the perfect job for her.

She heard the door slide open and close behind her.

"Hi May, it's me, Shirley Mac."

"Hi! I'm just putting this brain back in… come on in."

Shirley Mac stood opposite her just as May put the top of the skull in place. She commenced stitching the scalp down with Shirley as a rapped audience. "There! All as it should be," May announced, looking at Shirley for the first time. "How's the blue shoe case going?"

"It's going very slowly."

"Were those young men in the Porsche at the funeral of any help?"

"I met with them and their family yesterday and they said they went to school with Beth, then lost track of her."

"Were they hiding something?" asked May.

"I think the whole family was. There was some big argument going on. They clammed up when I got there."

"Who were they?"

"Adam Noble and his parents and a Marcel Lyon. Minor league pro hockey players for Laval."

"Was it hard to get their names?"

"Um, no. Ah... er... Beth's ghost told me their names the night before."

May raised her gaze to meet Shirley's. "A ghost told you?"

Shirley nodded. "I know you're medical doctor *and* a shrink. Saw your file. I thought I'd come and see if my marbles were escaping. I need to keep this on the Q.T. Smythe would love to lock me up."

May smiled. "Seeing ghosts with insider information, Inspector? You're positive it wasn't a dream?"

"Yes. Happened three nights in a row."

"And you are normally... normal?"

"Very much so. Rock solid. No measurable imagination."

"Drugs or alcohol?"

"No drugs. Some alcohol two of the nights but I stopped. Too spooked."

May took a breath and smiled, turning back to stitching the skull. "I've known you for thirteen years, Shirley. You're solid, dependable, efficient, adaptable, decisive and intelligent. Details and routine are your mantra. The perfect administrator. Shit happens *properly* under your watch."

"Is that good or bad?" Shirley Mac asked with a nervous smile.

"It's a good thing. I'd say you aren't a type who sees ghosts."

"There are types who do?"

"Yes. On a Myers Briggs chart there's a type who can channel ESP, extra sensory perception, and other mental powers. Introverted intuitive feelers. INFJ's like Beth are one type."

"Me?"

"God no. I'd say you were an ESTJ, an organized, bossy administrator—in a good way, of course."

"So, seeing a ghost is out of character for me, therefore possible?"

May smiled, snapping shut her sewing gear. "Who knows? Maybe you hide a well-developed sense of ESP or you're starting a series of psychotic episodes."

"I'll hope for the ESP part, May. Thanks!"

"No problem. I'm here if you start seeing anyone else, like Elvis or Michel Jackson."

"I wouldn't tell you about those, May." Shirley winked. Geez.

Shirley went back to her car and sat, thinking. I need to get organized!

She stopped at Staples and picked up a whiteboard, pens, tape, sticky pads and a stack of yellow paper pads. An under the radar, no budget, old school investigation without spread sheets, experts and tech! Hurrying home, she set up in the empty second bedroom. The whiteboard went on the wall and pictures and print outs were taped up in a flurry. She ignored the rum bottle and made a cup of instant coffee instead.

Focus without ghosts!

Beth's photo was top center. It was her training depot grad picture, Stetson and all. Shirley studied Beth's earnest, serious face. It always made her feel ill.

A voice behind her spoke.

"I was a good-looking babe, you know."

Beth's ghost. In daylight? She turned slowly and faced the ghost. The see-through Beth leaned comfortably on Shirley's folding table, minus one foot.

"Aren't you supposed to appear when I drink or at night or something? There's daylight out there."

"I'm not a vampire! I just appear for some, whatever, non-scientific reason. I don't even believe in ghosts."

"Yet here you are."

"I am what I am. Hey, nice 'Crazy Wall'. I heard that in old cop history. Isn't this supposed to be in a cave wall or something?"

"Funny. It's a 'Detective Relationship Chart' among other things. Who's who in the murder zoo. We solved crimes with these long before computers and spread sheets came along."

"Quaint."

There was an awkward silence as Shirley Mac turned to the "wall" and looked for clues. Once in a while she glanced back, checking to see if Beth was still there and she was, carefully perusing the clues as well. She always was a clever one.

"So, you're at the top as the murder victim, time and relative date. We don't have the actual day yet—just a shoe discovery. There's a list of faces below that are known persons of interest."

"I see Adam and Marcel, Ric, Bob, Zoo and the Carzoni's. I was involved with a lot more people than that."

"Like who?"

"Alfred for one. My handler. Saw him a lot."

"Are you saying he's a suspect? I'm not even sure how to contact him, anymore."

"I'd doubt he was involved but maybe he has something to add. Buy a Grape Fanta pop, drink it and put a rock into the can. Put it into the trash can in front of La Bistro Cinq. Next day go to Lesage Park at ten and wait for him to show up."

Shirley turned to the wall and added "Alfred X" with a yellow sticky paper. "How's that?"

Beth was gone. Apparently, for today, Beth's work was done.

In disguise, Shirley felt silly sitting on a bench, dressed in a yoga outfit, yellow hat and stupid large sunglasses. The pop can contact seemed ridiculous. Was Beth teasing her or was it her own mind stringing her along. Too weird.

It was now ten o'clock in the morning and she saw no Alfred. She spotted a young couple set up on a blanket nearby. They snuggled up on it and laid down, enjoying the sun. Cute guy and a plain girl. The girl didn't seem too keen to be spooned by the guy which struck Shirley as odd.

Aha! An old man hobbled up to the bench on a cheap walker. He unceremoniously flopped down on the bench. "Mind if I sit here, honey?"

"Suit yourself," Shirley answered without interest.

The man ignored her as he fumbled around in a battered paper bag, producing some bird seeds. He flung them in front of him, exciting the pigeons into a feed frenzy.

Shirley barely leaned toward him. "Your guard couple on the blanket aren't very convincing, Alfred."

He stopped, looking carefully at her. "Shirley Mac?"

"The one and only."

"What a get up! I had no idea it was you."

"That's the idea. I'm on vacation and this conversation is off the record. Smythe will have my ass if he knew I was talking to you."

"Smythe. What a useless bag of shit. He might have your ass just for fun," grumbled Alfred, resuming his bird feed tossing.

"Humph. You retired?" she asked.

"I am but I do a little work on the side. Undercover work is too stressful. I'm too old for this. What do you want?"

"The one who murdered Beth."

Alfred looked at her in shock. "I thought that was being swept under the table."

"It was. This is my own project."

"What will you do when you find the perp? Shoot them yourself?"

"I haven't decided. Let's find them first."

"So, you'll search the moon and stars in a big city, work your way through at least four crime organizations, find out who killed Beth and bring them to justice? Are you the Lone Ranger?"

"Let's get talking Alfred. Your bodyguards are getting tired of kissy face, at least she is. Who killed Beth?"

Alfred looked deflated and slouched as he sat. "You don't think I haven't agonized over Beth every hour of every day? She was killed under my watch, after *you* assholes in Head Office declared her fit and ready for undercover duty."

Furious, Shirley held her tongue with great effort. "I'm taking my share of the blame. I agree, she wasn't ready, but we passed her up and down the chain and nobody was willing to stop it."

Alfred looked at her, listening. "I get that. I could have said something, too, but didn't."

"So, let's at least get who killed her, if nothing else, so she can rest in peace."

"I'm in. I'm getting tired the nightmares."

She asked, "Do you see... ghosts?"

Alfred turned to her, eyebrows up. "Ghosts?"

"Just asking. Uh, look at the time. We have some information to exchange. Let's do it."

———

Adam and Marcel watched from the observation window as their Porsche rolled through Bubbles Car Wash. The sad bikini girls scrubbed and polished the car oblivious to their scanty outfits. It was all just dirty car wash work.

Adam and Marcel heard a couple of girls talking quietly at the reception desk behind them. They listened in, bored.

One cheerily said, "Hey, how's it going? This top is too fucking small!"

"Welcome back. Where ya been?" a second whined.

"Moved home for a while and it didn't work out, so I came back. What's new in shitty car wash world?"

"You haven't heard?"

"Heard what?"

"Ric's gone."

"Good riddance. He was the nastiest wash boss we ever had."

Bob and Zoo were happy to let him treat us like he did. Bastards!"

"So what happened?"

"Bob, Tammy and Zoo disappeared. Never found them."

"Nothing?"

"Cops said there was blood at Tammy's apartment... remember Tammy?"

"Yeah, she was okay."

"There was blood all over Tammy's apartment. Word is someone shot them all and deep sixed them."

Adam and Marcel exchanged uneasy glances and shifted their stance. They wanted to leave but were compelled to hear it all.

"Wow."

"And the best part of it all was a warning message left in the apartment by bikers telling these guys they were taking over the city."

"Holy shit!"

"And guess who wrote the note! Guess!"

"Tell me!"

"No, guess!"

"Just fucking tell me!"

Sounding a bit miffed, the second girl spelled out, "R – I – C."

"Ric killed them all? Oh my God."

"Yup, Ric did it."

"So's Ric's some big boss now?"

"Um, not so much. The Carzoni's went crazy! They grabbed Ric and tortured the shit out of him. There's pieces of him in biker bar doorways all over town with notes saying, 'This is what we'll do to you.'"

Marcel couldn't help a squeak of horror, turning it into a series of coughs.

Adam glared at him.

"Fuck! Now that's a warning! So, who's our new boss?"

"Not sure and I don't want to find out."

Adam's and Marcel's eyes drilled into one another. Who were they dealing with, here?

Alfred

Alfred talked to Shirley Mac almost non-stop, as if relieved to be asked about what led up to Beth's disappearance.

"In the beginning we set up Beth at the rooming house, similar to what we did for Tammy. Got her a job as a drug mule at Bubbles Car Wash. She worked day-to-day for Bob, Zoo and the guy before Ric... The guy called himself 'Peg'—no idea why."

"How was she doing?"

"At first she fit in well. Acted the drug mule part very well... too well."

"You had suspicions she was using something?"

"I did. Seemed like she was on something to relax her. Watery eyed, spoke a bit slower than usual. I called her on it, and she said it was just Xanax."

"Was she lying?"

"It may have been true. She was under enormous stress. The day-to-day stuff was wearing her down. I think she was having a hard time separating her real life from her undercover life."

"Terry... er... Tammy found the same, though I think she liked it. It was a big chess game to her."

"Not Beth. She hated it after six weeks. I told Smythe but he said it was too late to pull her. The information was starting to come in. He thought she'd settle."

"But she didn't settle?"

"No. She got worse. After three months she was a nervous wreck. Paranoid. Cried anytime I met with her. I should have scooped her up and just taken her away then."

"When did this all come to a head? What were the last few days like?"

"May third, I met with her. She seemed a bit cheered up. Said she'd seen couple of old friends but her clever disguise fooled them. That made her happy, gave her some faith in what she was doing."

"Seeing old friends when you're undercover is never a good thing."

"I'll say. Kill them or run away."

"She did neither. She swore up and down she'd fooled them with her drugged out car wash worker act. Then she didn't appear for our meeting a week later. We couldn't find a trace. I even chanced a break into her apartment and found she hadn't been there for days. I told Smythe but he said don't do anything. He said maybe she's sleeping with the boss or someone. Leave her alone."

"Then what did you do?"

"That would have been May 11. I got my guys together, looked around as much as we could. Nothing."

"Smythe wouldn't let you push the panic button?"

"He said nothing doing."

"What do you think happened to her, Alfred?"

"I've thought about this a lot. I think she bumped into her friends at the car wash… that makes them customers… they met her, then told someone about her. Somehow her real name came up which meant she was a cop and she had to be undercover. Then she vanished."

Shirley Mac shook his hand, standing up. "I'll be in touch. You've been very helpful."

He sat in a slump, without reply.

With new energy, Shirley updated her "wall", adding little yellow papers, arrows and a blank piece of paper.

"Who's the blank paper for?" asked a voice behind her.

Shirley didn't turn around this time. "Hi Beth. Talked to Alfred today."

"Oh, how's he doing?" Beth asked lightly.

"He's dandy. So, you met Adam and Marcel at the car wash, right?"

"Yes, but I fooled them."

"I don't think you did. I'm guessing they mentioned you to someone—someone connected, someone in the know. They mentioned your real name to the wrong person, the link was made, and it clicked you were an undercover cop at the car wash. Then that someone had you bumped off."

"Adam and Marcel wouldn't do that, would they?"

"Not sure if it was by accident or intentional. Whatever it was, they led you to your killer."

She was interrupted by a knock at the door. Beth vanished.

Another ghost at the door?

Shirley Mac warily opened her door a crack and was relieved to recognize her visitor. She swung the door wide. "Hi Dr. May. Come on in."

Dr. May smiled. "Coffee? I hear you talk to ghosts when you drink."

"Ah, thanks May. Come into my little 'Crazy Wall' room and sit down."

"A real Crazy Wall! Well done, Shirley Mac. All you need is the little colored knitting wool strings and you'd have it all. Has your favourite ghost been here for a look?"

"Yes. It seems I'm seeing her ghost in the daytime, too."

"Damn! This would make a decent novel if it wasn't true. I heard you talking to someone. Was it… Beth?"

Shirley held her palms out in mock surrender. "Yes. We were going over facts. I think Adam and Marcel were the trigger for this. They saw her and told someone."

They looked at the wall board and drank their coffee, trying to make connections with the murder.

"What's that news article about, Shirley? Bottom right."

"That's a bit of later news, after Beth's death. Terry Reid took over Beth's spot four months later and escaped when she was done. The news story said Bob and Zoo vanished along with Tammy, Terry's informant persona. No bodies of the trio were ever found."

"So Bob, Zoo and Tammy…Terry all vanished the same night?"

"Correct. Except Tammy…Terry had actually escaped. According to the article, Bob and Zoo vanished and a note was left in Tammy's room claiming Ric and the bikers killed them all as retribution for knocking off two bikers over a car theft ring. Looked like a tit-for-tat."

"Ric's dodged us for years."

"Apparently Ric didn't dodge anything, this time. Furious at the bikers, the Carzoni's grabbed Ric and cut him to pieces, literally."

May snorted, "Ah, Ric! His real name is Ricardo Marzetta Casetta. It's been weeks and I'm still getting bits and pieces of him turning up. Could've been an episode of Dexter."

"Zoo and Bob are missing and Ric gets sliced and diced over it." Shirley Mac thought to herself—all Terry needed to get rid of Ric was a well thought out note at the murder scene. Her pen was mightier than her sword, as they say. Good to know.

"Who's the boss of the Carzoni's these days?" asked May. "Who benefits from all this?"

"That's a very good question. As far as I know there was only a son… and a daughter."

———

Eva Carzoni was screaming. She threw an expensive vase against the wall, kicked the dog's water dish in its face and stomped around the room swearing.

Her ma sat impassively nearby. "Relax. What's the problem?"

Eva hissed at her, "Someone's snooping around, that's what!"

"They have no evidence."

"That snooper's shoe washed up on the beach and someone questioned Adam and Marcel."

"Did they say anything?"

"I don't know. That moron Wayne was supposed to knock her off and dump her somewhere. Then her fucking shoe washes up with her foot in it."

"Can they identify a person from a foot in a shoe," said Ma.

"Yes. DNA is the ultimate identifier! The cops will want to find out who killed the stoolie and trace it back to me! Fuck!" Eva kicked over a chair, then leaned against the wall, thinking.

Ma smiled. "You have the family temper."

Eva grinned back. "Sorry to rage at you Ma. You're the only one supporting me in gaining control of the family business. The men will never give it to me, us, especially if they think I'm connected to a cop stoolie."

"You gotta smother this shoe story, fast."

"Yes, I do. I need to make a call!"

———

Shirley Mac worked her home computer while May looked over her shoulder.

May focused on the police records. "Carzoni family… There were the two kids, Robert and Eva. She was the youngest. Any crime history with her?"

"It looks like she claims to be a legit social worker. Making the world a better place despite her scary family."

May pointed. "Let's see if she attended and graduated anywhere. I don't see a professional designation."

Shirley clicked around for ten minutes. "No record of her, anywhere. Not even a work experience placement."

"A cover! I'll bet she's bogus! What has she really been doing?"

"No arrests under that name, anyway," Shirley confirmed, getting excited. "Might have an alias or two. Interesting girl, this Eva, don't you think?"

———

Wayne's phone hummed over and over. He fumbled around for it with big clumsy fingers, struggling to see the phone number with seventy-five-year-old eyes. "Uh ya?"

"Wayne? Eva."

"Uh, Eva... who?"

"Eva Carzoni, you moron! Eva!"

"Uh, that Eva. Hiya..."

"Listen! What did you do with the cop stoolie's body?"

"Who?"

"The car wash girl? She's a cop, right? Remember?"

"Uh ya, the girl."

"Yes! What the fuck did you do with her body. Turns out her foot washed up in her shoe and the cops have had it all along."

"Uh, let me think here. Today's Thursday..." Wayne stumbled.

"Today's Monday! Monday! This was months ago! What did you do with her body?"

"Uh, I knocked her out at the wash with a poison dart, ya know. Deadly. Then I put a couple o' blocks on her ankles and dropped her in the channel, in the river, from the dock."

"The dock in the channel? The river current moves the bodies around so they come apart and the shoes float you idiot!"

"Uh, I had ta use the dock 'cuz of my sore back. I got sciatica and I can't bend much..."

Eva wasn't listening anymore, scrambling to think of a plan B.

"Shut up! Listen! I need you to bump off a couple of guys who can track that cop stoolie back to me. Can you do this? They drive an orange Porsche and they go to the Bubbles Car Wash every Monday, Thursday and Saturday. Got it? Knock them off!"

"Uh, let me find a pen and write this down…"

"Wayne! Are you even listening to me? Adam and Marcel, orange Porsche, at Bubbles Mondays, Thursday's and Saturdays! Don't screw this up!" Eva ended the call and turned her phone off.

"Uh, hello Eva? I got a pen. Hello?"

Blank.

Hanging up, Eva tried to get her temper in check. This was her time to take over the business. Under different names she'd been watching how it was done for years. Sure, Bob and Pa had grown up with the business but so had she. Eva snooped and watched every accounting sheet, personnel roster and list of which judges they had on the payroll. She just had to pull it together.

She hated having to use Wayne but he was elderly, kept his mouth shut and was counted out by everyone as past his prime. And they would be right—Wayne *was* old and forgetful to boot, but he was all she had. Shoot two people and tie up loose ends. Was that too much to ask?

He'd been her only hope when Adam and Marcel had pointed out their old McGill pal Beth at the car wash! A cop stoolie right under their nose! If Bob and Pa had found out, they'd have never let her have any part of the business and she was so ready!

She was proud of how she'd orchestrated Beth's demise. Wayne met her at the wash. Eva turned off the camera for five minutes and had the stoolie paged to meet Wayne's car, way in the back of the shop, had him shoot her in the leg with a poison dart, pushed her into his car and drive away. Wayne then tied blocks to the stoolie's feet and threw her off the dock and into the river. It had been swift, silent and the family had been none the wiser.

A well-done job. Or so she'd believed.

———

I t wasn't like Wayne hated Eva. He found her a very nice young lady. It was thanks to her he got the guarding job at Pa Carzoni's, which was a huge honour. Wayne had never anticipated getting a second chance like this at the age of seventy-five.

Old age irritated him. He remembered back in his mid-thirties when he was a giant—a vital and ruthless mob enforcer in his prime. He could shoot the eye out of an eagle at a half a mile. Those were the days. Then he retired.

The pen in his hand jarred him back to reality. Was it Monday, Wednesday, Friday? Blue Ferrari? Shit. He should've written it down while Eva yelled instructions at him. Bubbles Car Wash. Right. Something there.

The next morning, he picked up a large latte, two biscotti, and drove to the Bubbles Car wash, parking near the front entrance. He was pretty sure Eva wanted him to shoot a couple of guys. Here he enjoyed his breakfast and watched, telling himself he'd know them when he saw them. Both his pistols nestled in his pockets as always. He just needed that nudge to his memory to figure out who his target was.

He watched cars emerge from the wash, get the final rub down from the girls with the current supervisor making the final "drop" under the seat. It reminded him of that wash girl he killed. Normally killing someone didn't bother him but this girl was young and had seemed kind of sweet.

He watched an orange Porsche with two men in it approach Bubbles. That's it—an orange Porsche! It all came back to him now. They were the ones Eva spoke of. He waited, then followed them out the wash exit and watched where they went which was an empty arena parking lot. They both got out and dug hockey bags out of the little car's tiny trunk. Empty parking lot.

Wayne didn't want to get too close because theirs were the only cars in the lot. The men were already looking at him suspiciously. He had to move fast.

He hit the gas pedal and roared at the two men while fumbling with his gun in his pocket. The men were running. He pointed and shot out of his passenger side window which he'd forgotten to roll down. Damn! Glass flew everywhere and the bullet deflected away from harm. He had a piece of glass in his eye. Time to go.

Wayne roared away, a hand covering his bleeding eyeball, cursing.

He Shoots; He doesn't Score

Crouched down behind their car, shaking, Adam and Marcel watched with terror as the big old car emitting bullets roared away. There was a bullet hole in their car door to attest to the fact this was no hoax.

"What'll we do Adam? Someone's trying to kill us!"

"This has to be something to do with the dope from Bubbles and Beth's murder. Maybe we know something that's fatal."

"I'm not calling the cops about this. 'Hi, we're drug dealing hockey players who got one of your police undercover people killed.'"

"Let's call that cop who came to the house. I still have her card."

It wasn't twenty-five minutes later and a big unmarked cop car arrived, parking beside the orange Porsche.

Shirley Mac got out and asked, "What's up, boys?"

Adam pointed to the bullet hole in his car.

She nodded. "Nice. Any idea who?"

"Big old black sedan," Marcel answered. "Huge old guy driving. Shot once through his own side window, glass everywhere, lucky for us. He spooked and drove away."

"Good synopsis. License number?"

The men shook their heads.

Shirley Mac looked up and spied a parking lot camera nearby. She'd pull the tape and see what she could come up with. Might get the license number. She leaned back on her car, folded her arms like a pissed off teacher and asked, "No bullshit this time. Tell me why and how you know Bethany."

Adam looked down at his feet. "We knew Bethany from McGill. Just before she disappeared, we saw her at the Bubbles Car Wash."

Marcel added, "She looked like a crackhead, all drugged up and rough, but it was Beth! She pretended it wasn't her and sort of scurried away, but it was her for sure."

Adam continued, "What we didn't tell you was that the fourth one in our group back in school was Eva Carzoni."

"*The* Eva Carzoni of the crime family?"

"Yes. It never occurred to us that Eva was one of the real Carzoni's! It's a common name around here," said Adam. "Then a few days later we bumped into Eva at Bubbles and mentioned we saw Beth. She went white and walked away. Beth disappeared a few days later, according to the newspaper. We put it together and realized we might have got her killed."

"Will this information make the papers?" asked Adam.

"It will not. You both need to get your shit together and stay away from that car wash. Run while you can and never come back, got it?"

Adam and Marcel nodded. "We're packing our bags, tonight."

"Hopefully we'll never have to meet again. Ciao."

Just as she'd suspected, she was able to get the license number of the shooter's car from the tape and found it was owned by Wayne Deacon, an old and notorious hit man and muscle for the Carzoni's.

It was a sleepless night for her. She had the evil people who killed Beth along with probably dozens of others. The Carzoni's were hidden from their enemies. There was no chance of prosecution—Beth's killers would go free. A thought came to her. She jumped out of bed and sat with her computer.

Perhaps the enemies of the Carzoni's could follow a trail of breadcrumbs or cake crumbs as the case may be. With a slow smile, she typed up a very nice fiftieth wedding anniversary party announcement. It wasn't often these days that couples could endure marriage for that long. This was to celebrate a couple who did.

Open bar, cake, formal, kids welcome. She included an original wedding picture of them on the invitation so there would be no mistaking them. Looked legit.

She carefully noted the correct address and handy hints as to how to find the place. She would make it the easiest-to-find creepy black mansion with the high steel fence on a secluded block, ever. After all, it was the only house on that road.

Two weeks from today. Lots of time to plan for it. That's if the bikers could follow the clues to the Carzonis.

The biker gang, the Shadows, longed to find out where the Carzonis lived. Pa had had dozens of them killed or 'pruned' as he called it. After so many attempts on Pa's life Ma and Pa Carzoni were hidden in plain sight after a bullshit plea deal. They'd made a deal, had been turned to burn the Montreal biker gangs for police prosecution. Then had come the showy move out scene for all to witness, followed by a clandestine move back in when no one was around. It was brilliant. The Carzoni's had been living in relative peace right here in the family home for years, with no one the wiser. Witness protection at its finest. Safe, fat and happy until the end of their days while their kids ran the crime business.

Ironic.

Shirley only sent this invite to one gang in particular—the Shadows, who hated the Carzoni family the most. Here they are on a silver anniversary cake platter. Now Eva and her hired killer would pay for killing Beth, Terry Reid vengeance style. Shirley knew retribution would be swift.

———

Buster enjoyed riding his bicycle on occasion. If the road was flat and didn't have much traffic, he was happy. There were always new things to see and smell when he rode his bike, especially when he planned to blow something up. The Shadows paid him a bundle for this job and Buster had learned from the best in the mines of northern Quebec.

His bike chain squeaked as he pedaled along the drive. The pavement looked good and there was a decent approach from the road to the fence and up to the ugly mansion, both on the level.

The rusty high steel fence wouldn't be a problem. He saw the brick pillars were crumbling after decades of neglect. The corners where the steel fence attached were cracked. One good bump and the showy barrier would all fall down.

He slowed his bike and looked over at the mansion. What a neglected eyesore. The vegetation was dead and the big old building stones were black with dirt, dead ivy and age. Must have been grand in its day. Now the Shadows knew it for what it was—the Carzoni's self-imposed prison.

Buster was a bit out of breath as he passed the end of the yard. There must been eight surveillance cameras on that place. He heard it had a vintage Billboard pool table, too. A pity he'd never see it.

He picked up the little downhill that tracked back where he came from. This road was lower than the one he came in on. There it was! A little rocky alcove where he could see the mansion and duck in relative safety. Bomb shelter.

It was time to head home for a beer, to play a little pool if his technical guy Maynard wasn't quite done packing the explosives, then he'd wire it all together in the bus before he went for a little drive.

———

Wayne looked out the peephole of the Carzoni Mansion. He hadn't yet told Eva the shooting of the two Porsche guys didn't go well and wasn't looking forward to the coming exchange. The Carzoni's never even asked him why he had a patch over his eye where the doc picked out the piece of glass from his car side window. "Lucky you didn't poke your eye out, Mr. Deacon," said the nice lady doctor while she'd worked on him in the clinic.

He had a hard time seeing with one bleary eye. It'll be good to get this patch off.

———

B uster enjoyed driving the bright yellow school bus. Everyone waved at him, so he smiled and waved back. Maynard had stolen him a nice one this time. He'd said it wasn't every day you get to crush your arch enemy.

The bus was diesel, had air brakes and the little stop signs to flip open and closed to control traffic. The seats looked quite comfy, at least the ones they hadn't removed. He steered with his left hand while gently touching his cell phone with his right to make sure he had it handy.

It was all for nothing without this trigger phone.

The big yellow bus picked up speed as it neared the Carzoni Mansion. Buster watched the fence section he wanted, jerked the steering wheel to the right and the fifteen-ton machine flattened the steel fence with ease. It roared towards the old building. The problem was now to get it stopped so he wasn't injured when it hit the stone mansion.

Buster slammed on the air brakes as the bus sped to the near stone wall, the tires squealing as they skidded. He needed to get off this bus before the shooting started. He hopped away from the seat and backed away from the front, clinging tightly to a chrome hand-hold when the bus connected with the mansion wall. The impact rattled him down to his teeth but he was still in one piece—shaken but uninjured, just as they'd planned. The side door was crushed, barring his exit. Well shit. .Quickly he turned and stepped gingerly over the giant tarped bags littering the back. Don't damage the wires!

At last he pushed open the little escape door on the end of the bus, climbed out and jumped down. He ran as fast as his stumpy little legs could carry him, across the road and over the bank. Buster found the little rock alcove and snuggled in closely, pulled out his phone and pushed an app Maynard had thoughtfully marked "Kaboom" and covered his ears.

———

Wayne heard a sound of crashing out in front of the mansion. He saw something come through the fence and wondered if it was a big lawn mower. It had been a long time since they had their grass cut. After trying the peephole and giving up with his bad eye he opened the door for a closer look.

The earth shook in a big way. Three tons of top quality stolen DND explosives blew the big yellow school bus and the ugly old mansion to smithereens. The ground shook for miles. Car sized pieces of rock scattered around the area. The bus vanished along with any evidence of who did it. Awesome was an understatement.

Goodbye to the Carzonis.

———

Beers all around would be the order of the day when he got back to the bar, for sure. Buster darted from his hiding place immediately, congratulated himself on a job well done and ran back to the getaway car. Being the expert on billiard tables that he was, Buster would have appreciated the irony of having an expensive, well made two-ton slate Luxury Billboard Gold Leaf Model coming down from the sky, crushing him as flat as cheap carpet from Wal-Mart. It even landed right side up with its trademark bullet hole from the Carzoni's.

The police would find the evidence of who the bomber was as soon as they got a tow truck to lift the table up and find Busters pulverized corpse and incriminating phone. Very traceable back to the Shadows.

———

Dr. May Hall opened her newspaper and read— "Huge explosion wipes out the infamous Carzoni Clan".

"Martin, Eva and Josia Carzoni believed dead".

"Unidentified victim found crushed under a pool table nearby. Police suspect he was the bomber."

"Wayne Deacon, the security man with ties to the Carzoni family found dead, impaled almost at the top of a tall tree two blocks away".

May raised her eyebrows. "Hmmm. I'm going to be busy over the next few days."

———

S hirley Mac snored like a saw in a mill. After a month's holiday she felt more relaxed than she had in years.

"Hey Shirley Mac. What's up?" asked the ghost of Beth.

Shirley snorted and sat up sleepily. "Oh, hi Beth."

"So what did you find out?"

Shirley Mac turned on her bedside light, rubbing her eyes. "You were ID'd by old friends who mistakenly told one wrong person. Chance."

"How did it all shake out?"

"It's a long story. Turns out Adam and Marcel told Eva they saw you at the car wash, thinking Eva wasn't part of the family business—but she was, even back then—and especially now that Bob's gone. Eva thought herself a contender. She had bumbling Wayne knock you off with a poison dart in the back of the wash. We got it on video when Eva screwed up and didn't turn off the camera."

"So, when I leaned into his car I got the poison dart? Dead, Amazon jungle style. Bizarre."

"Correct. Then you were dropped off in the river near the docks because Wayne had a sore back. The river current let one of your shoes get away and it was sheer luck we found it."

"So, my shoe was the reminder."

"Barely. The media got the initial tip off about the shoe then Head Office buried the story."

"Assholes!"

"And the shoe led you to tell me about Adam and Marcel, connecting me to Eva Carzoni," Shirley Mac said, nodding. "Eva wasn't on our radar."

Beth added, "And Terry Reid killed Bob and Zoo, opening a

splendid opportunity for Eva to finally take over."

Shirley Mac's eyes popped open wide as she jolted awake at this revelation. "Terry... Bob... what?"

"Oops... already said too much. Thanks boss!" Beth blew Shirley a kiss and vanished, forever.

"Damn!" Shirley Mac fell back to her pillow, absolutely shocked. "Terry killed Bob and Zoo and framed Ric—and it was a ghost who told me all about it. Who'd believe it?"

She rolled over in bed, closing her eyes, mumbling to herself. "Who said, 'The dead tell no tales'?"

ABOUT THIS COMPILATION

S ome are old, some are new, some refurbished and some are true. Short stories and novelettes are handy vehicles to test out an idea or thought process. It can tell us where the limits of a story line or a character are. They are trial balloons to see where the story goes. Even if they lead no-where, that is a statement of direction.

Sometimes they are pure fun…hatching an idea. Imagining what a character's life was really like after the story closed. Perhaps Dr. May Hall goes on to solve a murder on her own. Unlimited possibilities.

This is a selected group of stories I had on the shelf, hidden in the basement or in the 'for deletion' bin. A few were left untouched while some were vastly changed. Ramblings forced to become coherent.

Not all made the cut. Maybe they'll be resurrected at a future date. A few were inspirations and thought processes for my later novels. They started the boulder rolling down the hill. A few were novel story line spin offs. Most mention a connection to either the 'Gypsy' or Disciples' series. Did you spot the lonely motorcyclist?

I must return to finishing Terry Reid's books 4 and 5.

Thank you all for your kind support. Read and enjoy.

Patrick D. Ferris

ALSO BY PATRICK D FERRIS

Larry and Giselle Series:

A Gypsy Romance

A Gypsy Engagement

A Gypsy Haunting

Terry Reid Mystery Series:

His Disciples Watch

His Disciples Sleep

His Disciples Deceive

Short Story Collection:

Fragmented Thoughts Random Directions

ABOUT THE AUTHOR

Born in Winnipeg, Manitoba in 1954, Pat Ferris grew up in Victoria and moved to Fort St. John in 1975 to pursue his trade in the rapidly expanding natural gas industry. His high school English skills were worthy of note, as were his mechanical skills, but working with his hands paid the bills. Pat retired from the gas industry and a subsequent bicycle shop in 2015 to spend more time with writing.

In the mid-nineties he turned his hand to writing once again. After much tinkering and experimenting he utilized his cycling experiences in his first novel 'Gypsies' published in 2014. A year later came 'A Gypsy Engagement' with a third edition 'A Gypsy Haunting' following.

Another of his projects is the dystopian Terry Reid novel series 'His Disciples Watch', 'His Disciples Sleep', and His Disciples Deceive', all set in a future ruled by Trump-like demagogues set on controlling the world. Political murders and a sweet poem from an adolescent girl could upset their whole program. Book four and five are in the works. There's always more coming. As they say…*Stay tuned!*

Contact Pat at https://patrickdferris.com

www.ingramcontent.com/pod-product-compliance
Lightning Source LLC
Chambersburg PA
CBHW060401260626
47160CB00006B/2393